Songs of Resistance

Songs of Resistance

Challenging Caesar and Empire

R. ALAN STREETT

CASCADE *Books* · Eugene, Oregon

SONGS OF RESISTANCE
Challenging Caesar and Empire

Cascade Books
An Imprint of Wipf and Stock Publishers
199 W. 8th Ave., Suite 3
Eugene, OR 97401

www.wipfandstock.com

PAPERBACK ISBN: 978-1-7252-6999-6
HARDCOVER ISBN: 978-1-7252-7000-8
EBOOK ISBN: 978-1-7252-7001-5

Cataloguing-in-Publication data:

Names: Streett, R. Alan, author.

Title: Songs of resistance : challenging Caesar and empire / by R. Alan Streett.

Description: Eugene, OR: Cascade Books, 2022 | Includes bibliographical references and index.

Identifiers: ISBN 978-1-7252-6999-6 (paperback) | ISBN 978-1-7252-7000-8 (hardcover) | ISBN 978-1-7252-7001-5 (ebook)

Subjects: LCSH: Hymns in the Bible. | Bible. New Testament—Criticism, interpretation, etc. | Hymns, Early Christian. | Rome—In the Bible. | Politics in the Bible.

Classification: BS2545.H94 S774 2022 (paperback) | BS2545.H94 (ebook)

VERSION NUMBER 103122

To my daughters-in-law:

Katie, Allison, and Renée

And to:

Emrys, my last (?) granddaughter

Contents

Abbreviations

Old Testament Pseudepigrapha

2 Bar.	2 Baruch
1 En.	1 Enoch
4 Ezra	4 Ezra
Jub.	Jubilees
Pss. Sol.	Psalms of Solomon
Sib. Or.	Sibylline Oracles
T. Benj.	Testament of Benjamin
T. Jud.	Testament of Judah
T. Levi	Testament of Levi
T. Sim.	Testament of Simeon
T. Zeb.	Testament of Zebulun

Greek and Latin Works

Augustine

Civ.	*De civitate Dei*

Cicero

Div.	*De divination*
Rep.	*De republica*
Flac.	*Pro Flacco*
Rab.	*Pro Rabirio*

Clement of Alexandria

Strom.   *Stromata*

Dio Cassius

Hist.   *Historiae Romanae*

Dio Chrysostom

Nicom.   *Ad Nicomedienses*

Dionysius

Ant. or.   *De antiquis oratoribus*

Euripides

Bacch.   *Bacchae*

Eusebius

Hist. eccl.   *Historia ecclesiastica*

Homer

Il.   *Ilias*   *Iliad*

Horace

Carm.   *Carmina*
Ep.   *Epistulae*

Irenaeus

Haer.   *Adversus haereses*

Josephus

Ant.   *Jewish Antiquities*
J.W.   *Jewish War*

Justin

Dial.   *Dialogus cum Tryphone*

Juvenal

Sat.   *Satirae*

Livy

Hist.   *History of Rome*

Martial

Epigrams

Minucius, Felix

Oct.   *Octavius*

Origen

Cels.   *Contra Celsum*

Ovid

Metam.   *Metamorphoses*
Fast.   *Fasti*

Petronius

Satyr.   *Satyricon*

Philo

Cher.	*De cherubim*	*On the Cherubim*
Conf.	*De confusion linguarum*	*On the Confusion of Tongues*
Contempl.	*De vita contemplativa*	
Embassy	*On the Embassy to Gaius*	
Leg. 1, 2, 3	*Legum allegoriae* I, II, III	*Allegorical Interpretation*
Opif.	*De opificio mundi*	*On the Creation of the World*
QE 1,2	*Quaestiones in Exodum* I, II	
Spec.	*De specialibus legibus*	

Plato

Symp.   *Symposium*

Pliny the Elder

Nat.   *Naturalis historia*

Pliny the Younger

Ep. Tra.   *Epistlulae ad Trajanum*
Epistulae   *Ep.*

Plutarch

Ant.   *Vita Antony*
Praec. ger. rei publ.   *Praecepta gerendae rei publicae*
Quaest. conv.   *Quaestionum convivialum libri IX*
Rom.   *Romulus*

Seneca (the Younger)

Ben.   *De beneficiis*

Suetonius

Aug.   *Augustus*
Claud.   *Divus Claudius*
Dom.   *Domitianus*
Jul.   *Divius Julius*
Vesp.   *Vespasianus*

Tacitus

Ann.   *Annales*
Hist.   *Historiae*

Tertullian

Nat.   *Ad Nationes*

Virgil

Aen.   *Aenid*
Ecl.   *Eclogae*

Apocrypha and Septuagint

Bar	Baruch
Jdt	Judith
1–2 Macc, 3–4 Macc	Maccabees
Sir	Sirach/Ecclesiasticus
Wis	Wisdom of Solomon

Apostolic Fathers

Did.	Didache

CHAPTER 1

New Testament Songs in Historical Context

Music is the universal language.
—ATTRIBUTED TO HENRY WADSWORTH LONGFELLOW

MUSIC SPEAKS TO PEOPLE of all ages, backgrounds, nationalities, cultures, and times. Everyone, regardless of musical knowledge or aptitude, can appreciate and enjoy beautiful melodies.

While music may be universal, *lyrics* are not. They are specific to a particular culture and social context, especially protest songs. Woody Guthrie's "This Land is Your Land" is a case in point. His poignant lyrics called attention to the plight of migrant farmworkers and those on the margins of society in the 1940s and 50s, who had little or no hope of achieving the American dream. Negro spirituals, birthed in the Antebellum south, expressed the sadness and aspirations of those enslaved by their masters. Abel Meerpool wrote the metaphorical lyrics of "Strange Fruit" to depict the horrors of lynching during the Jim Crow era and prick the consciences of white listeners. Thousands of black Americans marched hand-in-hand through city streets singing "We Shall Overcome" in their struggle to gain civil rights and equal justice under the law.

1

In their original context, medieval nursery rhymes were instruments of sedition. Their lyrics contained hidden transcripts designed to ridicule or lampoon British royalty and the politics of their day.[1]

Hip-hop first hit the airwaves in 1973 and served as an outlet for impoverished blacks living in the borough of The Bronx, New York to vent their anger against governmental authorities, who deemed them insignificant and invisible.

The advent of reggae music coincided with the rise of widespread political and social unrest in Jamaica in the late 1960s and early 1970s, when American companies gained control of the tourism, farming, and mining industries. They siphoned off the large profits and made sure a percentage found its way into the coffers of the Jamaican Labor Party and its leaders. Reggae, a combination of calypso tunes and protest lyrics, was created to voice opposition to economic injustice and corrupt politics.

These songs, like many others not mentioned, had one thing in common. They were songs of resistance that spoke to the times and culture in which they were written. They protested various injustices and offered hope to the oppressed and disenfranchised that someday things would be different.

When removed from their initial political and social contexts, the original impact and meaning of the lyrics are often lost. In fact, they can be interpreted to mean the exact opposite of what the writer intended. For example, "This Land is Your Land" has been transformed into a patriotic song that celebrates free enterprise.[2] Nursery rhymes are now viewed as children's literature. Hip-hop has become a popular genre for people of all classes and social backgrounds.

1.1 Context, Context, Context

Likewise, when we encounter songs in the New Testament, the issue of context comes to the forefront. The songs were not written in a socio-religious or political vacuum, but were created by minority members of an oppressive society, and their lyrics reflected the beliefs of Christ followers on certain subjects and proposed a vision of the future that differed from Rome's

1. Hazlett, "Use of British Nursery Rhymes," 8–9.

2. In order to transform "This Land is your Land" into a mainline patriotic song, its two most controversial and subversive stanzas opposing private property and railing against the church had to be expunged from most versions.

social agenda. Without understanding the circumstances in which each writer lived, it is easy to miss the meaning of a song's lyrics. Therefore, we must familiarize ourselves with the Roman world of the first century CE.[3]

Some scholars analyze New Testament (NT) songs in order to uncover theological content. This approach might be feasible if the lyricists were trained theologians rather than lay people, or if the apostle Paul, a towering intellectual, wrote most of the hymns. This was not the case. The first-century church, particularly in its early years, had no settled theology. Theology was in flux. Therefore, when a NT song makes a theological statement, it likely reflects the narrow beliefs of a particular writer and not necessarily those of all believers of the first century.

This book examines NT songs in light of the historical and the cultural milieu in which they were created. New Testament songsters lived at different times under different emperors and resided in different locations across the empire. Therefore, the Christ movement was as diverse as its people and the location where it found itself. Some followers were messianic Jews and others were converted pagans; some were preachers and others were maidens. Life for a believer in Asia Minor differed from that of a believer in Corinth; yet, each was born and existed under an oppressive regime. With limited rights and freedoms, they wrote songs that were relevant to them and their listeners. And like many songs written while living under the heavy hand of authoritative regimes throughout history, NT songs protested their lot in life and hoped for a brighter future. In essence, they were songs of resistance that challenged Caesar and the empire.

This leads us to look first at the nature and function of NT songs in light of their sociopolitical context.

1.2 The World Before the Christ Movement

In the first century BCE, Rome became a military juggernaut and conquered one Greek stronghold after another until finally in 88 BCE the Macedonian Empire succumbed to death. A quarter-century later (64 BCE), Pompey, Rome's great military general, marched into northern Syria, disposed of Antiochus XIII, and sent an envoy southward to Judea to negotiate a

---

3. As Carter observes, "Every chapter and every pericope of the New Testament are products of empire. Every text must be investigated in this light. The New Testament calls followers of Jesus to active discipleship that resists imperial abuses" (*Empire Then and Now*, 149).

surrender.[4] His soldiers laid siege of Jerusalem and the independent Jewish state came under the authority of Rome.

Unlike other nations who worshiped a pantheon of gods and were able to find an approved equivalent among the Roman deities, Israel was monotheistic. It recognized the existence of other gods but did not worship them; Jews uniquely worshiped one god only, Yahweh, whom they claimed created the world. By special arrangement Pompey agreed that Israel could continue its practice. He hand-selected and appointed the high priest, who pledged to carry out Rome's agenda, while serving as Israel's highest-ranking political figure. The balancing act was difficult at best.

In the years that followed, a struggle for power erupted between generals Pompey and Julius Caesar over who would rule the Roman Republic. Caesar emerged victorious in 44 BCE and took the title *Dictator perpetuo* ("Dictator in perpetuity"). The following year he was assassinated by Brutus and Cassius. In 42 BCE Mark Antony and Gaius Octavian successfully hunted down and defeated the assassins at the battle of Philippi, but eventually turned on each other. The republic was thrown into chaos and a civil war ensued. Octavian defeated Antony at the Battle of Acton, and was hailed *savior* of the republic. He ascended the throne in 27 BCE and under his leadership Rome became an empire.

Octavian's official title was *princeps*, meaning "first among equals." In reality, he was *imperator* (emperor) over the *imperium* (empire). The Senate dubbed him "Augustus" or magnificent one.[5] Despite his apparent self-effacement, he gladly accepted the title. Soon he was answerable only to Jupiter, head of the pantheon of gods.

By the time of Jesus' birth, Rome had spread its tentacles to the far reaches of the Mediterranean. Rome's reach was so vast that Luke in describing the birth of Jesus, writes, "In those days a decree went out from Emperor Augustus that *all the world* should be registered" (Luke 1:26).

1.3 The Roman World at the Time of the Jesus Movement

John the Baptist and Jesus preached the "gospel of the kingdom" to Palestinian Jews and announced that God was about to restore the kingdom to Israel under a new divinely appointed king. Disciples of Jesus took this message beyond the borders of Israel and invited gentiles to join the

4. Josephus, *Ant.* 14.46–75; *J. W.* 1.127–58.

5. Virgil, *Aen.* 6.793.

kingdom. Christ followers—far and wide, Jews and gentiles, all subjects of the empire—formed themselves into small assemblies where they sought to live according to kingdom principles. In doing so, they embraced a sociopolitical vision that opposed Rome's ideology and agenda for the world.

Christ's kingdom-focused churches proclaimed Jesus Lord of all creation and lived in peaceful noncompliance with the empire's core values. Their subversive songs resisted the "great tradition," i.e., the official version of society as constructed by the rulers.[6]

In the next few pages, we will examine the bedrock beliefs of empire to discover how the kingdom of Christ and the kingdom of Caesar were in conflict.

1.3.1 Manifest Destiny

Caesar Augustus claimed that Jupiter chose him and Rome to rule the world, carry out the gods' will, and spread their blessings among the nations. To fulfill this divine mandate, Augustus sought to conquer the nations surrounding the Mediterranean.

Jesus' mission was no less extensive. He told his disciples to "Go and make disciples of all nations" (Matt 28:18). In issuing his mandate, he defied Rome's exclusive claims of world-domination.

According to Roman tradition, the gods made their will known through the use of avian signs.[7] Romulus (771–716 BCE) was chosen and confirmed to be Rome's first leader when an eagle landed on his shoulder, marking him and not his twin brother Remus, as the choice of the gods. Augustus insisted the gods selected him in like manner to rule Rome and the entire world.[8] Others pointed to an avian sign as divine proof that they were next in line to serve as emperor. Tiberius (14–37 CE), who reigned at the time of Jesus, was confirmed after an eagle landed on the roof of his house, and Claudius (41–54 CE), who ruled during the ministry of Paul, after "an eagle swooped down and perched on his shoulder."[9]

According to the Gospel accounts, God in similar manner called Jesus to be his earthly representative and provided an avian sign; a dove descended at Jesus' baptism and a voice from heaven announced, "*This* is

6. Herzog, "Onstage and Offstage," 42.

7. Cicero, *Div.* 1.48; Livy, *Hist.* 1.6.4—7.7.

8. Suetonius, *Aug.* 7.2; 95; Dio Cassius, *Hist.* 46.46.2.

9. Suetonius, *Tib.* 14; *Claud.* 5.7.

my beloved son in whom I am well pleased" (Matt 3:17; Mark 1:11; Luke 3:22). The message was clear: the god of Israel also had a son, destined to rule over a universal kingdom. Several of the christological songs we will examine in the chapters ahead contain lyrics that contest Rome's claims of manifest destiny and Caesar's unique role.

1.3.2 Pax Romana

Caesar Augustus commissioned his troops to spread the good news of *Pax Romana* (Roman peace) to all the world.[10] When the army, dressed in full combat gear, reached the edge of a foreign nation, an envoy entered the capital, met with the leaders, and brought good news from Caesar. If the nation's leaders willingly pledged their allegiance to the empire, Caesar guaranteed "peace and security" to their nation.[11] In turn, their native leaders were allowed to retain their government posts, but now under the emperor. Their king became a client king and paid homage to Caesar as the "king of kings."[12] As part of the empire, they taxed their people to support Rome's interests and adopted its social agenda. As toadies of Rome, these native elites continued to fare well, but their citizenry less so.[13]

The emissaries of the Christ movement also promoted a "gospel of peace" that contradicted Rome's version. The alternative *pax* originated with Jesus: "Peace I leave with you; my peace I give to you. I do not give to you as the world gives. Do not let your hearts be troubled, and do not let them be afraid" (John 14:27). They recognized Jesus, not Caesar, as God's son and "prince of peace" (Isa 9:6). The apostle Paul called Jesus "our peace" (Eph 2:14).

---

10. For the definitive treatment of *Pax Romana* see Wengst, *Pax Romana*.

11. Horace, *Carm.* 4.15.

12. Dio Cassius recounts how king Tiridates of Armenia made the long journey to Rome to kneel and lay his crown at Emperor Nero's feet. He said, "Master . . . I have come to you, my god, worshiping you as I do Mithra. The destiny you spin for me shall be mine, for you are my Fortune and my Fate." In return, Nero invited Tiridates to ascend the royal platform and placed the crown back on his head, signifying he was a client king to Nero, himself the "king of kings" (*Hist.* 63.2.1; 63.5.2–3).

13. The arrangement reminds one of the armistice between Hitler and France during WWII. The Vichy government (July 10, 1940–August 9, 1944) under Marshal Philippe Pétain was allowed to run the civil administration of France. In reality, because of compromises, the officials of the Vichy government ended up serving goals of Hitler.

Paul also spoke of Jesus as the "only Sovereign, the King of kings and Lord of lords" (1 Tim 6:15). In describing an end-time war against "the Lamb," John the visionary, writes, "the Lamb will conquer them, for he is Lord of lords and King of kings" (Rev 17:14). And again, "On his robe and on his thigh, he has a name inscribed, King of kings and Lord of lords" (Rev 19:16). The writers of Scripture took Rome's words and applied them subversively to Jesus. Additionally, they composed songs that proclaimed Jesus alone worthy to receive "glory, honor, and power" because of his position as creator and ruler of the universe (Rev 4:11). Hymns served to counteract Roman propaganda.

1.3.3 Violence

When nations spurned Rome's diplomatic efforts, troops seized valuable property, burned the capital city, raped its women, slaughtered thousands in battle, and enslaved captives. They set up martial law until a new government was installed. The spoils of battle were carried back to Rome along with their ousted leaders who were chained and marched through the streets of the capital to display Rome's superiority over the nation and its gods.

Violence was the engine that drove the empire.[14] Like all dictatorships before or after, Rome also used brutal force to keep its own subjects in line.[15] The military "assured compliance."[16] They established and maintained the fragile *Pax Romana*.[17] Crucifixion was the ultimate "imperial weapon of terror."[18] It was reserved for non-citizens and lowly provincials who committed the most serious crimes against the state. Citizens could also be crucified if found guilty of treason.[19]

Native retainers and Roman provincial authorities were charged with maintaining law and order. If they failed to do so, Rome acted swiftly and aggressively and removed them from office.

14. Vearncombe et al., *After Jesus*, 35.

15. Vearncombe et al., *After Jesus*, 35.

16. Carter, *Empire Then and Now*, 153.

17. The Jewish rebellion of 66–70 CE was met with the full force the Roman army with devastating results.

18. Elliott, "Anti-Imperial Message," 167.

19. Carter, *Empire Then and Now*, 154.

Christ followers were often the objects of Roman cruelty, especially at the hands of regional and local authorities who did Rome's bidding. Christian heralds, like Stephen, Philip, Peter, John, James, Paul, Silas, and John the revelator, were hauled into court, jailed, threatened, tortured, or exiled. Several letters containing embedded songs to Christ were written from prison.

Many Jewish Christ followers were expelled from synagogues or beaten (Matt 10:17; Mark 13:9: John 9:22; Acts 9:22–25; 17:1–9; 18:4–7, 18), disowned by their families for breaking with Jewish tradition, and lost their livelihood. Just as Eastern European Jews were terrorized or murdered under Hitler, or the Uyghurs of China, or slaves in pre-Civil War America, so believers were similarly persecuted under Rome.

John, the Apocalyptic visionary, did not readily accept Rome's labeling of the executed persons as enemies of the State or lawbreakers, but reclassified them in martyr-like terms. Many modern-day Christians in the West cringe when they watch a news report that features an Islamic spokesperson calling a slain terrorist "a martyr." Yet, John did the same thing. He recast those murdered by Rome as victims, not culprits. Rome slaughtered and beheaded the faithful, showing no reluctance whatsoever to use violence to accomplish its ends.

In a later vision John hears the departed saints cry out, "Sovereign Lord, holy and true, how long will it be before you judge and avenge our blood on the inhabitants of the earth?" (Rev 6:10–11). At the end he finds them raised from the dead, reigning with Christ, and singing his praises (20:4).

1.3.4 Economic Control and Domination

Rome dominated people. Only two kinds of people lived in the empire: rulers and the ruled. The rulers were composed of a minority elite class of people starting with the emperor at the top of the power pyramid, answerable to Jupiter head of the pantheon of gods, and followed by the nobles who included senators, equestrians, and councilors in descending order. The ruling class, composed of the wealthiest men in the empire, served in the Senate or positions of authority in the provinces and colonies. They controlled nearly all assets of the empire, including money supply, landholdings, agriculture, commerce, and trade. All profits flowed up the economic ladder with each taking his designated share.[20] The aristocracy accounted for approximately 2 percent of the total population.[21]

Native elites living in annexed lands retained their power and ruled their respective nations on behalf of Rome. The high priestly family and members of the Sanhedrin fit into this category in Palestine. Native elites accounted for about 8 percent of the population of the empire and were people of material means.

The remaining 90 percent of the people (the ruled) lived at a subsistence level and had no political power. The majority were rural peasants and worked the land of the rich without benefitting from their labors. They were essentially day laborers and got paid daily after working from dawn to dusk. Others were slaves, manual laborers, artisans and merchants, beggars, and prisoners. Everyone except the elites lived on the edge of poverty. There was no middle class, as we think of it in the twenty-first century, although those in the military came the closest. The masses were heavily taxed and exploited, and the economic fruit of their labors moved up the pyramid and ended in the hands of the elites.[22]

Completely marginalized and oppressed, the masses lived in silent desperation. They kept their faces toward the ground in public, submitted to authority, paid taxes, and went about their business without recourse. Most lived in one room tenements without a kitchen or bathroom facilities. The nobles, by comparison, lived in mansions, some that spanned 6–8,000 square feet with multiple rooms, running water, private baths, gardens, and enclosed courtyards.[23]

In his first synagogue sermon Jesus took up the mantle of the Isaianic savior and declared:

> The Spirit of the Lord is upon me,
>   because he has anointed me
>   to bring good news to the poor.
> He has sent me to proclaim release to the captives
>   and recovery of sight to the blind,
>   to let the oppressed go free,

20. Caesar was considered the sovereign over land and sea. In essence, a portion of the profits from working the land or fishing in the waters went into the imperial treasury. Fishermen, for instance, were required to pay taxes and percentages of their income to Rome. See Juvenal, *Sat.* 4.51–55, 83–84.

21. Stegemann and Stegemann, *Jesus Movement*, 14.

22. Stegemann and Stegemann, *Jesus Movement*, 72–73.

23. Thompson, *Handbook*, 66.

to proclaim the year of the Lord's favor (Luke 4:18–19).

Jesus' message and mission were a direct assault on the domination system. He called on his Jewish listeners to adopt a new social agenda and announced the kingdom of God was at hand. Those who heeded his message formed themselves into small societies that met in homes and entered into a covenant relationship with each other. They sang about Jesus and the kingdom of God.

1.3.5 Male-Dominated, Family-Focused

The empire was male-dominated and functioned as a large family. Caesar considered himself the head of this family (*paterfamilias*). As "the father of the fatherland," he controlled the family and was responsible for meeting its needs.[24]

To implement his social agenda, the emperor depended on each male to rule his own family in accordance with the will of the emperor.[25] Each father was like a god over his own house just as Caesar was a god to his family.[26] As the family priest, each husband led his family in devotion to Roman deities, thus ensuring them divine protection. Women, children, and slaves had no rights, except those granted by the husband, father, and master. They obeyed and carried out his demands.

While assuming the traditional Roman family structure with the man as head of the family, the Christ movement developed household codes that subverted male dominance. Paul, the apostle, instructed the man to relate to his wife, children, and servants in the same way as Christ does to the church (Eph 5:22—6:9). Members in a redeemed household defined their identity as being "in Christ." They saw God as the ultimate *paterfamilias* of the family.

When believers came together as the church, they regarded all as equals—male and female, Jew and Greek, slave and free, Roman and barbarian. Women functioned in significant roles, slaves might be elders of a congregation, and children were considered part of the kingdom.[27]

24. Suetonius, *Aug.* 2.58.

25. Rome considered the family an essential social institution that reinforced its values and social hierarchy. Each head of household was the ruler over his own domain. If the family structure failed to hold, it would undermine and weaken Rome's social agenda.

26. Vearncombe et al., *After Jesus*, 153.

27. Origen, *Cels.* 3.44, 55, 59, answered accusations by Celsus who ridiculed

Jesus excoriated James and John, the sons of thunder, after they sought positions of authority in God's kingdom: "You know that the rulers of the Gentiles lord it over them, and their great ones are tyrants over them. It will not be so among you; but whoever wishes to be great among you must be your servant, and whoever wishes to be first among you must be your slave; just as the Son of Man came not to be served but to serve, and to give his life a ransom for many" (Matt 20:25–28). The Gospels present Jesus as a leader who did not seek or demand honor, but earned it through servitude.

The Christ communities stood in stark contrast with Rome's social structure. They practiced an alternative lifestyle and sang of a day when equality would spread throughout the earth under the reign of Christ.

1.3.6 The Political Nature of Worship

In ancient societies, unlike modern democracies in the West, worship was a political act. Religion and politics functioned like Siamese twins, organically and practically, co-joined at the hip.[28] Rome was a political entity wrapped in religion. Likewise, ancient Israel was a "kingdom of priests" and operated as a theocracy (Exod 19:6). The terms "kingdom" and "priests" were inseparable. All kingdoms in biblical times implemented the will of their respective deities.

Jesus' kingdom message was just as political as Rome's. It was about God restoring his kingdom on earth. It was about regime change. Christ followers rejected Rome's right to conquer the world. Their songs presented Christ as God's designated sovereign over the cosmos and themselves as citizens (Phil 2:9–11; 3:20); "a royal priesthood, a holy nation" (1 Pet 2:9); "a kingdom," and "priests serving his God and Father, to him be glory and dominion forever and ever. Amen" (Rev 1:6).

Christianity as an inferior religion because its converts were mainly ignorant women, children, and slaves, and it lacked masculinity.

28. In modern times, a few countries still operate as theocracies, especially in the Middle East. The Islamic Republic of Iran, Pakistan, Mauritania are all "Muslim" states and follow the rule of Islamic law.

1.3.7 The Imperial Cult

The cult of the emperor "was the product of the Augustan cultural revolution.[29] Although the imperial cult permeated the entirety of the empire it was not "one size fits all."[30] It had no central headquarters that handed down directives how people should worship the emperor; nor was it exclusive in its demands. People throughout the empire worshiped other gods, but not without also paying homage to the emperor. As deSilva points out:

> The imperial cult was embedded in the cults of the traditional deities. Frequently statues of the emperor and the traditional deities shared the same space, emphasizing their connectedness. The emperor was not simply a god but a vessel by which the traditional gods established order and showered their gifts on humanity. As the chief priest (*Pontifex Maximus*) of the Roman world, he stood as mediator between the gods and the human race.[31]

Cities erected temples to Jupiter, Apollo, Venus, Asclepius, and others, depending on their needs and locations. Ephesus erected a temple to Diana, patron goddess for the silversmith guilds. A coin minted in Corinth depicts the goddess Fortuna crowning Emperor Nero. Many other coins carry a picture of the emperor on the front side with the title *divi filius* and on the back side a picture of a local deity. Worship of the deity was not possible apart from recognizing and honoring the emperor.[32]

Everyone related differently to Caesar. In Asia Minor, seventy imperial temples and shrines were built in honor of the emperor.[33] The masses, especially throughout the Lycus Valley, worshiped him as a full-fledged deity and offered sacrifices in his name.[34] But even in this region, Caesar was not worshiped exclusively.

Many living in the western part of the empire, considered Caesar divine, but not fully god. As Jupiter's earthly representative on earth, Caesar undertook a divine mission and held divine status. He was highly esteemed. Regardless of one's opinion of the emperor, everyone in the empire supported and joined in imperial cult events, private and public, including

29. Crenshaw, "*Roman Worship*," 293.
30. Beard et al., *Religions of Rome*, 348.
31. DeSilva, *Introduction*, 800.
32. DeSilva, *Introduction*, 800.
33. Price, *Rituals and Power*, 162.
34. Dio Cassius, *Hist.* 51.20; Tacitus, *Ann.* 4.37.

singing paeans of praise to Caesar, offering him sacrifices, praying to him or for him, eating meals, and attending parades in his name. Olympic style games, festivals, and holiday celebrations were held in his honor. Caesar was exalted above all in the empire.[35]

One may liken participation in imperial cult activities to American citizens standing as the flag passes in front of them or when the National Anthem is played or sung, regardless of the person's religious beliefs. Patriotism is the common denominator that links all citizens.[36] The emperor cult served the same purpose. It was the "superglue" that held the empire together.[37]

Imperial cult observance presented difficulty for Christ followers. To what extent should they honor Caesar? Should they use coins bearing Caesar's image, consider him divine, participate in festivities held in his name? When believers abstained from cult-sponsored activities, Roman authorities logically suspected the Christ movement of subversion.

There is evidence suggesting that some Christ followers never fully abandoned their involvement (1 Cor 10:14–22). This was a matter of concern for the apostle Paul who expected believers to separate from these alliances. The author of Revelation urges his charges in the Lycus Valley to desist from all cultic participation, lest they compromise their commitment to Christ. Instead, they were to acknowledge and sing that Christ alone was worthy of worship (Rev 4–5).

1.3.8 Associations/Guilds

Based on the similarity between first-century churches and synagogues, most scholars until recently assumed the former was modeled on the latter. But in the past two decades a new consensus has emerged that Greco-Roman voluntary associations/guilds served as the template.[38] Words usually associated with the church, i.e., *ekklēsia, koinonia, diakonos, presbyteros,*

---

35. Virgil, *Aen.* 6.791–96; Horace, *Ep.* 2.1.15–16.

36. Some Americans believe the United States is a divinely created nation. Others do not. But most show a modicum of respect as noted above. When NFL player Colin Kaepernick protested and "took a knee" as the "Star Spangled Banner" was sung, he was ostracized and lost his job.

37. Crossan and Reed, *In Search of Paul*, 142.

38. Ascough, "What Are They Saying," 207.

epískopos, were first used in conjunction with guilds and associations.[39] Documentary evidence strongly suggests that churches in the first century were viewed and treated as associations.[40]

An association was essentially a local club whose members had a common interest. Some focused on a particular occupation or trade. Others were philosophical and provided a venue for intellectual debate. Still others were comprised of those with common ethnic roots or cultic beliefs. Regardless of their purpose, they were religious and dedicated to favored gods.[41]

Nearly everyone, even the poorest of the poor, belonged to one or more voluntary associations, which ranged in membership from less than a dozen to ten times that amount. Depending on its financial stability, the wealth of its sponsors, and the size of its membership, its meetings were held in homes, rented quarters, a local temple, or an association-owned building. Clubs convened on a monthly basis. Associations offered their members a sense of belonging and identity, and connected them with patrons.

Regardless of their respective focus, all groups had one thing in common—they were "supper clubs." Their banquets, which lasted three to four hours each, included two major sections: 1) the full course meal called a *deipnon*, and 2) a *symposion*, known as "second tables," a prolonged period of leisurely drinking, desserts, entertainment, group singing, and conversation on a favorite subject. The two segments were joined together by a ceremonial libation, i.e., a drink offering of unmixed wine, that was poured out to the emperor and the club's patron deities. Singing a hymn of praise accompanied the libation and paved the way for the *symposion* activities.[42] Petronius mentions that community singing took place during the meal and solos were offered during the *symposion*.[43]

---

39. Corley, *Maranatha*, 12.

40. The reader is referred to three essential and groundbreaking publications that make the case for the associations serving as the model for local churches, based on extensive research of primary sources, including recent translations of inscriptions, association manuals, minutes of meetings, and titles: Harland, *Associations*; Ascough, et al., *Associations*; Kloppenborg, *Christ's Associations*.

41. Kloppenborg and Wilson, *Voluntary Associations*, 18–22.

42. See Smith, *From Symposium*, 191–214 for an excellent discussion of voluntary associations and banquets.

43. Petronius, *Satyr.* 23.1–2; 70.7; 109.6.

One's status in society determined which banquet one attended. Elites ate with elites and peasants with peasants. Each table had an imputed ranking attached to it and an invitee reclined accordingly with the host and patrons having the best seats and the others in descending order. Since a person's identity was linked to an association and where he reclined, the banquet reflected and reinforced one's status in society.

Rome imposed two obligations on all associations: 1) They must honor the emperor with a libation at its meals, and 2) They must not participate in any subversive actions against the state. Rome viewed banquets as another tool to keep members in line with the empire's social agenda. If an association did not follow the rules, it might be dismantled and its officers disciplined.

Mimicking the structure of the voluntary association, Christ groups met regularly to eat a meal and participate in after dinner activities. But instead of pouring out a libation to Caesar, they raised a cup in Jesus' name and sang praises to him, not to Caesar and the Roman gods. In doing so, they offered themselves fully to the Lord. Emulating their master, they saw themselves as being poured out for Christ like a drink offering, (Luke 22:17–20; Phil 2:17; 2 Tim 4:6). During the symposion they sang more songs to him and ministered as the Spirit moved (1 Cor 14:26).[44] By their nature they were songs of resistance that challenged Caesar and the empire.

Most church members had previously held membership in pagan associations and some continued to do so. When Paul discovered this, he demanded that they stop immediately, believing Christ deserved undivided loyalty: "You cannot drink the cup of the Lord and the cup of demons. You cannot partake of the table of the Lord and the table of demons" (1 Cor 10:21). Their new identity was "in Christ." They had a new fictive family, not based on common ethnicity, nationality, trade, or status. All were welcomed to attend and recline at the Lord's table, Jews, gentiles, slave, free, male, female, rich, poor, saints, and sinners.

1.3.9 Honor and Shame

Honor and shame were two fundamental values that dominated and shaped behavior in the Mediterranean world. Honor was determined by cultural standards and was not self-ascribed. It was based on the court of public opinion, i.e., how others perceived and esteemed a person. Consequently, it

44. Taussig, *In the Beginning*, 104.

was precarious and could be lost. Most strove to maintain their reputation, status, and family name. Honorable activities included showing respect to elders, being courageous in battle, supporting one's patron, following decorum, marrying within one's own class, and bowing to images of the emperor.

Shame was the opposite. Activities and behaviors that did not conform to cultural expectations brought disgrace to an individual and their family. For example, it was considered a shame for a man to wear his hair long or to take a seat of honor without an invitation, or for an adult woman to go outdoors with her head uncovered. Such actions brought shame and loss of respect. One might liken shame to the modern equivalent of "losing face" or finding oneself in an embarrassing situation. Once reputation was soiled, it was hard to reclaim.[45]

Not wanting to suffer shame, people were motivated to conform to societal expectations. Rome took advantage of this value system and used it as a tool to dominate their subjects.

To join the Christ movement brought shame on the person and his/her family. To turn away from one's family traditions, religion, gods, patrons, meals at the pagan temples, and to proclaim unqualified allegiance to Jesus and his kingdom and not to Caesar and the empire, stained one's reputation among peers and brought reproach upon one's kin. It marked the Christ follower as someone out of step with the norms.

Worst yet, Christ followers pledged their loyalty to one whom Roman and Jewish authorities considered to be an insurrectionist and deserving of crucifixion, the most disgraceful and humiliating form of punishment. Nothing was more shameful than hanging naked in public view.[46]

45. Eastern cultures continue to observe honor and shame protocols. For example, I recently read of a father who murdered his daughter because she had a sexual relationship with a non-Hindu. It was dubbed an "honor killing." Based on Western standards of right and wrong, he committed an egregious felony and was deserving of arrest, trial, and punishment. Based on his native culture, however, his daughter shamed the family. To regain the respect of his peers he performed an honorable act. Likewise, we might think back to WW II and kamikaze pilots who committed suicide missions by crashing their planes into an enemy target rather than return to base in disgrace without a kill. According to their culture they did the honorable thing.

46. It was not that Christ had died like everyone else, but he was crucified. This carried imperial connotations. He was shamed and humiliated as an enemy of the state. As the well-known hymn suggests, "On a hill far away stood an old rugged Cross the emblem of suffering and shame."

The idea of a Jew following a crucified messiah was scandalous, and the thought of a gentile following a debased convict was absurd (1 Cor 1:23; Heb 12:2).

Christ followers, however, turned the honor and shame concept on its head. Jesus' disciples were not to seek honor for themselves like the gentiles (Luke 22:24–26) or to be conformed to the world's standards (Rom 12:1–2). Instead, they sang about Jesus' crucifixion as his finest hour that should be celebrated not shamed. The lyrics portrayed Rome as a bully that used force to silence its opposition, which touched a chord with the oppressed who themselves were victims of Roman brutality. The songs did not stop with Jesus' crucifixion; they sang how God raised Jesus to life and thus, reversed Rome's actions. The resurrection called into question Rome's power over life and death.

1.3.10 Roman Propaganda

Rome's imperial publicity campaign continually promoted the idea that it had favored status with the gods and was on a god-given mission.

In contrast, Christ followers painted a different picture of the empire. Matthew's Gospel depicts Satan as the authority behind the empires of the world, including Rome (Matt 4:8). The book of Revelation (ca. 95 CE) identifies Rome as "Babylon" because Rome destroyed Jerusalem and its temple in 70 CE just as ancient Babylon had done in 586 BCE.[47] Using political satire John's apocalyptic vision exposes Rome as an agent of Satan and includes songs with satirical lyrics to lampoon and depict the empire in the worst possible light.[48] Vearncombe labels Rev 17–18 an epic song in which an angel takes the visionary on a journey where he sees a giant sex worker (a harlot) riding the back of a grotesque monster (beast) with seven heads. The angel identifies the giant woman as Babylon the Great, the city that holds sway over the nations of the world.[49] John's songs in Revelation

---

47. Kraybill, *Apocalypse*, 29. First Peter also uses the cryptic reference in his letter to the suffering Jewish Christ followers. In more contemporary times, Rastafarians used the term "Babylon" to describe the corrupt government of Jamaica in the 1960s. They believed chanting Reggae lyrics broke the power of "Babylon" over the oppressed.

48. One might say that Revelation was the first-century equivalent of the popular "Babylon Bee."

49. Vearncombe et al., *After Jesus*, 277–78.

are like a modern-day editorial cartoon that uses caricatures to ridicule a politician, dictator, or rogue state.[50]

This song mocks Rome's military power, its assertion of manifest destiny, and economic control over the world. It likewise rails against the city's violence and reminds the hearers that nothing escapes the eyes of God who will avenge his people. The lyrist imagines Rome on fire and watches as an angel announces, "Babylon the Great is fallen." And again, "Alas! Alas! Great city! City clothed in fine linen, purple and scarlet cloth! City adorned with gold ornaments, and precious stones, and pearls! In a single hour your vast wealth has vanished!" (Rev 18:2, 16–17).

In the vision God's long-suffering people are delivered and then rewarded as genuine peace prevails on the earth under Christ's reign.[51]

Since these events never actually happened except in the imagination of the visionary, how should one interpret Revelation and its songs? What did the recipients think when the messenger delivered the Apocalypse to the house churches and possibly sang these passages to them? A. Y. Collins believes the songs were intended to provide a catharsis experience for those who had suffered so much at the hands of imperial powers.[52] They were a way of escaping violence—if only momentarily—as they were read or performed.[53]

1.4 Closing Thoughts

The old adage, "the winners write history" was certainly true in the first century. The "majority report" is the official record that makes it into the history books. The masses coalesce around this narrative and find their identity in relationship to it.

Rome, the world's most powerful empire, propagated the myth that it was under divine orders to bring peace to the world and that Caesar was the savior. It used all means possible to promote its story, including social stratification, patriotism, patronage, the values of honor and shame, military might, propaganda, events, voluntary association meetings and banquets, songs, inscriptions, coinage, and the imperial cult, among others.

50. Koester, *Revelation*, 155.

51. Vearncombe et al., *After Jesus*, 277; Kraybill, *Apocalypse*, 21.

52. Collins, *Crisis and Catharsis*, 152–54, 161, 166.

53. Many of the pre-Civil War slave songs included hidden transcripts or symbolic lyrics that gave slaves hope of a better future.

While the winners "write" the official version of history, it is not always the most correct or complete version. Take for example, the American story. Until relatively recent times, it contained glowing accounts of American conquests. Columbus, the Pilgrims, presidents Washington, Jefferson, Lincoln, and JFK, generals Custer, Lee, Grant, and MacArthur, and a host of others were portrayed as bigger than life and true heroes who fought for "truth, justice, and the American way." They were more like supermen than mere mortals.

The official report, however, only contained part of the story. Other narratives were told and passed down by the losers, marginalized and the disenfranchised—Native Americans, slaves, migrant farmworkers, Chinese laborers, Welsh and Scottish miners, blacks under Jim Crow, and women suffragettes, among others—who recounted experiences of disease, confiscation of land and property, poor wages and living conditions, racism, persecutions, and lynching, sterilization, police brutality, and voter suppression, often enforced on the orders of the winners.

Each group shared its respective version of history through the use of long recitations, poems, and songs.[54] After generations, a "people's history" emerged that eventually found its way into print as a "minority report."

Similarly, the Gospels, Epistles, and Apocalypse, and the songs embedded in them, constituted a minority report that offered a counter-narrative to Rome's version of events. The songs, in particular, with their rhythmic lyrics, kept the alternative truth alive in the hearts and minds of Christ followers. Although Rome executed Jesus as reported, Israel's God raised him back to life and exalted him to a position of supreme authority. The empire did not have the last word. As a result, Jesus and not Caesar was Lord of all. The songs invited people to switch allegiance and declare their fidelity to Jesus who was bringing a new world order. He alone had the divine prerogative to speak and rule on God's behalf.

The early church communities embraced egalitarianism, ate meals together, and sang songs that praised Christ and his kingdom. The Christ movement gave birth to christological songs, which sustained the

---

54. Thomas Faltysek, a former student, recently told me about Te Ata (1895–1995). A member of the Chickasaw Nation, she was the earliest songster and storyteller to share publicly the unknown version of her people's history, which at many points conflicted with the "official" government account. In 1933, she performed at the first state dinner given by President Franklin Roosevelt. Over the next four decades, Te Ata used songs and drama to carry her message throughout the United States, Europe, and South America.

movement. As believers sang these songs of resistance that challenged Caesar and empire, they were emboldened to live for Christ no matter the cost.

CHAPTER 2

In the Beginning Was the Song

When you come together, each has a song . . . (1 Cor 14:26)

SOON AFTER THE BIRTH of the Jesus movement believers sang praises to him as their exalted Lord (Acts 2:47; 16:25). As Powell observes,

> Before the Gospels, before the Epistles, before Josephus, even before Q, Christians were writing hymns about Jesus. A few of them even get quoted in the Bible. The hymns were there before anyone tried to write a narrative of Jesus' life or reflect systematically about his identity or message.[1]

We might say, "In the beginning was the song." Nothing preceded the song, except word-of-mouth stories told about Jesus by his followers, beginning at Jerusalem and spreading throughout the Roman Empire. Based on these oral accounts, believers composed lyrical hymns and spiritual songs that reflected their heartfelt devotion to Jesus and their beliefs about him.

By the time the Epistles and the Gospels were penned (mid-50s to mid-90s CE), the churches had been singing christological songs for decades. Several NT writers quoted and embedded portions of these lyrics in their correspondence for illustrative purposes or to drive a point home. These lone references give us access to the more popular songs that survived the test of time.

---

1. Powell, *Jesus as a Figure*, 184.

21

Hymns found in Luke's Gospel focus mainly on the events surrounding the birth of Jesus (*Magnificat*, Luke 1:46-55; *Benedictus*, 1:68-79; *Gloria Excelsis*, 2:14; and *Nunc Dimittis*, 2:29-32). The Prologue of the Gospel of John (1:1–18) is a song that speaks of Christ's preexistence and earthly glory. Other embedded hymns appear in several Epistles (Phil 2:6-11; Col 1:15-20; 1 Tim 3:16; Heb 1:1-4; 1 Pet 3:18-21), and even more find their way into the Apocalypse (Rev 4-5; 15; 17–18). We will examine each as it appears in the canonical text and not in the chronological order in which it was written.[2] This approach will be more familiar to a wider audience, but still allows this author to deal with scholarly issues in the footnotes.

Christian hymns were not sung strictly in private since they were part of mealtime and symposium activities, to which outside guests were invited. Therefore, a hymn's lyrical content did not remain behind four walls since attendees carried them out the doors. One must ask, "Did peasant Christ followers sing hymns while they worked in the fields?" If so, they reached the ears of unbelievers, opening opportunities to share the gospel and also leading to confrontations with opponents.

Christological hymns asserted that the god of Judaism was the highest god and that Jesus was his unique son who alone was authorized to speak on his behalf. Their subversive lyrics challenged the empire's authority and Caesar's boast that he owned the prerogative to rule the world.

Christ followers were not the first to use songs in worship. For centuries Jews and pagans sang to their respective deities. The church simply adopted and adapted the custom for themselves.

The pattern or structure of their songs was no different than others; only the lyrics were unique and focused on Jesus, rather than Caesar; thus, they were considered dangerous and seditious.

In this chapter we will examine the various kinds of music the church used to worship Christ.

2.1 Singing as an Early Church Practice

In his Letter to the Corinthians, Paul discusses how believers should conduct themselves in worship and then gives them some guidelines to follow: "When you come together, each has a hymn, a lesson, a revelation,

---

2. The undisputed Pauline Epistles were the first written texts about Christ and the church, followed by the remaining Epistles, the Gospels, the Acts account of Christianity's spread, and the book of Revelation.

a tongue, or an interpretation. Let all things be done for building up" (1 Cor 14:26). One notices immediately that singing leads the list of various worship practices.[3] The phrase "each has a hymn" (ἕκαστος ψαλμὸν ἔχε) can be translated, "one has a psalm".[4] Since Hellenized Jewish Christ followers were a part of the Corinthian church, one would expect them to sing psalms from eschatological and christological perspectives. Psalms were usually accompanied by instrumentation and "cast in poetic form," making them "easy to memorize and put to music."[5]

Likewise, Paul instructs another congregation, traditionally identified as Ephesians, to maintain civility at the Lord's Supper, and avoid excess and rowdiness during worship:

> Do not get drunk with wine, for that is debauchery; but be filled with the Spirit, as you sing psalms and hymns and spiritual songs among yourselves, singing and making melody to the Lord in your hearts, giving thanks to God the Father at all times and for everything in the name of our Lord Jesus Christ. (Eph 5:18-20)

The Spirit's infilling, Paul advises, is the path to God-honoring praise. The list of worship songs includes psalms (ψαλμός), hymns (ὕμνοις), and spiritual songs (ᾠδαῖς). As with 1 Cor 14:26, "psalms" is listed first among the expressions of worship.

In his letter to the "twelve tribes in the dispersion," James closes with a series of commands, including, "Are any cheerful? They should sing songs (ψαλλέτω) of praise" (5:13). The setting is clearly a worship service where activities such as prayer, confession of sin, laying on the hands, and church discipline take place (5:13-20). The term ψαλλέτω, translated "sing songs," likely refers to singing lyrics with musical accompaniment, i.e., psalms.

2.2 The Nature of Psalms, Hymns, and Spiritual Songs

No scholarly consensus exists over the precise meaning of the terms "psalms," "hymns," and "songs" but all agree that Christ followers were not

---

3. Paul personally practices his own advice: "What should I do then? I will pray with the spirit, but I will pray with the mind also; *I will sing* praise with the spirit, but *I will sing praise* with the mind also" (1 Cor 14:15). Singing was part of Paul's worship experience.

4. Hengel, "Hymn and Christology," 174, asserts that Hellenized Jewish believers understood *psalmos* to refer to songs from the LXX edition of the Psalter.

5. Anderson, *Out of the Depths*, 21.

the first to use them in worship. This begs the question, "What forms of music do these terms represent, and where did they originate?"

2.2.1 The Synonymous Theory

According to F. F. Bruce, the apostle Paul used these terms interchangeably without intending any clear distinction between them.[6] Lincoln observes the LXX uses all these same words to describe songs in general and do not represent three separate genres.[7] Thielman asserts "it is probably a mistake to distinguish the terms sharply from one another" especially in Ephesians where redundancy is common.[8] Josephus remarks that King David taught the Levites to sing "hymns," but this was an obvious reference to Psalms.[9]

An example of how one term can be used synonymously for another is found in the account of the Last Supper. Jews sang sections of the "Hallel" (Pss 113–118) as part of their Passover ritual. They closed each feast with Pss 115–118 before leaving the table and departing. Jesus and his disciples followed this tradition; yet, the Gospel accounts say, "When they had sung the hymn, they went out to the Mount of Olives" (Matt 26:30; Mark 14:26). Here psalm and hymn are the same.

2.2.2 The Distinction Theory

Other scholars, however, believe psalms, hymns, and songs, at least in Eph 5:19, designate three different kinds of lyrics.[10] According to this view, a "psalm" refers to a selection from the Psalter with musical accompaniment.[11] Since the first Christ followers were Jewish, they continued worshiping according to tradition and sang psalms both in the synagogue and the house church.

---

6. Bruce, *Colossians*, 158–59. Moo, *Colossians*, 289; O'Brien, *Ephesians*, 394; Dunn, *Epistles*, 238–39 also hold to this view.

7. Lincoln, *Ephesians*, 346, also notes that these three terms are used without distinction to translate Hebrew Psalm titles into Greek (LXX). For instance, Ps 92, "A Psalm. A Song for the Sabbath Day."

8. Thielman, *Ephesians*, 361.

9. Josephus, *Ant.* 7.12.3.

10. Arnold, *Ephesians*, 353.

11. Hengel, "Hymn and Christology," 174.

By contrast, the term "hymn" (ὕμνοις) speaks of a musical paean of praise or prayer offered by pagans, traditional Jews, and Christ followers to their favorite god(s).[12] Hymns were not exclusive to Yahweh's chosen people and were common to the Greco-Roman culture.

Odes (ᾠδαῖς), or poetic songs, convey a lyricist's thoughts and passions about a particular person or subject, and address directly the person or subject of the ode.[13] Christ followers likely composed odes that were similar to modern-day odes and folk songs but focused on Jesus and his kingdom. Long before the Christian era, others employed the same genre to express their heartfelt emotions. Pindar (517–437 BCE), one of the great Greek odists, wrote a series of victory odes to honor the heroes of the Olympian-style games associated with four Panhellenic festivals.[14]

Most educated people in the Roman Empire during the reign of Augustus were familiar with Horace's Odes—four volumes of Latin lyric poems written between 23–15 BCE—that dealt with popular topics, e.g., ethics, virtue, sociopolitical issues, and development of the spirit.[15] Some odes were addressed directly to Mercury (1.10), Bacchus (2.19), Augustus (3.5), Apollo (4.6), among other deities. But most were simply stories or commentary on a popular topic.

2.2.3 Meaning Based on Context

While none of the earliest Christian odes are found in the NT text, the discovery of the Odes of Solomon, containing forty-two songs and written toward the end of the first century CE, provides some examples.[16] They are

12. Arnold, *Ephesians*, 353.

13. The famous poet John Keats (1795–1821) wrote six lyric odes in 1819, including the "Ode to a Nightingale" and "Ode on a Grecian Urn." On a lighter and more contemporary note, who of a certain age can forget *The Ode to Billie Joe*, the story-song about Billie Joe McAllister's suicidal plunge off the Tallahatchie Bridge that occurred after he and his unnamed girlfriend (the narrator of the ode) toss something into the river? Although written and sung in 1967, those who heard it played on the radio that year still remember its tune and refrain. The power of an ode is its simplicity, making it easy to be retained in memory.

14. Baker, "Some Aspects of Pindar's Style," 100–110, discusses Pindar's fame and his odic style of writing.

15. See Lyons, *Music in the Odes*, for a full-length discussion of the musical performances of Horace's Odes and their popularity during the age of Augustus.

16. Corwin, "St. Ignatius," 71–80, notes that Ignatius of Antioch (ca. 100 CE) quotes eleven of the odes, dating the Odes of Solomon to the late-first century or early-second

essentially Jewish in tenor and recount events and attitudes surrounding Messiah Jesus' life, death, and exaltation.[17] They also offer God praise, speak of suffering, perseverance, fruit of holiness, God's love, judgment, salvation, and an array of other topics. Each ends with the word "Hallelujah."[18]

Which position is the correct one? Most scholars agree that the NT often uses the terms psalms, hymns, and songs synonymously.[19] However, at other times, depending on the audience and context, they were used in a narrower sense to describe a specific kind of song. Toward the end of the second century, for example, Clement of Alexandria mentioned that hymns, psalms, chants, and doxologies were distinct from each other, but all were part of corporate worship.[20]

Context and audience are the key considerations when interpreting the terms. Jews and gentiles often used the same term differently. In the Last Supper scenario mentioned above where hymn and psalm seem to be synonymous, another explanation is possible. The Markan account, likely written to gentile converts in Rome (ca. 70 CE), with little understanding of Jewish Passover customs, might have used "hymn" instead "psalm," because his audience was familiar with singing a hymn to a deity at the close of a typical gentile cultic meal.[21]

Context is also important when it comes to identifying odes. Christ followers obviously wrote songs that mimicked the traditional odic style (e.g., *Odes of Solomon*). But odes may additionally refer to songs composed spontaneously as the Holy Spirit moved upon worshipers. In his letter to the Ephesians Paul labels these songs as ᾠδαῖς πνευματικαῖς ("spiritual songs"). One finds another occurrence in Revelation, when the heavenly worshipers break into extemporaneous praise: "They sing a new song [*ode*]" (Rev 5:9). The twentieth-century charismatic movement of the 1960s and 1970s was characterized by such phenomena. To an outsider a typical gathering may have resembled a Corinthian celebration or a drunken Ephesian songfest.

---

century CE. Charlesworth, *Pseudepigrapha* 2, 725, 727, agrees.

17. *Ode* 42:11 speaks specifically of God raising Jesus out of *sheol*.

18. Charlesworth, *Pseudepigrapha* 2, 725–71, offers an excellent background on the *Odes of Solomon* and a complete and excellent translation of the odes.

19. Some Psalms are described as songs of praise in their superscriptions. Many of the *Odes of Solomon* fall under the same category. 1 Macc 4:54 uses the word "songs" to describe Psalms and 2 Macc 10:7–8 uses the word "hymns" for the same.

20. Clem. Al., *Strom.* 6.113.3.

21. Lührmann, *Das Markusevangelium*, 24.

In conclusion, one must be careful to interpret the terms "psalms," "hymns," and "spiritual songs" with the context in mind.

2.3 The Origin of Jewish Songs

Since the beginning of time, God's creatures, heavenly and earthly, have raised their voices in praise to Yahweh. According to Hebrew Scriptures, singing can be traced to angelic worship at the time of creation. God asks Job, "Where were you when I laid the foundation of the earth? . . . When the morning stars sang together, and all the sons of God shouted for joy?" (Job 38:4, 7).

In his heavenly vision Isaiah describes seraphim raising their voices in praise, singing, "Holy, holy, holy is the Lord of host; the whole earth is full of his glory" (Isa 6:3). John, the revelator encounters similar angelic worship scenes in his Patmos visions (Rev 4–5).

Among God's earthly people, Moses and the Hebrews sang during the Exodus as they passed through the Red Sea (Exod 15:1–19). The song begins:

> I will sing to the Lord,
> for he is highly exalted.
> Both horse and driver
> he has hurled into the sea.
> The Lord is my strength and my defense;
> he has become my salvation.
> He is my God, and I will praise him,
> my father's God, and I will exalt him. (vv. 1–2)

Subsequently, Miriam and the women joined the chorus and danced for joy as they marched to freedom (Exod 15:20–21).

During their trek across the wilderness, the Israelites arrived at a place called Beer, where God instructed Moses, "Gather the people together, and I will give them water. Then Israel sang this song:

> Spring up, O well!—Sing to it!—
> the well that the leaders sank,
> that the nobles of the people dug,
> with the scepter, with the staff." (Num 21:17–18)

After their devastating defeat of the Canaanites, Deborah and Barak, two of Israel's judges, marched victoriously through the city with captives in tow and sang, "Hear, O kings; give ear, O princes; to the Lord I will sing, I will make melody to the Lord, the God of Israel" (Judg 5:2, 12). Judges 5 includes the entirety of the lyrics of this ode-like song (Judg 5:1–12).

When young David slew Goliath, King Saul sent him into battle with the Philistines. His success led to fame. Upon his return, the townspeople greeted him with "songs of joy and with musical instruments. And the women sang to one another as they made merry, 'Saul has killed his thousands, and David his ten thousands'" (1 Sam 18:6).

Not all songs in the Hebrew Bible spoke of victory; some warned of defeat. After transferring leadership to Joshua before the Israelites entered the promised land, God dictated a song to Moses and instructed him to write it down and recite it to his people.

> The Lord said to Moses, "Soon you will lie down with your ancestors. Then this people will begin to prostitute themselves to the foreign gods in their midst, the gods of the land into which they are going; they will forsake me, breaking my covenant that I have made with them. My anger will be kindled against them in that day. I will forsake them and hide my face from them; they will become easy prey, and many terrible troubles will come upon them. In that day they will say, 'Have not these troubles come upon us because our God is not in our midst?' On that day I will surely hide my face on account of all the evil they have done by turning to other gods. Now therefore write this song, and teach it to the Israelites; put it in their mouths, in order that this song may be a witness for me against the Israelites." (Deut 31:16–19)

Moses did as instructed. The lyrics, found in Deut 32:1–43, served a prophetic function and warned the nation of judgment should they break covenant with God.

2.4 Israel's Three Song Books

The Hebrew Scriptures contain three hymnbooks: Psalms, Song of Solomon, and Lamentations.

2.4.1 The Psalter

Several composers—David, Asaph, Solomon, Korah and his sons, among others—penned the Psalms during the time of the monarchy (ca. 1040–537

BCE). Psalms are mainly Hebrew poetry put to music and written for every occasion: Passovers, sabbath celebrations, and deaths. They include praises to God, cries for deliverance, prayers of repentance and mercy, requests for God to judge their enemies.

The collected and collated songs became Israel's basic hymnbook, the Psalter. These musical numbers kept God's vision alive for his people even in the hardest of times.

Several Psalms exhorted God's people to "Sing to the Lord a new song" for his mighty work in creation, or delivering them from enemies, or keeping covenant with the nation despite its transgressions (Ps 33:3; 96:1; 98:1; 149:1; 105:2). In anticipation of victory in battle, King David prayed, "Put a new song in my mouth, a song of praise to our God" (Ps 40:3). New songs were composed for every kind of occasion and sung "in the assembly of the faithful" (Ps 149:1).

Singing was a corporate affair. "Praise the Lord! Praise God in his sanctuary!" the Psalmist commands (Ps 150:1a).

> Praise him with trumpet sound;
>   praise him with lute and harp!
> Praise him with tambourine and dance;
>   praise him with strings and pipe!
> Praise him with clanging cymbals;
>   praise him with loud clashing cymbals!
> Let everything that breathes praise the Lord!
> Praise the Lord! (vv. 2–6)

On another occasion the people are instructed to:

> Make a joyful noise to the Lord, all the earth;
>   break forth into joyous song and sing praises.
> Sing praises to the Lord with the lyre,
>   with the lyre and the sound of melody.
> With trumpets and the sound of the horn
>   make a joyful noise before the King, the Lord. (Ps 98:4–6)

Of the 36,000 Levites chosen to minister to God's people, 4,000 were musicians (1 Chr 15:16; 23:5). Some were specifically songsters: "These are the men whom David put in charge of the service of song in the house of the Lord" after the ark came to rest there. Serving in the tabernacle until a permanent house of God was built in Jerusalem (1 Chr 6:31–32), they formed choirs to sing in the presence of God and lead the people in singing

(1 Chr 13:8; 15:16–24; 16:4–6). Once the temple of Solomon was completed, the tradition continued (2 Chr 5:11–14).

During the time of the divided kingdom temple worship was in disarray (2 Chr 20:22–24, 26–28), until Jehoiada "assigned the care of the house of the Lord to the Levitical priests whom David had organized to be in charge of the house of the Lord, to offer burnt offerings to the Lord, as it is written in the law of Moses, with rejoicing and with singing, according to the order of David" (2 Chr 23:18). During the national revival under King Hezekiah, worship was once again restored:

> He stationed the Levites in the house of the Lord with cymbals, harps, and lyres, according to the commandment of David and of Gad the king's seer and of the prophet Nathan, for the commandment was from the Lord through his prophets. The Levites stood with the instruments of David, and the priests with the trumpets. Then Hezekiah commanded that the burnt offering be offered on the altar. When the burnt offering began, the song to the Lord began also, and the trumpets, accompanied by the instruments of King David of Israel. The whole assembly worshiped, the singers sang, and the trumpeters sounded; all this continued until the burnt offering was finished. When the offering was finished, the king and all who were present with him bowed down and worshiped. King Hezekiah and the officials commanded the Levites to sing praises to the Lord with the words of David and of the seer Asaph. They sang praises with gladness, and they bowed down and worshiped. (2 Chr 30:25–30)

2.4.2 Song of Solomon

According to Israel's archival history Solomon wrote 1,005 songs (1 Kgs 4:32). The Hebrew Scriptures contain only a few of them, but the most famous—the Song of Solomon or Canticles (Song 1:1)—is considered the greatest love song of all time and metaphorically speaks of God's unconditional love for Israel, his wife.

2.4.3 Lamentations

The story of Judah's moral decline and exile to Babylon reminded Israel of the warning song God gave to Moses (Deut 32:1–43). They were now facing judgment.

An unknown lyricist recalls those desperate years in his song of despair:

> By the rivers of Babylon—
> > there we sat down and there we wept
> > when we remembered Zion.
> On the willows there
> > we hung up our harps.
> For there our captors
> > asked us for songs,
> > and our tormentors asked for mirth, saying,
> > "Sing us one of the songs of Zion!"
> How could we sing the Lord's song
> > in a foreign land? (Ps 137:1–4)

The book of Lamentations contains five mournful songs that reflect Israel's emotional state after its fall to Babylon. The title in Hebrew is 'ekah and means "how." It is the first word in three of the five dirges (1:1; 2:1; 4:1). The LXX translates 'ekah into the Greek qinot, meaning "lamentations" from which it derives its title. Despite numerous cries of woe, Lamentations is not without hope and anticipates that God will deliver his people. His faithfulness is great, and his mercies are fresh every morning (3:21–26). Acknowledging God's eternal reign, the last lament cries out for God to restore the kingdom to Israel (5: 19, 21).

2.5 Second Temple Worship

When Persian King Cyrus defeated Babylon in 538 BCE, he called on Jews to return to their homeland and rebuild the Jerusalem temple (2 Chr 36:22–23). Led by Zerubbabel, 42,360 exiles made the journey, including "two hundred male and female singers" (Ezra 2:64–65).[22]

---

22. Nehemiah later discovered a genealogy listing those who returned in the first wave. They included 148 singers who were "the descendants of Asaph" (Neh 7:44) and another group of 245 male and female singers (Neh 7:67).

When the builders laid the foundation of the temple of the Lord, the priests in their vestments were stationed to praise the Lord with trumpets, and the Levites, the sons of Asaph, with cymbals, according to the directions of King David of Israel; and they sang responsively, praising and giving thanks to the Lord, "For he is good, for his steadfast love endures forever toward Israel." (Ezra 3:10–12)

A second wave returned during the reign of King Artaxerxes and included "some of the priests and Levites, the singers and gatekeepers, and the temple servants" (Ezra 7:7).

A third wave returned with Nehemiah to build a wall around Jerusalem. After its completion the people gathered to dedicate it to the Lord and celebrate "with rejoicing, with thanksgivings and with singing, with cymbals, harps, and lyres. The companies of the singers gathered together from the circuit around Jerusalem and from the villages of the Netophathites; also from Beth-gilgal and from the region of Geba and Azmaveth; for the singers had built for themselves villages around Jerusalem" (Neh 12:27–29; see 45–47).

Singing songs in worship was built into the fabric of Israel's history. The remnant that returned to Palestine continued to live under Persian rule. Nehemiah and the other native leaders served at the pleasure of the king.[23] Alexander the Great defeated the Persians and Palestine became part of the Macedonian Empire (333 BCE).

During the intertestamental period, the Jews continued to use Psalms in their temple.[24] Ben Sira (ca. 180 BCE) speaks of the importance of Psalms of David for temple worship (Sir 47:9–10) and adds how they were still used in his day: "Then the singers praised him with their voices in sweet and full-toned melody" (Sir 50:18).

The Qumran community treasured the Psalms. This is attested to by the discovery of the DSS, which contained 39 different manuscripts or fragments of Psalms, the largest number of any canonical books, e.g., Deuteronomy with 31 and Isaiah with 22 manuscripts, respectively. Scroll 11 QPsa contained nearly one-third of the Psalter.[25]

---

23. Most Jews did not return to Palestine. Their story is recorded in the book of Esther.

24. Charlesworth, *Jesus*, 105–6.

25. Flint, "Psalms and Psalters," 233–72.

Many Psalms included cries for God to right injustices against his people. Imprecatory Psalms railed against Israel's leaders and its enemies. While under domination of foreign powers, Jewish writers produced a wealth of apocalyptic literature (including poems/hymns) that resisted and challenged the grand narrative of the oppressor and spoke of a day when God would restore the kingdom. These songs motivated covenant keepers to remain faithful, despite hardships and persecution. Deliverance was always just around the corner.

God's people took solace by turning to their three hymnbooks: Psalms, Song of Solomon, and Lamentations. Whatever their circumstances—joy, sadness, victory, defeat, feast, famine, freedom, bondage—their songs provided ways to express their feelings and help them move on with God.

2.6 Christ Followers and the Psalms

The NT never quotes or cites the Song of Solomon or the Book of Lamentations; however, the first Jewish Christ followers continued to sing Psalms. From NT texts one discovers that certain Psalms were sung more than others, particularly ones that announced God's reign over the nations and identified the king of Israel as God's son and earthly representative. The first believers interpreted these songs of Israel from a messianic perspective and recognized Jesus as the one whom God anointed and set over his universal kingdom.[26] The writers of the Gospels, Letters, and Apocrypha quoted frequently from certain Psalms, e.g., Ps 2 (nine times), Ps 69, (twelve times), and Ps 110 (thirty-two times), among others. They cited Psalms to support their theological claims about Jesus. By adopting these songs as their own, early believers set themselves on a collision course with Rome. They took lyrics that were written a thousand years before and interpreted them as if they spoke of the superiority of Jesus over all others, including Caesar and the pantheon of gods. This was an act of resistance.

The book of Acts gives the first glimpse how Christ followers in Jerusalem sang and interpreted Psalms. After the Sanhedrin released Peter and John from jail, the disciples reported back to the church and the gathered saints broke into a spontaneous rendition of Ps 2:1-2 (Acts 4:23-31).

---

26. Chilton, *Pure Kingdom*, 31–55. Jesus' own understanding of the kingdom was drawn partially from the Royal Psalms.

Psalm 2 is divided into four stanzas and describes: 1) Yahweh's rule over the nations, 2) his anointed king, 3) a pagan rebellion, and 4) God's response.

Stanza 1 opens with the surrounding nations conspiring to plan a surprise attack against Israel and its ruler. The Psalmist ponders their rationale for launching an unwinnable assault, and concludes they wanted to be free of the restrictions that Israel had placed on them.

> Why do the nations conspire,
>> and the peoples plot in vain?
> The kings of the earth set themselves,
>> and the rulers take counsel together,
>> against the Lord and his anointed, saying,
> "Let us burst their bonds asunder,
>> and cast their cords from us." (Ps 2:1–3)

In stanza 2 God initially laughs in scorn at their folly, but his amusement turns to holy anger. An attack against Israel and her anointed king is an attack against God.[27]

> He who sits in the heavens laughs;
>> the Lord has them in derision.
> Then he will speak to them in his wrath,
>> and terrify them in his fury, saying,
> "I have set my king on Zion, my holy hill." (vv. 4–6)

In stanza 3 Israel's king speaks up and confirms his favored status with God, and then recalls how God adopted him as a son (v. 7) and offered him carte blanche rule ("ask of me") over all nations (v. 8). They are the son's inheritance, but he must fight to get what is rightfully his (v. 9). If the son acts, God promises a decisive victory.

> I will tell of the decree of the Lord:
>> He said to me, "You are my son;
>> today I have begotten you.
> Ask of me, and I will make the nations your heritage,
>> and the ends of the earth your possession.
> You shall break them with a rod of iron,
>> and dash them in pieces like a potter's vessel." (vv. 7–9)

In stanza four the Psalmist counsels the nations and their leaders to fall in line (vv. 10-11), reconcile with the king ("kiss the son"), or face the

---

27. God told Samuel to anoint David king (1 Sam 16:3–13).

devastating consequences (v. 12a). Those who heed the Psalmist's commands will be blessed (12b). Conversely, those who refuse will be destroyed.

> Now therefore, O kings, be wise;
>   be warned, O rulers of the earth.
> Serve the Lord with fear,
>   with trembling
> kiss his feet ["Kiss the Son"-NIV]
>   or he will be angry, and you will perish in the way;
>   for his wrath is quickly kindled.
> Happy are all who take refuge in him. (vv. 10–12)

In historical context Ps 2 deals specifically with David's monarchy and a gentile plot against him. By the second century BCE, Ps 2 took on messianic overtones. Israel had been without a monarch for nearly 800 years, and gentiles now controlled the Jewish homeland. Most Jews were not living in Israel but were scattered throughout the empire. Many had intermarried and adopted Greco-Roman lifestyles. Literature of the era anticipated the arrival of a new Davidic king who would deliver Israel from gentile oppression:

> See, Lord, and raise up for them their king, the son of David, to rule over your servant Israel in the time known to you, O God. Undergird him with the strength to destroy the unrighteous rulers, to purge Jerusalem from gentiles who trample her to destruction. (Ps of Sol 17:21-22)

4Q521 also refers to a coming "Messiah whom heaven and earth will obey." Under Roman domination, Jewish hopes arose as they waited the appearance of the mighty deliverer, a new king David. Reading Ps 2 and old Hebrew texts (e.g., 2 Sam 7:14; Ezek 36–37; Isa 26:19; 35:5-6; 61:1-2) through eschatological eyes, many covenant-keeping Jews looked forward to the day when their champion reclaimed his inheritance and restored the kingdom to Israel.

By mid-first century CE, Jews associated with the Jesus movement read the same texts, including Ps 2, through an additional christological lens. As they sang Ps 2, they envisioned the exalted Jesus reigning over the universe from his heavenly throne.

When Peter and John suddenly showed up at the house church and Peter recounted the story of their arrest and release, the assembled believers "raised their voices together to God and [sang], 'Sovereign Lord, who made the heaven and the earth, the sea, and everything in them, it is you who said by the Holy Spirit through our ancestor David, your servant:

> Why did the Gentiles rage
>   and the peoples imagine vain things?
> The kings of the earth took their stand,
>   and the rulers have gathered together
> against the Lord and against his Messiah.'" (Acts 4:23-26)

Although the Christ community sang the ancient hymn, they gave it an anti-imperial twist by identifying Rome and its Jewish conspirators as enemies of God. This becomes evident in the verse that follows:

> For in this city, in fact, both Herod and Pontius Pilate with the Gentiles and the peoples of Israel, gathered together against your holy servant Jesus, whom you anointed. (v. 27)

God's enemies were still around. They simply had different identities. The "Gentiles" were now the Romans. The "kings," the Herods. The "rulers," Pilate and native elites doing Rome's bidding. The "peoples" were both gentiles and Israelites. Their common enemies were "the Lord and his Messiah." Jesus, not David, was now identified as God's "holy servant" and "anointed" one, whom they sought to destroy. God laughed at their feeble efforts to thwart Jesus' mission. Their murderous acts were "predestined" and used by God to effectuate his plan of redemption (v. 28). He then raised Jesus from the dead and set him on the Davidic throne as reigning king.

A new political entity had been established and many identified with it. King Jesus, not Caesar, was destined to usher in a new world order of peace. Rome, its client kings, and its native surrogates, including the Jewish priesthood in Jerusalem, unable to defeat Jesus, turned their wrath against Christ followers who met regularly to sing praises to Christ as Lord and trust him, and not Caesar, to protect and provide for them.

The church carried on Christ's mission and called people to turn away from old alliances and pledge their loyalty to Christ, i.e., "kiss the son" or face the judgment to come (Ps 2:12; Acts 4:12).[28]

The Jerusalem believers concluded their Psalm with a prayer:

> And now, Lord, look at their threats, and grant to your servants
> to speak your word with all boldness, while you stretch out your

---

28. Goldingay, *Psalms*, 93, provides various interpretations of *nasaq* ("kiss the son") in its original context.

hand to heal, and signs and wonders are performed through the name of your holy servant Jesus (Acts 4:29–30).

Immediately God responded: "The place in which they were gathered was shaken; and they were all filled with the Holy Spirit" (v. 31a). Encouraged by this divine manifestation, they confidently "spoke the word of God with boldness" (v. 31b).

This account provides insight into the early church's use of Psalms in worship.

2.7 The Origins of Greco-Roman Songs

Christ followers not only drew upon ancient Jewish musical traditions but also followed the hymnic practices of non-Jews. In ancient Greece hymn singing was a regular part of all association and temple banquets. Along with the meal proper and the pouring of a libation, people offered musical tributes to deities in hopes that the gods would intercede on their behalf.[29] Homer, the revered seventh-century Greek poet, describes how "the sons of the Achaeans" worshiped by "hymning the god who works from afar; and his heart was glad, as he heard."[30] The Greeks continued the tradition of hymn singing and the Romans adopted it.

Additionally, many Greeks belonged to one of the popular mystery religions devoted to Demeter, Dionysus, Serapis, Cybele, or some other god. When Rome conquered Greece, many of its people were attracted to the mysteries. They gathered in temples to receive instruction, make sacrifices, eat cultic meals, and participate in mythical dramas about their respective god(s). Every meeting included singing hymns to the gods.[31]

Orphic hymns were a prominent feature of Bacchus (Gk., Dionysus) worship in Pergamum. In Phrygia worshipers gave their devotion to the Great Mother (the Roman equivalent of goddess Cybele). They referred to themselves by the title "hymn singers" (*hymnōdoi*).[32] At Ephesus, hymn singers played a significant role in the mystery cult of Demeter, considered the Olympian goddess of the harvest.[33] Worship of deities, however, was

---

29. Harland, *Associations*, 72.

30. Homer, *Il.* 471–75.

31. Harland, *Associations*, 46, 48, 71.

32. Harland, *Associations*, 72.

33. Harland, *Associations*, 131.

not a solitary endeavor. Rome required cult members to pay homage to the emperor. Harland provides numerous examples of inscriptions that describe altars being dedicated to Caesar or the goddess Roma by groups of hymn singers.[34]

Choral societies and professional choirs were created to sing praises to Caesar.[35] Their hymns were called *carmina* (Lat.). Virgil links hymn singing directly to worship.[36] Many cities throughout the empire, especially in the region of Asia Minor, formed youth choirs that sang at civic and cultic festivals honoring the emperor, Roman heroes, and patrons.[37]

The *Ludi Saeculares* or Secular Games were held every 110 years throughout the history of the Roman Republic. They included athletic competitions designed to display Rome's greatness and were accompanied by lavish festivities, performances, entertainment, and sacrifices to the gods. Over time they were discontinued. When Augustus rose to power and transformed Rome into an empire, he chose to resuscitate the lapsed games in honor of the past and the dawning of a new era.[38]

In 17 BCE he commissioned Horace, his unofficial Poet Laureate, to write a hymn for the next set of games. In compliance, he wrote the *Carmen Saeculare*, translated "Secular Hymn" or "Song of the Ages," which extolled Caesar as the one who ushered in the new age.

The lyrical poem in the form of a prayer hymn addresses the gods Apollo and Diana, along with Venus and Jupiter, and asks them to bless the empire and its capital city, protect all mothers of child-bearing age, ensure fruitful harvests, and champion Rome's military endeavors.

Hymn singing was popular and people lifted their voices in song to Caesar and the gods in both private and public venues.

Rome encouraged hymn singing and used it as a propaganda tool.[39] Hymns made teaching accessible and memorable.[40] Singing songs extolling emperor and empire was considered one's patriotic duty. As individuals sang, they formed a social identity, felt a sense of civic pride, thought of

---

34. Harland, *Associations*, includes scores of inscriptions that speak of hymn singers and hymn singing and their significance to emperor worship.

35. Harland, *Associations*, 128–40.

36. Virgil. *Aen.* 8.268–305.

37. Josephus, *Ant.* 19.30; 1 *Eph* 18d.424.

38. Putnam, *Horace's Carmen Saeculare*, 1.

39. Medley, "Subversive Song," 428.

40. Gordley, *Christological Hymns*, 68–69.

themselves as the most blessed people on earth, and the beneficiaries of divine blessings. To be part of a powerful empire was something to sing about.[41]

As mentioned in chapter 1, most people, regardless of status, belonged to voluntary associations and raised paeans to Caesar and their patron gods, including Diana, goddess of fertility; Ceres, the goddess of corn; Vulcan, the god of craftsmen; Minerva, the goddess of wisdom; Saturn, the god of agriculture; and a host of others.

Associations operated freely as long as they supported Rome's social agenda and promoted unity. Rome became suspicious, however, if an association encouraged practices contrary to social norms or promoted beliefs that conflicted with Roman ideology. Consequences soon followed. Jewish synagogues and temples were exempt. Under a special arrangement Rome allowed Jewish priests and rabbis to lead their members in worshiping Yahweh apart from worshiping Caesar. However, they were required to offer sacrifices on behalf of the emperor (but, not to him) and to pray for him (but, not to him) three times daily.

As long as Rome considered the Christ movement a part of Judaism, it escaped scrutiny. Jewish Christ followers preached from the porticoes of the temple and attended local synagogues where they were free to argue with and seek to persuade their non-messianic Jewish brethren that Jesus was the anointed son of God.

As the gospel spread throughout the empire, especially under the preaching of the apostle Paul, many gentiles joined Christ communities. As pagans they attended association meetings and sang hymns to Caesar as a god. Now they gathered with Christ followers in home groups that functioned as unofficial voluntary associations, where they ate meals and worshiped Jesus. They linked their new social identity to a kingdom other than Rome. They sang about a man whom Rome executed as a seditionist, and claimed that he rose from the dead and was now alive. Their intent was not to cause a public ruckus, but the lyrics of their songs boldly contradicted Rome's interpretation of history, announced the arrival of a new savior, promoted an alternative worldview and vision of the future, and declared that Jesus, not Caesar, was Lord of all.[42]

41. See Gordley, *Christological Hymns*, 41–45 for further discussion.
42. Gordley, *Christological Hymns*, 55.

2.8 The Church Sings to Christ

The christological hymns found in the NT were composed and sung long before they ever made their way onto the pages of Scripture. Their lyrics focused on Christ and were based on the oral stories that had circulated about him.

When the gospel heralds raised their voices in the synagogues and marketplaces to announce that Jesus had emerged from the chamber of death and ascended to heaven in bodily form, how was their message received? What would cause a rational person to listen and consider such outlandish claims? More importantly, what convinced Jews and gentiles to join the Christ movement and begin to sing hymns to Christ? Unlike moderns, who are children of the Enlightenment, first-century Jews and gentiles heard the gospel message through unique filters linked to their ancient myths and beliefs.

CHAPTER 3

The Exalted Christ

The Object of Praise

While he was blessing them, he withdrew from them and was carried up into heaven. And they worshiped him. (Luke 24:51–52b)

CHRIST'S FOLLOWERS LAVISHED MUSICAL tributes on the exalted Jesus, believing he had overcome death. They claimed that God not only overturned Roman justice and raised Jesus from the dead, but according to the Lukan oral tradition, lifted him bodily into heaven where he reigned as Lord over the cosmos (Luke 24:50–51; Acts 1:9; 2:29–36; 3:12–16; 4:1–10; 7:55–56; 13:22–33; 17:22–31). Based on this unofficial and contrarian version of events, believers congregated to praise Jesus in songs that addressed him as a god above all other gods. On this basis, their hymns sounded subversive.

To moderns, the idea of a bodily resurrection and subsequent ascension into heaven seems more like science fiction than reality. This was not the case for people in the first century. Stories of humans overcoming death and even floating upward into heaven, although rare, were part of Jewish and Roman traditions.[1]

---

1. Cotter, "Greco-Roman Apotheosis," 130. Romans had long told stories of kings and heroes who returned from the dead to instruct their followers how to live in their absence. They were then exalted to a status of godhood through the rite of apotheosis. Gentile recipients of the gospel likely interpreted Jesus' resurrection and exaltation in this context, while Jewish hearers interpreted it in light of the Old Testament (OT) and

3.1 Jewish Resurrection Traditions

Most first-century Jews were familiar with the *Assumption of Moses*, a pseudepigraphal work quoted in Jude 9 that tells of a dispute between Satan and archangel Michael over the body of Moses, which supposedly happened as Moses rose into heaven after death.[2] Philo of Alexandria (ca. 20 BCE–50 CE) held that God lifted Moses bodily into paradise because he was Israel's foremost prophet, empowered to perform divine signs and wonders before the eyes of Pharaoh and God's people (Deut 34:10–14). Philo writes, "Afterwards came the time when he had to make his pilgrimage from earth to heaven, and to leave this mortal life for immortality, summoned thither by the Father who resolved his twofold nature of soul and body into a single unity."[3]

According to Christian tradition Moses and Elijah appeared on the Mount of Transfiguration to three of Jesus' disciples (Matt 17:1–3). Hence, Jews in the first century had a literary tradition of certain humans ascending to heaven.[4] So when they heard the story of Jesus' exaltation, it may not have sounded outlandish.

3.1.1 The Testaments of the Twelve Patriarchs

Jews also held to a literary tradition that spoke of an *end-time* resurrection and the establishment of God's kingdom on earth.

Written in the second century BCE, *The Testaments of the Twelve Patriarchs* claims to be the last words of Jacob's twelve sons. The subject matter

---

their own Jewish traditions.

2. See Stokes, "Not over Moses' Dead Body," 192–213, for various views of Moses' ascension.

3. Philo, *Moses*, 2.288, implies that when Moses transitioned from mortal to immortal, God gave him a new body fit for heaven.

4. *Exagoge*, a five-part drama written in the third century BCE by Israel's first playwright, Ezekiel the Tragedian, tells of Moses on Mount Sinai when he is transported to heaven and sees a "noble man was sitting on [the Mount], with a crown and a large scepter in his left hand." Moses, the main character in the play, says, "He beckoned to me with his right hand, so I approached and stood before the throne. He gave me the scepter and instructed me to sit on the great throne. Then he gave me a royal crown and got up from the throne. I beheld the whole earth all around and saw beneath the earth and above the heavens. A multitude of stars fell before my knees and I counted them all. They paraded past me like a battalion of men. Then I awoke from my sleep in fear." Such literature and dramas influenced how Jewish people interpreted ascension stories.

covers personal ethics, Israel's sin as a nation, exile and judgment, and the end–time restoration of the kingdom to Israel. Several of the accounts speak of a future resurrection. Judah writes,

> And after this Abraham, Isaac and Jacob will be resurrected to life and I and my brothers will be chiefs (wielding) our scepter in Israel. Levi, the first; I, second; Joseph, third; Benjamin, fourth, Simeon, fifth; Issachar, sixth; and all the rest in their order . . . And those who died in sorrow shall be raised in joy; and those who died in poverty for the Lord's sake shall be made rich; those who died on account of the Lord's sake shall be awakened to life. (*T. Jud.* 25.1-4)

Likewise, Zebulun comforts his children with these words: "And now my children, do not grieve because I am dying, nor be depressed because I am leaving you. I shall rise again in your midst as a leader among your sons, . . . But the Lord will bring fire down on the impious and destroy them to all generations. I am now hurrying to my rest, like my fathers." (*T. Zeb.* 10:1-4)[5]

Simeon speaks of the restoration of the earth, the judgment of evil, and of his own destiny, "Then I shall arise in gladness and I shall bless the Most High for his marvels." (*T. Sim.* 6.6-7)

In his parting words to his family Benjamin likewise speaks of the end-time judgment and the resurrection of the just, and warns his children to live in the fear of God:

> And then you will see Enoch and Seth and Abraham and Isaac and Jacob being raised up at the right hand of great joy. Then shall we also be raised, each of us over our tribe, and we shall prostrate ourselves before our heavenly king. . . . . You, therefore, my children, may your lot come to be with those who fear the Lord. (*T. Benj.* 10.6-10)

These statements about resurrection reflect popular beliefs of Jews during the late Second Temple period, including those who heard the gospel of Christ. An announcement that God raised him from the dead fell within the realm of possibility.

---

5. Charlesworth, *Pseudepigrapha* 1, 807, notes this is a reference to the resurrection of the just.

3.1.2 Sibylline Oracles, Book 4

Sibylline Oracles 4, a Hellenistic Jewish document, written in the fourth century BCE during the time of the Alexandrian era, speaks of four worldly kingdoms to be followed by the kingdom of God (cf. Daniel 2, 7, and 12). Jewish writers redacted and revised it in the late first century CE for God's people living under Roman oppression. The newer version mentions the destruction of the temple (116), describes "a leader" (Nero) who escapes in disgrace to the land of the Parthians (119-124), and interprets the eruption of Mount Vesuvius as a sign of God's judgment on Rome for destroying Jerusalem (136).[6] Book 4 concludes with a reference to a final judgment and resurrection:

> But when everything is already dusty ashes, and God puts to sleep with unspeakable fire, even as he kindled it, God himself will again fashion the bones and ashes of men and he will raise up mortals again as they were before. And then there will be judgement over which God himself will preside, judging the world again. (Sib. Or. 4.179-183)

The final resurrection appears to be inclusive with some raised to condemnation and others to life in a restored earthly paradise. Jews envisioned this scenario as a possible way God might reconstitute his kingdom.

3.1.3 Second Baruch

Based on internal evidence (e.g., *2 Bar.* 32. 2-4; 67.1-5, 7) scholars believe 2 Baruch was written after the destruction of Jerusalem (post-70 CE) and likely during the early-second century, since it was dependent on 4 Ezra.[7] That makes it contemporary with Revelation.

Second Baruch suggests immortality is progressive and takes place in two stages. First, the survival of the soul at death (2 Bar. 21.13, 23). Second, the ultimate state of existence: "And it will happen after these things when the time of the appearance of the Anointed One has been fulfilled and he returns in glory, that all who sleep in hope of him will rise" (30.1). When Baruch asks about the nature of the resurrected body (49.1-5), the Lord responds:

---

6. J. J. Collins, "Sibylline Oracles," 382, in Charlesworth, *Pseudepigrapha* 1.

7. Charlesworth, *Pseudepigrapha* 1, 616-17. Fourth Ezra was written around 100 CE.

For the earth will surely give back the dead at that time; it receives them now in order to keep them, not changing anything in their form. But as it has received them so it will give them back. And as I have delivered them to it so it will raise them. For then it will be necessary to show those who live that the dead are living again, and those who went away have come back. And it will be that they recognize each other, . . . (50.1-4).

3.1.4 Hebrew Bible

Many Jews were also familiar with passages in the Jewish Scriptures that spoke of Israel's return from exile in metaphorical terms as a bodily resurrection (Ezek 37:1-14; Isa 26:19; Dan 12:1-3), when the kingdom would be restored to Israel under a new King David and headquartered in the New Jerusalem. When Jewish Christ followers spoke in temple and synagogue settings, they identified Jesus as God's anointed one and claimed his death and resurrection marked the beginning of God's kingdom restoration project.[8] He was the first among the nation to be raised.[9] Using a midrash method to interpret Scriptures such as Pss 2, 8, 68, 69, 110, and Isa 52:12-13, they declared that Jesus was the Suffering Servant and promised eschatological David who now ruled from a heavenly throne at God's right hand.

Except for the Sadducees, most Jews would not cringe over the concept of a resurrection, even if they rejected that God had raised Jesus from the dead. It was simply easier for them to believe the "official" line as espoused by their leaders.

The same is true with the idea of an ascension. Jews were familiar with the stories of Enoch (Gen 5:21–24) and Elijah (2 Kgs 2:1, 11–12) ascending into heaven without facing death. So, an ascent into heaven was feasible. The gospel, at least according to Luke's version, wedded resurrection and ascension and applied them to Jesus.

---

8. This may be the literary intent of Matt 27:52–53. Jesus' death and bodily resurrection are connected to Israel's eschatological resurrection: The "tombs also were opened, and many bodies of the saints who had fallen asleep were raised. After his resurrection they came out of the tombs and entered the holy city and appeared to many." It may also serve to let the post-70 readers know that their suffering will be vindicated. They too will be raised from the dead.

9. In Matthew's account when Jesus was resurrected, others were raised with him (Matt 27: 6–8, 52). The restoration of the kingdom to Israel had begun.

Jewish Christ followers in Israel were free, at least initially, to proclaim their message in the synagogues or from the portico of the temple without recrimination. Many listeners accepted the gospel of Christ, including some priests, and joined others of like mind in worshiping Jesus as their heavenly king. And thus, christological hymns were born.

3.2 Gentile Traditions

Compared to Jews, how did gentiles throughout the empire construe the message of Jesus' resurrection and/or ascension? While not familiar with Hebrew Scriptures or Jewish apocryphal writings, gentiles had their own stories and traditions of kings and heroes who rose to heaven and received the status of a god. The metamorphosis from human to divine was called apotheosis. The most notable example was Romulus, the father of Rome.

3.2.1 The Apotheosis of Romulus

According to legend, Romulus (753-715 BCE), the founder and warrior king of Rome, was the first of the nation to receive divine status. While moderns debate the historicity of Romulus, people in the first century CE were less skeptical. Many intellectuals, especially Roman writers and poets told and retold the story of Romulus and how he attained apotheosis. Plutarch (ca. 46-120 CE), the well-known Roman philosopher and author, tells how Romulus died under mysterious circumstances.[10] While reviewing his troops from the elevated dais at the Campus Martius (aka, the "Field of Mars"), the sun suddenly turned black, and the noonday became as night. As lightning cracked and ominous clouds descended, a driving rain caused much of the crowd to scatter. Only the senators seated on the platform and the troops below remained in place. According to Roman historian Livy (ca. 59 BCE–17CE), as the storm subsided and daylight returned, the "[r]oyal seat was vacant" and Romulus was gone. When the common people inquired of the king's whereabouts and started to search for him, the ranking nobles forbade them and proclaimed that the king "had been snatched away to heaven by a whirlwind."[11] He was now Rome's immortal benefac-

---

10. Plutarch, *Rom. Lives* 27.6-7. Although Plutarch considered the apotheosis of Romulus a likely myth, he wrote the most complete account of the event.

11. Livy, *Hist.* 1.16.2; Dionysius, *Ant. or.* 2.56.2 mentions that Romulus was caught up into heaven by his father, Mars. Plutarch, *Rom. Lives* 27.1-7.

tor.[12] They hailed him as "a god, the son of a god, the King and Father of the City of Rome."[13] Others, however, believed that a group of senators and aristocrats, who opposed the king's peace treaties with enemy nations, murdered him. The violent storm provided them a cover of darkness and an opportune time to carry out their dastardly deed. They disassembled his body, each carrying off a body part hidden under his toga.[14] Over time, this version of Romulus's apotheosis became the accepted tradition.

The Reappearance of Romulus

According to Plutarch:

> [A] man of noblest birth, and of the most reputable character, a trusted and intimate friend also of Romulus himself, and one of the colonists from Alba, Julius Proculus by name, went into the forum and solemnly swore by the most sacred emblems before all the people that, as he was travelling on the road, he had seen Romulus coming to meet him, fair and stately to the eye as never before, and arrayed in bright and shining armour.[15]

In Livy's account, Proculus declares:

> At break of dawn, to-day, the Father of this city descended from heaven and appeared to me. Whilst thrilled with awe, I stood rapt before him in deepest reverence, praying that I might be pardoned by gazing on him, "go," he said, "tell the Romans that it is the will of heaven that my Rome should be the head of all the world."[16]

Romulus closes his discussion with Proculus in this manner:

---

12. Plutarch, *Rom. Lives* 27.1-7. As the masses adopted this official version, they began to worship Romulus and request that he favor the nation with his benevolence.

13. Livy, *Hist.* 1.16.3. Plutarch, *Rom. Lives* 27.7-8.

14. Livy, *Hist.* 1.15.1-5; 1.16.4. Plutarch, *Rom. Lives* 27:5-6, places the dismemberment at the Temple of Vulcan. While the idea of mutilation seems wildly speculative at first glance, a modern-day example is Washington Post reporter Jamal Khashoggi, a vocal critic of Saudi Arabia's Crown Prince Mohammed bin Salman. Khashoggi entered the Saudi Arabian consulate in Istanbul, Turkey, on October 2, 2018, but never came out. A Turkish government investigation determined he was murdered and dismembered by a fifteen-man Saudi hit squad in retaliation for opposing the policies of the Crown Prince.

15. Plutarch, *Rom. Lives* 28.1.

16. Livy. *Hist.* 1.16.5-7. Romulus' post-resurrection instruction to Proculus became a foundation for Rome's claim of manifest destiny. Also see Ovid, *Fast.* 2:49-51.

It was the pleasure of the gods, O Proculus, from whom I came, that I should be with mankind only a short time, and that after founding a city destined to be the greatest on earth for empire and glory, I should dwell again in heaven. So farewell, and tell the Romans that if they practise self-restraint, and add to it valour, they will reach the utmost heights of human power. And I will be your propitious deity, Quirinus.[17]

The masses of Romans accepted the testimony of the most esteemed Proculus and thereafter prayed to their new god whose new name was now Quirinus.[18]

At the time of the Christ movement most people in the empire accepted the apotheosis of Romulus as an established tradition. Christians were also familiar with the story. By the second century CE some believers were commenting on it.[19]

Preaching the Gospel to Gentiles

Because of the apotheosis legends, the gospel may have received a positive hearing among gentiles. They believed that ascent to godhood was reserved only for heroes and good men. Luke certainly presents Jesus in this light. He writes, "how God anointed Jesus of Nazareth with the Holy Spirit and with power; how he went about doing good and healing all who were oppressed by the devil, for God was with him (Acts 10:38). But Luke, of the four Gospel writers, goes one step farther. He alone speaks directly of Jesus' ascent into heaven.

Is it possible Luke wished to portray Jesus' exaltation in terms of an apotheosis? The comparison between Romulus and Jesus is obvious. The resurrected Jesus was seen by witnesses. He interacted with a couple on a road and taught them. When gathered with his disciples he commissioned them to expand his mission to all the world and promised them the divine means to complete it. They then observed him ascend bodily into heaven.

17. Plutarch, *Rom. Lives* 28.2.

18. Plutarch, *Rom. Lives* 28.3.

19. Cotter, "Greco-Roman," 139. While most Christ followers believed the account of Romulus' ascension was a fable, some drew clear–cut parallels between the ascent and divination of Roman heroes and that of Jesus. See Tertullian, *Nat.* 3.2.9; Minucius, *Oct.* 4.23; Arnobius, *Seven Books*, 6.1.41; Augustine, *Civ.* 2.483.

Matthew adds that Jesus promised to be with his followers forever. And John and Paul reveal the exalted Lord was given a new name.

Possibly these storytellers strategically used familiar language and similar stories to contextualize the gospel to get a hearing from their non-Jewish audiences. For gentiles the resurrection of Jesus must have sounded, at least initially, like an apotheosis.

3.2.2 Lesser Apotheosis Accounts

One can argue that the apotheosis of Romulus set the standard by which all future accounts were judged.[20] When compared with the prototype they fell short. A new paradigm emerged.

The Apotheosis of Julius Caesar

When Julius Caesar, ruler of the Roman Republic, succumbed (March 15, 44 BCE) to 27 stab wounds inflicted by the hands of assassins Junius Brutus and Cassius Longinus, his enemies rejoiced. But Octavian Gaius Caesar, his adopted son and heir to the throne, along with Marc Antony, petitioned the Senate to declare him a god. With no credible witnesses to Caesar's revivification, the Senate refused to act.[21] Once enthroned as emperor, Octavian announced by fiat that Caesar had been apotheosized. To celebrate the occasion, Octavian reserved The Forum for a week of festivities and Olympic-style games. On the opening day to everyone's amazement, a long-tailed comet appeared in the northern sky and slowly followed a seven-day path.[22] It was visible to all.[23] Octavian declared the comet was the sign from the gods that Caesar was now one of their own.

Yet, Caesar's *body* still lay in state on a pyre in the center of The Forum. What kind of apotheosis was this? Octavian explained that the gods had

20. Cotter, "Greco-Roman," 134.

21. Caesar's body lay in repose for three days at the Domus Publica before his State funeral service, which was followed by cremation. The ashes were gathered and placed in an urn. Today, Julius Caesar's grave is located in "The Temple of Caesar" at The Forum; although, an altar is all that remains of the ancient gravesite.

22. Pliny the Elder, *Nat.* 2.93–94. Octavian used the symbol of the comet as a propaganda tool. He broke ground in 42 BCE for the temple of the divine Caesar and dedicated it in 29 BCE. It became known as the "Temple of the Comet Star."

23. Virgil, *Ecl.* 9.47.

carried his *spirit* into heaven. He was now *Divus Julius*. The Roman poet Ovid (43 BCE–18CE) confirmed this version. He describes how Caesar's celestial mother, the goddess Venus, watched in horror as the plot unfolded to kill her son. Despite her pleas for the gods to intervene, they advised her to let fate take its course. In consolation, Jupiter instructed her to "take up Caesar's spirit from his murdered corpse, and change it into a star, so that the deified Julius may always look down from his high temple on our Capitol and forum."[24]

Ovid adds,

> He had barely finished, when gentle Venus stood in the midst of the senate, seen by no one, and took up the newly freed spirit of her Caesar from his body, and preventing it from vanishing into the air, carried it towards the glorious stars. As she carried it, she felt it glow and take fire, and loosed it from her breast: it climbed higher than the moon, and drawing behind it a fiery tail, shone as a star.[25]

Ovid tells that the exalted *Divus Julius* prophetically looked into the future and saw his son ruling in his stead. In response, Jupiter announced that one day Augustus, too, would be apotheosized.[26]

Julius Caesar's *spiritual* ascension became the new standard of apotheosis, replacing *physical* revivification. Ritual enactment or symbolic endorsement became the only criterion now needed for the Senate to declare that a human had been elevated to divine status. The dead body of the hero or ruler was now placed on a funeral pyre and set aflame. As smoke and ashes rose, an eagle was released that soared high into the heavens; thus, signifying ascent to godhood.

Augustus Caesar

During the first century CE the Senate elevated four Roman emperors to godhood upon their deaths.[27]

At the beginning of his reign,—with Julius Caesar elevated to the status of a god,—Augustus (Octavian) began referring to himself as "son of

24. Ovid, *Metam.* XIV: 842.

25. Ovid, *Metam.* XIV:843-48.

26. Ovid, *Metam.* XIV: 849-70.

27. Tiberius, Caligula, Nero, and Domitian were not among those who received the honorific.

god," an appellation the public soon employed when speaking of the emperor. This designation, along with rumors surrounding his superhuman conception, elevated Augustus to a level of semi-divinity.[28] Augustus ruled from 39 BCE to 14 CE. Upon his death, senators carried his body and laid it on a funeral pyre to be burned. As his mortal remains were set afire and the smoke and ashes ascended, a senator and former imperial administrator, avowed he had witnessed the emperor's "spirit soaring up to Heaven in the flame."[29]

In an elaborate public rite of consecration, the Roman Senate affirmed that Augustus had indeed made an ascent and now sat among the pantheon of gods. Once officially divinized, coins were struck, which displayed his image on one side and divinized title on the other. Temples were built in his honor, monuments erected with inscriptions of tribute, and new frescoes painted that depicted a hero ascending into heaven or seated among the gods.

Claudius Caesar

The anti-Semitic Emperor Claudius (10 BCE–54 CE), whose mother dubbed "a monster" and "a fool," was the next to be deified.[30] After giving Claudius a "lavish funeral," the new Emperor Nero and the Senate declared him to be a god, a designation that Nero later rescinded.[31] Emperor Vespasian restored the honor and built a temple honoring Claudius as a god.[32]

Vespasian (9–79 CE)

On the night of his death, sickly yet still cognizant, Vespasian glanced toward the heavens and saw a bright comet crossing the sky. He remarked,

28. Suetonius, *Aug.* 2.94, tells of discovering a story in the book *Theologumena* by Asclepiades of Mendes that speaks of Octavian's divine conception in the temple of Apollo. While his mother Atia slept, a serpent impregnated her and she dreamed "her intestines were carried into Heaven" suggesting "a divine paternity." This supranatural account was widely accepted by the masses.

29. Suetonius, *Aug.* 100.7. Dio Cassius, *Rom. Hist.* 56.46.1–3, wrote nearly two centuries later that Livia, Augustus' widow, had awarded one million sesterces to Numerius Atticus to say he witnessed her husband's apotheosis.

30. Suetonius, *Claud.* 5.2.

31. Suetonius, *Claud.* 5.45; Suetonius, *Nero* 6.9.

32. Suetonius, *Vesp.* 10.9.

"Look at that long hair!" Then joked, "The king of Parthia must be going to die," before he sighed "Dear me! I must be turning into a god."[33] The Senate concurred and granted him apotheosis.

Titus (39–81 CE)

Prior to ascending the throne of his father, Titus was a young successful general who soundly squelched the Jewish uprising. In the course of his victory, he captured Jerusalem, burned the temple of Herod, and left widespread carnage in his wake. His imperial reign was short-lived and only lasted June 79–September 81 CE. He died at the age of 41. Domitian, his younger brother and successor, promoted him to godhood.[34]

Of all the apotheosis accounts, the Romulus legend stands supreme for various reasons.[35] He ascended in bodily form into heaven, not in spirit only. He completely disappeared; he was not cremated. An eyewitness attested he had met Romulus on a road. Romulus received the full status of deity and not that of a minor deity. He obtained a new name—Quirinius. He gave post-resurrection instructions to Proculus that Rome's expansion throughout the world was divinely sanctioned. Cicero (106–46 BCE), the famed equestrian statesman and scholar, connects Romulus' apotheosis to the Romans being a "chosen people."[36] Romulus promised to be with the Roman people always and protect them as they carried out their mission.[37]

3.3 Concerns Related to Worshiping the Exalted Jesus

Since both Jews and gentiles in the first century had their own resurrection and/or ascension stories, what made the Christian claim so controversial and marked it as counter-imperial? It was *not* that Jesus ascended into

---

33. Suetonius, *Vesp.* 10. 23.

34. Suetonius, *Dom.* 12.2.

35. Cotter, "Greco-Roman," 134.

36. Cicero, *Rep.* 2.2.

37. There is an obvious similarity between the apotheosis of Romulus and the exaltation of Jesus. According to Luke's unique perspective, the parallels stand out. Both were killed by government officials; came back to life in a physical body; had a post–resurrection encounter on a road; gave instructions to expand the mission to all the world. Other writers mention Jesus' promise to be with his people (Matt 18:18–20) and that he was given a new name (Phil 2:6–11).

heaven. Many believed other heroes and emperors before and after him did the same.

3.3.1 Jewish Concerns

For Jews, the hullabaloo was manifold. First, Jesus and his disciples made exclusive claims for him; namely, he was superior to Moses, Joshua, David, Solomon, Isaiah, and all the Hebrew prophets.

Second, Jesus characterized Israel's current leaders as false shepherds (John 19:13-16, 40; Ezek 34), who were leading the nation to destruction (John 10:1, 8-10, 15). He intimated that they were like thieves, murderers, and hirelings, whose motives were primarily monetary (John 10:10-12), and that he alone was Israel's legitimate "good shepherd" (the anticipated eschatological King David) whom God sent to restore the kingdom to Israel.[38] Israel—still in exile and under occupation—was like a flock of sheep without a shepherd.

Third, Jesus was executed for blasphemy and being a false messiah (Matt 26:64–65). Why should a Jew believe God raised a convicted criminal?[39] According to Mosaic law:

> When someone is convicted of a crime punishable by death and is executed, and you hang him on a tree, his corpse must not remain all night upon the tree; you shall bury him that same day, for anyone hung on a tree is under God's curse. You must not defile the land that the Lord your God is giving you for possession (Deut 21:22–23).

Since Israel was now subservient to Roman authority, its native leaders could not carry out capital punishment; so, they delivered Jesus to Pilate who ordered him crucified.

38. Carter, "Jesus the Good Shepherd," 97, shows that both Jewish and Roman political leaders (kings and emperors) were lauded as "good shepherds" who provided security and abundance for their subjects. The Gospel of John presents Jesus alone as "the good shepherd" who opposes the false shepherds, including Caesar, Pilate, Herod, and the Jewish native retainers (John 19:12, 15). *Psalms of Solomon* 17:1-46 speaks of an eschatological shepherd-king, who will heal the nation and restore the kingdom forever. Carter provides strong evidence for the inter-connection between Ezek 34 and John 10 and shows that God's agent of rescue and restoration of Israel is the "one shepherd, my servant David" (Ezek 34:23-24).

39. At Jesus' tribunal, Pilate asked mockingly, "Shall I crucify your king?" The chief priests cried out, "We have no king but Caesar."

This gets to the heart of the matter. Interpreting Jesus' death in light of Mosaic law, Jesus was cursed by God. If anything, this was proof that he was not Israel's eschatological king. For Christ followers to intimate that God reversed their judicial action, raised Jesus from the dead, and set him over the cosmos, did not make sense. Surely, Jesus was not the long-awaited messiah as his followers proclaimed. The idea of a crucified messiah was an oxymoron, equivalent to a "good devil" or "fried ice."[40] The concept was a stumbling block to Jewish belief. Why should Jews worship and sing songs to a condemned criminal?

When Christ's followers formed messianic associations where they worshiped Jesus, ate meals together in his name, and invited others to join them, they faced opposition from the Jewish leadership. From the time of Stephen's death, "a severe persecution began against the church in Jerusalem" (Acts 8:1–2). Many of the believers scattered. As the Christ movement expanded beyond Palestine, the Jewish opposition grew. The book of Acts is rife with stories of Christ followers hunted down, flogged, imprisoned, and put to death.

The *possibility* that God raised a man from the dead was feasible. He did it in the past; he could do it again. The claim that he raised the crucified Jesus from the dead was *outlandish*, despite the claims of so-called eyewitnesses. Still, some believed and the movement grew (Acts 2:47; 6:7; 9:31; 12:24; 16:5; 19:20; 28:31).

3.3.2 Gentile Concerns

Because many gentiles were familiar with stories of apotheosis, the account of Jesus' resurrection may not have seemed far-fetched. Three major obstacles, however, stood in the way of gentiles becoming believers in the first century.

First, Jesus was a Jew! Why would a gentile want to become a follower of a Jew, a member of an oppressed people whose nation Rome had conquered? What could be more scandalous than to worship a Jew whose own leaders dubbed a messianic pretender and Roman officials labeled an insurrectionist? What did it mean for gentiles to follow one convicted and executed for crimes against the state? It was a fool's errand (1 Cor 1:23).

Second, the good news of Jesus' resurrection and exaltation as ruler over heaven and earth, carried anti-imperial overtones. Rome had

40. Fee, *First Corinthians*, 78.

successfully executed this self-proclaimed, unauthorized king of the Jews. Now, his followers were saying that the God of Israel subverted Roman power and overturned Roman justice.[41]

Christ's disciples were calling Roman subjects to be baptized in Jesus' name, to pledge loyalty to God's empire, and align with an association whose members conduct their lives according to a new set of social ethics. To pledge loyalty to Christ one had to acknowledge that Rome wrongly executed a person destined for apotheosis (exaltation) and that Rome's ultimate expression of imperial power—crucifixion—could not withstand the resurrection power of the Jewish God. The message was an affront to Rome and its pantheon of gods.

Christ followers depicted Jesus' ascension as superior to the apotheosis of Romulus. Jesus appeared to hundreds of people over a six-week period (1 Cor 15:1–5), while Romulus appeared only to one person. Jesus was placed over the entire cosmos, while Romulus became the heavenly benefactor of Rome only. All human rulers and gods, including Jupiter (Zeus) the father of the Roman pantheon, owed allegiance to Jesus.

That the gospel of Christ undermined the social and political structure of the empire is not an overstatement. The wider the movement spread, the more dangerous it became. Choices had to be made. One had to accept either the official position that Rome crucified Jesus as usurper and political revolutionary or, that Israel's god overpowered the Roman gods and raised Jesus from the dead.

Third, for a gentile to align with the Jesus movement likely meant loss of patronage. Survival depended on healthy relationships with benefactors. Following Jesus often resulted in loss of income and social status. Was it worth it?

When the *ekklēsia* met to praise Jesus in song as the unique and exalted Lord, local and regional political leaders viewed them with suspicion. Their songs sounded familiar, but their lyrics were disturbing. It was common knowledge that songs should heap praises on Caesar and the Roman gods alone!

---

41. For an excellent analysis of how and why the resurrection of Jesus was considered anti-imperial, see Pillar, *Resurrection as an Anti-Imperial Gospel*.

3.4 Pliny the Younger Reports to Emperor Trajan (ca. 110 CE)

When Pliny (61–113 CE), the governor of Bithynia, received information that some of his subjects had become Christ followers, he took swift action. Charges were filed against those who "meet on a fixed day before dawn and sing responsively a hymn to Christ as to a god, and . . . bind themselves by oath." Pliny, who had no previous experience in prosecuting Christians, sought advice from Emperor Trajan. His letter addresses three concerns:

1. Should he punish the weak as severely as the more robust?

2. Should he punish or pardon those who recant?

3. Should he punish those who take the name of Christ if they are otherwise law-abiding citizens?

He explains to the emperor the actions he took thus far:

> In the meantime, this is the plan which I have adopted in the case of those Christians who have been brought before me. I ask them whether they are Christians; if they say yes, then I repeat the question a second and a third time, warning them of the penalties it entails, and if they still persist, I order them to be taken away to prison. For I do not doubt that, whatever the character of the crime may be which they confess, their pertinacity and inflexible obstinacy certainly ought to be punished. There were others who showed similar mad folly whom I reserved to be sent to Rome, as they were Roman citizens. Subsequently, as is usually the way, the very fact of my taking up this question led to a great increase of accusations, and a variety of cases were brought before me.
>
> A pamphlet was issued anonymously, containing the names of a number of people. Those who denied that they were or had been Christians and called upon the gods in the usual formula, reciting the words after me, those who offered incense and wine before your image, which I had given orders to be brought forward for this purpose, together with the statues of the deities - all such I considered should be discharged, especially as they cursed the name of Christ, which, it is said, those who are really Christians cannot be induced to do.
>
> Others, whose names were given me by an informer, first said that they were Christians and afterwards denied it, declaring that they had been but were so no longer, some of them having recanted many years before, and more than one so long as twenty

years back. They all worshipped your image and the statues of the deities, and cursed the name of Christ. But they declared that the sum of their guilt or their error only amounted to this, that on a stated day they had been accustomed to meet before daybreak and to recite a hymn among themselves to Christ, as though he were a god, and that so far from binding themselves by oath to commit any crime, their oath was to abstain from theft, robbery, adultery, and from breach of faith, and not to deny trust money placed in their keeping when called upon to deliver it. When this ceremony was concluded, it had been their custom to depart and meet again to take food, but it was of no special character and quite harmless, and they had ceased this practice after the edict in which, in accordance with your orders, I had forbidden all secret societies.[42]

I thought it the more necessary, therefore, to find out what truth there was in these statements by submitting two women, who were called deaconesses, to the torture, but I found nothing but a debased superstition carried to great lengths. So I postponed my examination, and immediately consulted you.

The matter seems to me worthy of your consideration, especially as there are so many people involved in the danger. Many persons of all ages, and of both sexes alike, are being brought into peril of their lives by their accusers, and the process will go on. For the contagion of this superstition has spread not only through the free cities, but into the villages and the rural districts, and yet it seems to me that it can be checked and set right. It is beyond doubt that the temples, which have been almost deserted, are beginning again to be thronged with worshippers, that the sacred rites which have for a long time been allowed to lapse are now being renewed, and that the food for the sacrificial victims is once more finding a sale, whereas, up to recently, a buyer was hardly to be found. From this it is easy to infer what vast numbers of people might be reclaimed, if only they were given an opportunity of repentance.[43]

In response to the inquiry, Trajan praised Pliny for his measured actions and instructed him not to chase down Christians, but "if they are brought before you and the offence is proved, they are to be punished." Those who deny the accusations or recant should "be pardoned" if they willingly prove it "by offering prayers to our deities."[44]

42. This is a reference to voluntary association meetings.
43. Pliny, *Ep. Tra.* 10.96–97.
44. Pliny, *Ep. Tra.* 10.97.

This correspondence reveals what it was like for Christians to meet and worship at the turn of the second century CE in the region north of Asia Minor. Since Pliny outlawed unsanctioned voluntary associations, including the church, "baptized" Christ followers rose before daybreak and gathered in an isolated location in order to avoid drawing attention to their singing and praise.[45] Later in the evening they met to eat an agape feast.

3.5 Summary

Some Jews joined the Jesus movement after hearing and believing Gospel accounts that God raised Jesus from the dead and lifted him into heaven. Based on their traditions and sacred writings, the story of Jesus' resurrection and ascension resonated with them. In like manner, gentiles had their own popular traditions of apotheosis; hence, the story of Jesus' ascension sounded plausible.

Nevertheless, most rejected the gospel (if they ever heard it) and sided with the majority report that Jesus' death was justified and his resurrection a fantasy.

The christological songs with their subversive lyrics were an assault on Jewish and Roman sensitivities. Taking the form of odes, hymns, spiritual songs, and elevated poetry, they told an alternative story, namely that God placed Jesus as ruler over heaven and earth, and placed humankind's future in his hands. As a result, he alone was worthy of worship.

The exclusive claims that Christ followers made for Jesus divided Jewish and gentile families, friends, and neighbors. The gospel, if embraced, had the potential to disrupt politics, religion, the economy, and the social fabric of the empire.

In the remaining chapters we will take a careful look at several embedded NT songs and analyze their controversial lyrics.

45. Did. 9.5 (ca. 110–120 CE).

CHAPTER 4

Mary's Song

The Magnificat (Luke 1:46–55)

My soul magnifies the Lord, and my spirit rejoices in God my Savior.
(Luke 2:46)

SEVERAL THEMES DISTINGUISH THE Gospel of Luke from the other Gospels: Jesus' teaching during mealtime, its travel motif, emphasis on the poor, promise and fulfillment, just to name a few. Additionally, music plays a significant role in the Lukan account. The first two chapters of the storyline are "repeatedly interrupted by poetry and hymns. A modern reader might think that Luke's Gospel was a musical: every time something important happens in the prologue, a character seems to burst spontaneously into song. Christian tradition has assigned Latin names to these hymns, . . . "[1]

Elizabeth sings of Mary's pregnancy in the *Ave Maria* (Luke 1:42–45).

Mary praises God in the *Magnificat* (1:46–55).

Zechariah celebrates his son's birth in the *Benedictus* (1:67–79).

Angels sing the *Gloria in Excelsis* (2:14).

Aged Simeon exalts God in the *Nunc Dimittus* (2:29–32).

1. Powell, *Introduction*, 170.

In four of the five songs one finds an individual responding to God's intervention on Israel's behalf and his promise to restore the kingdom to Israel. The canticles portray God's son as the agent of change. Uttered by Jewish songsters living in Roman-occupied Palestine or travelling messengers to the inhabitants, these lyrics speak of opposition to the current Roman government and its oppressive policies. They do not explain how God's eschatological purposes will be fulfilled, but they set the stage for the rest of the Lukan story that flows out of the musical prologue and informs readers that God's purposes are unfolding as predicted.

We will limit our discussion in Luke's Gospel mainly to Mary's *Magnificat*. This will enable us to focus our discussion on the counter-imperial nature of NT songs.

4.1 A Blessed Event

When a woman receives news that her firstborn will be a son, her joy often gives way to moments of deep reflection and heart-wrenching questions about his future. The nature of these quandaries is usually related to the new mother's social, racial, and religious status. If she is privileged, she may wonder if her son will go to Harvard like his father; marry into a good family; or become a partner in his father's law firm. If she is from rural Middle America, she might ask if the boy will move to the big city; worry he will fight in a war; or bless her with grandkids. But what if the expectant mother is African American or a poor Latin American immigrant? She wants to know if her son will receive an adequate education at the underfunded inner-city school; or if the cops will stop his car and frisk him because of his skin color; or worse yet if he will ever reach the age of adulthood in a culture of drive-by shootings. A Muslim mother living in a majority Hindu nation may ponder whether her son will face religious persecution; be overlooked for a good job; relegated to living in a shack on the slum side of town.

Twenty-first century mothers, however, are not the first to contemplate or worry about their offspring's future. Throughout the ages moms have prayed for, prophesied over, and sung to their children even before their birth. Some claim that God revealed their son would one day become a pastor or he would die as a martyr for Allah. Such stories make sense in the context of a particular culture.

What about Jewish mothers-to-be living at the turn of the first century CE under the oppressive rule of the Roman Empire? Were their fears and aspirations different from modern-day women? The Gospel of Luke opens with two birth narratives. The first tells how infertile Elizabeth, the wife of a Jewish priest, unexpectedly conceives and praises God for his favor. The shame of her barrenness has been removed (Luke 1:5–24). The second tells of Mary, a teenage peasant girl living in a depressed, rural village in far north Galilee. According to the Lukan account an angel appears and informs this virgin that she soon will be a mother.

Unwed and confused, she asks, "How can this be, since I do not know a man?" (Luke 1:26–34). The heavenly messenger explains, "The Holy Spirit will come upon you, and the power of the Most High will overshadow you; therefore the child will be holy; he will be called Son of God" (Luke 1:35). For Jews the phrase "Son of God" carried significance and referred to a Davidic king. When interpreted eschatologically it took on messianic overtones. What must Mary have thought? Did God intend to use her pregnancy to restore the Davidic throne to Israel? Was she to be the mother of Israel's deliverer? Luke wants his readers to think so.

As a sign that all will unfold as predicted, Gabriel informs Mary that Elizabeth, her "barren" relative is also pregnant (v. 36). Both pregnancies are miracles. This may have been designed to embolden Mary and strengthen her faith. Gabriel then proclaims, "For nothing (ῥῆμα, *rhēma*) will be impossible with God" (v. 37). The Greek term (*rhēma*), translated "nothing" (NRSV) may also be translated "word" and carries the idea that nothing God says is without results. His words are accompanied by divine action and are thus self-fulfilling. They do not return void (Isa 55:11).

We glimpse this meaning from Mary's response: "Here am I, the servant of the Lord; let it be with me according to your word (*rhēma*)" (v. 38). Mary submits to God's will and makes herself available for his use.[2]

---

2. Despite personal sacrifice and sorrow to follow, Mary says, "Yes" to God. As a result, God blesses her and through her blesses the world. Arguably, just as Jesus is viewed as a second Adam, so Mary can be seen as a second Eve. Both Jesus and Mary have significant roles in reversing the consequences of the cosmic tragedy in the Garden.

EVE	MARY
Doubts God—"Did God say?"	Believes God—"So be it according to your word"
Disobeys God—"Thou shalt not eat"	Obeys God—Conceives, carries, and gives birth
God curses Eve	God blesses Mary
Indirectly brings sin to world	Indirectly brings deliverance

According to Irenaeus, "The knot of Eve's disobedience was untied by Mary's obedience; what the virgin Eve bound through her unbelief, the Virgin Mary loosened by her

The narrator concludes his account of the annunciation with Mary making a hasty trek to Jerusalem to visit Elizabeth (Luke 1:39). Just as God poured out his favor on Elizabeth, he has done the same for Mary. But there is a difference. God's grace removed the shame of Elizabeth's infertility, but it will lead to scandal and shame for Mary. What will her friends and relatives think?

By placing these two birth narratives at the beginning of his Gospel, Luke shows that God *conceived* and *gave birth* to the Christ movement as part of his plan to restore the kingdom to Israel. Written to a post-70 CE audience, Luke may have included these stories to show that all humanly-conceived schemes and efforts to bring in the kingdom through force were doomed to fail from the start. By the time the Gospel of Luke was written, Zealots had attempted to liberate Israel by violent uprisings for more than a century. Their last effort (66–70 CE) ended in total defeat. The Roman troops destroyed Jerusalem, burned the temple, and slaughtered over 200,000 Jews.

God's plan to restore the kingdom happens without resorting to force. Rather than calling for an angelic army to overthrow Rome, Jesus trusted God to restore the kingdom to Israel according to his design. Jesus faced Rome in silence and faith. Rome, in turn, humiliated, victimized, and executed him as an "Enemy of the State." Israel's divinely appointed king hanged on a cross. Jesus' death, shameful to Jews and despicable to Romans, was designed to put an end to his messianic claims and scatter his followers. To all rational observers, Rome succeeded. No one understood at the time that God's kingdom initiative centered on the crucifixion.

John the Baptizer and Jesus, both conceived through divine intervention, were part of God's strategy to restore the kingdom to Israel. They called God's people back to covenant obedience and faithfulness. Some heeded and joined their movement, which had spread far beyond Palestine and was still advancing when Luke wrote his Gospel in 85 CE. Yet, the kingdom had not arrived as expected. In fact, it looked like Rome had dealt the kingdom agenda a death blow when it executed John, Jesus, and many of its leaders. Caesar continued to rule supreme, which begs the question, "How or in what manner had the kingdom been restored to Israel?" The Gospel of Luke seeks to clear up the confusion.

---

faith" (*Haer.*, 3.22.4)." Pope Paul VI, "Lumen Gentium," 56, in the *Dogmatic Constitution of the Church* (1965), addressed this theory.

4.2 The Magnificat

Following the two conception accounts, the narrator says Mary visits her cousin Elizabeth in Jerusalem (Luke 1:39). Surprised by Mary's arrival, Elizabeth breaks into a Spirit-inspired ode, and pronounces a blessing over her pregnant visitor and her unborn child (vv. 40-42).[3] She inquires of Mary the reason of her visit and addresses her as "the mother of our Lord" (vv. 43-44). This "is the first time 'Lord' is applied to Jesus" in the Gospel of Luke (cf. Luke 2:11).[4] Elizabeth explains that Mary is blessed because she believed the angelic promise would come to pass (Luke 1:45).

In response, Mary spontaneously breaks into song as well (vv. 46-55). According to Raymond Brown, Mary's refrain "resembles in many ways the psalm type known as a hymn of praise."[5] The song has a dual emphasis: 1) Verses 46-50 speak of God's favor toward Mary—the personal benefits of salvation ("for me," v. 49). 2) Verses 51-55 speak of corporate benefits of salvation ("his servant Israel," v. 54). Hence, God acts on behalf of the individual and the nation. Delivered in a poetic cadence, Mary's lyrics are both prophetic and subversive, and can be divided into two strophes or stanzas with verses 46-50 and 54-55, respectively, serving as a summary of each stanza.[6]

4.2.1 Stanza One

My soul magnifies the Lord,

---

3. In announcing, "Blessed are you among women," Elizabeth is echoing the refrain found in the Apocrypha of Uzziah given to Judith, after the latter beheaded Holofernes, Assyria's general (Jdt 13:18). Uzziah explained he gave Judith his blessing because "you risked your life when our people were being oppressed, and you averted our disaster, walking in the straight path before our God" (Jdt 13:20). Judith was God's instrument used to deliver the nation (Jdt 14-15). The narrative ends with Judith praising God in song for liberating his people and reversing their social status (Jdt 16:1-17). Mary receives the same designation, but she will be remembered for her faith, not her use of force. She believes the angelic promise and will give birth to the "Son of the Most High" who will inherit David's throne (Luke 1:32), restore the kingdom to Israel, and "reign over the house of Jacob forever" (Luke 1:32-34).

4. Garland, *Luke,* 93.

5. Brown, *Birth,* 355. Psalms of praise (Pss 8, 19, 29, 33, 100, 103, 104, 111, 113, 114, 117, 135, 136, 145, 146, 147, 148, 149, 150) are divided into distinguishable parts: introduction, praise to God, motives for praise, and conclusion.

6. Green, *Luke,* 101.

and my spirit rejoices in God my Savior,
for he has looked with favor on the lowliness of his servant.
Surely, from now on all generations will call me blessed;
for the Mighty One has done great things for me,
and holy is his name.
His mercy is for those who fear him
From generation to generation. (Luke 2:46–50)

The opening lines (vv. 46-47) take the form of a Hebrew parallelism.
The second line mimics the first; only it uses different words.

Verse 46	Verse 47
my soul	my spirit
magnifies	rejoices
Lord	God my Savior

In this psalm of praise Mary magnifies or boasts of God's greatness;
hence, the title *Magnificat*, the Latin term meaning magnificent. Her use
of the phrase "my Savior" (σωτῆρί μου), however, seems to contradict the
facts on the ground. After all, God certainly has not saved her from poverty
or political oppression.[7] At the time of her visit to Elizabeth, Augustus Caesar was universally acknowledged as "savior." Under the banner of "good
news," he claimed to bring universal peace and security to the world. But
for most Jews under the heavy hand of Roman rule, peace was an illusion.
They were an oppressed people who still awaited liberation. When Mary
first sang the opening line of this hymn ("My soul magnifies the Lord, and
my spirit rejoices in God my Savior") her Jewish friends must have thought
she was delusional. But from a gentile perspective, Rome had already established peace! (*Pax Romana*) Through military conquests and negotia-
tions, Augustus Caesar brought all civilized peoples under the banner of
the empire and offered them protection from outside forces. What further
peace was needed?

Nearly a century later (ca. 85 CE), when Luke committed Mary's lyrics
to a sheaf of papyrus, social conditions had worsened for traditional Jews
and Christ followers. Emperor Claudius expelled Jews from Rome (53CE);
Nero blamed Christians for burning Rome, the capital city of the empire
(67 CE); Roman troops invaded and destroyed Jerusalem, slaughtering

---

7. In 63 BCE Pompey marched into Jerusalem and claimed the land for Rome. The
Jews put up little resistance and Rome brought Israel and its god to their knees. Things
had not changed at the time of Mary's song.

thousands, and burning the temple to the ground (70 CE); and Emperor Domitian (85–96 CE), the latest Roman savior charged with safeguarding the world, was more tyrannical than most of his predecessors. For Luke's audience Mary's lyrics did not seem to match reality. God had not saved them. Why should he be praised?

The answer lies in the way the readers interpreted the lyrics. From their vantage point God indeed was the Savior. Through the conception and birth of Mary's son, God had already put into motion his eschatological salvific plan to restore the kingdom to Israel and eventually redeem humankind.[8] They now read and sang Mary's song in light of the Christ event, including his ministry, death, resurrection, and exaltation. For them salvation was a present reality and the kingdom realized at least in part (Luke 4:21). Christ now reigned at God's right hand. But the end had not yet arrived. At the Parousia all God's enemies would be destroyed and the kingdom would encompass the world. While it appeared that Rome was in control of the world, Christ followers believed the arc of history had been altered and was now bending toward justice. The deliverance of God's people was at hand and already happening.

When Luke's readers gathered together to eat a meal and worship, they did not pour out a libation to Caesar as the rest of the empire, but raised a cup to a man whom Rome executed as a political revolutionary. Their symposium songs exalted Jesus, not Caesar, as Lord. Hence, they challenged Rome's "great tradition," i.e., the official narrative of events, and replaced it with an alternative account and vision for the future.

Mary now gives a twofold purpose for praising God as her savior.[9] First, she explains: "for he has looked with favor on the lowliness of his servant" (Luke 1:48a). As a Galilean peasant woman living far from Jerusalem—the center of Jewish political and religious power—Mary possesses no social status. Yet, she is not invisible to God. He is mindful of her existence and plight and elevates her status in the eyes of Elizabeth and those who know of God's intervention, including the community of Christ followers who read this account. As a result, Mary adds, "All generations (in perpetuity) will call me blessed" (v. 48 b).[10] "To implement his plan of

---

8. Green, *Luke*, 100.

9. Verses 48–49 form a second parallelism, each beginning with the word "for."

10. Garland, observes, "Mary is one of the lowly in Israel, but that situation has been reversed so that she has become the most blessed among women" (*Luke*, 94).

salvation, God did not choose a rich woman of high social ranks, but chose a humble girl from a village."[11]

Mary gives a second reason for calling God *magnificat*: "for the Mighty One (μεγάλα ὁ δυνατός) has done great things for me" (v. 49a). The "Mighty One" speaks of God as a powerful warrior who fights for his people. This is likely another parallelism and simply expands on the first reason. Now he has done "great things" for Mary. He not only raised her standing in the community of faith but gave her a prominent role bringing salvation to Israel and the world. He chose her as his vessel to bring the Davidic king into the world. Thus, Mary pronounces of God, "holy is his name" (v. 49 b).

The recipients, who first read the Lukan version of God's benevolence to Mary and her faithfulness to the angelic vision, are among the generations who will call Mary "blessed."

This first stanza of the Magnificat concludes, "His mercy is for those who fear him from generation to generation" (v. 50) and serves to summarize stanza one. Mary is not the only one to receive God's kindness. His mighty acts of mercy are done on behalf of all the lowly in Israel and include Luke's audience and beyond.[12] The only caveat is they must "fear God," i.e., both Jewish and gentile Christ followers are required to give unrestrained obedience to the Lord as they dwell in a culture that reverences the emperor and worships Roman gods. The fear of God must exceed the fear of the authorities. And like Mary, Christ followers must make a choice.

4.2.2 Stanza Two

Stanza two switches gears. It moves from speaking about God's mercy toward Mary and future generations to his covenant interventions on Israel's behalf in the past. It concludes with a promise that God's ongoing mercy extends "forever" into the future (v. 55).

The next few verses are some of the most grammatically difficult to interpret in the Gospel of Luke:

> He has shown strength with his arm;
>> he has scattered the proud in the thoughts of their hearts.
> He has brought down the powerful from their thrones
>> and lifted up the lowly ones;

11. Buffa, "Magnificat," 378.
12. Buffa, "Magnificat," 379.

he has filled the hungry with good things,
    and sent the rich away empty.
He has helped his servant Israel,
    in remembrance of his mercy,
according to the promise he made to our ancestors,
    To Abraham and to his descendants [seed] forever" (Luke 1:51–55).

The hymn now veers in a new direction and mentions explicitly three ways God has acted on behalf of his oppressed people. Each verse (vv. 51–53) takes the form of a contrasting or antithetical parallelism and describes ways God had been merciful to his people. First, with a strong "arm" he defended Israel and defeated her enemies. Israel's opponents were no match for him (v. 51), whether Egypt or Babylon. Second, he dethroned "the powerful" rulers and promoted the lowly (v. 52). He brought about a political and social reversal. Third, he provided food for the famished and conversely caused "the rich" to scavenge for food (v. 53).

The theme of stanza two is clearly about liberation and covenant justice. But how and when, if at all, did God free his people and reverse their fortunes?

At the time of Luke's Gospel, Jews are still in exile and under bondage to a foreign power. Luke's Jewish readers are scattered throughout the empire and their leaders did not take seriously the call to repent in preparation of the kingdom's arrival. While temporary reversals occurred, certainly none were permanent. A more appropriate stanza might have been: "He sets a table before me in the presence of mine enemies" (Ps 23:5).

The song continues in the same tenor: "He has helped his servant Israel in remembrance of his mercy" (v. 54), and reintroduces "mercy" first mentioned in stanza one (v. 50). It thus unites both stanzas and serves as a theme for the song with implications for Luke's audience. God had acted compassionately toward the nation throughout its bumpy history. The basis for his mercy is his ongoing covenant faithfulness: "the promise he made to . . . Abraham and to his seed" (v. 55).

As long as Abraham's seed survives, the promise remains in effect. But who exactly is Abraham's seed? At a surface level it speaks of the Jewish people as a whole. But Jesus narrowed the focus and limited the seed only to Jews faithful to God's covenant. Paul expanded the definition, identified Jesus as "Abraham's seed" (Gal 3:16), and included all those "in Christ," i.e., baptized Christ followers—Jews and gentiles—as beneficiaries of the promise. This means that God fulfilled his covenant promise to Abraham in Christ and his mercy extends to all, including those of Luke's day and ours.

We will fail to grasp the revolutionary nature of the Magnificat until we realize these lyrics were sung originally by those under Roman domination. The song acknowledges only one supreme God who sides with the oppressed. His actions in the past have set in motion a plan that will bring political strongmen to their knees, replace the present social structure with his kingdom, and install one who will rule righteously on his behalf. In the end, justice will prevail. Wickedness will be banished. The world will be united under the reign of God.

The Magnificat is a prophetic call for God's people to acknowledge Christ as Israel's eschatological king and give him, not Caesar, their allegiance. The subversive message opposes every authoritative regime that has ever existed, and has awakened people's imaginations of a preferred future. As a result, oppressive governments throughout history have banned the Magnificat from public use, citing its revolutionary message.[13] For Christ followers living under the heavy hand of a dictator, Mary's Song was a rallying call for non-violent resistance.

Excursus: The Elusive Aorist Tense

Six aorist tense verbs control the action in verses 51–53. Aorist verbs can function in several different ways. How we choose to interpret them in this context will determine our understanding of the passage.

Aorist verbs often—but not always—translate as simple past-tense verbs. If the rule holds true in our text, then Mary is referring to God's mighty acts in Israel's history. In the context of the Lukan narrative, his latest achievement is the miraculous conception of Mary's son, who will also be "called 'Son of the Most High.'"[14] This event sets in motion "the decisive

13. British officials in colonial India, recognizing the subversive nature of its message, ordered agitated Indian natives to stop singing The Magnificat, even during church services. Likewise, when the poor and marginalized of Guatemala adopted the song, which spoke of hope for deliverance and regime change, the government outlawed singing or reciting it in public. When mothers of kidnapped and murdered children in Argentina posted the lyrics of Mary's song in the Plaza de Mayo of Buenos Aries, the military junta of Argentina banned any public display of Mary's song ("The Subversive Magnificat: What Mary Expected The Messiah To Be Like," http://enemylove.com/subversive-magnificat-mary-expected-messiah-to-be-like).

14. Green, *Luke*, 99–100.

eschatological work of God" and marks the beginning of Israel's kingdom restoration.[15] Salvation for God's people has arrived.[16]

The aorist tense, however, may also function idiomatically like the Hebrew perfect tense (popularly called the prophetic perfect) and points to the future.[17] If this is the case, and Mary is the inspired composer of the Magnificat, she may be confident that the events (vv. 51-53) are forward looking and speaks of them imaginatively as if they have occurred already. In her mind Mary's unborn child ("God's son") "has already put down the mighty from their thrones."[18] It is as good as done. In real time, he will become the instrument to bring about the sociopolitical reversal.

But as Garland observes, "the aorist tense may also reveal the perspective of Luke and the reader[s]."[19] In this scenario the verbs point to specific past actions, i.e., what God did in Christ when he raised him from the dead and placed him on the throne of David (Acts 2:29-36). In doing so, God set his people free and inaugurated his ever-expanding kingdom. When Luke's audience comes together and sings the Magnificat during their symposium meetings ca. 85 CE, they remember the "salvific work of Christ in the past."[20] This lyrical "praise for what God *had done* could be retroverted and placed on Mary's lips because Luke is interpreting the conception of Jesus" from a post-resurrection point of view.[21] Christ followers believed that Jesus' death and resurrection marked an end to Rome's universal rule. The church became the locus where (for a few hours a week, at least) the faithful exercised their freedom, overcame social class distinctions, filled their empty stomachs, and praised Jesus as Lord over all.[22]

15. Green, *Luke*, 100.

16. Salvation does not speak primarily of a spiritual salvation, but of an earthly deliverance. The Magnificat, however, is not a call to launch a violent revolution against Rome, but a recognition that God's faithfulness to his covenant promises will bring about the desired change.

17. Bruce, *Colossians, Philemon, Ephesians*, 287 notes other examples include Eph 2:6 and Jude 14.

18. Brown, *Birth*, 362.

19. Garland, *Luke*, 95.

20. Green, *Luke*, 100.

21. Brown, *Birth*, 363.

22. The Gospel of Luke and Acts place great emphasis on the good news to the poor and reversal of social status (Luke 4:18-19; 6:20, 24-26; 7:18-23; 14:13-21; 16:19-26; 18:18-30; 19:1-10; 21:1-4; Acts 2:41-47; 4:32-39; 5:11; 6:1-7; 11:27, 30). Luke says a sea change has begun. Salvation has arrived "Today" (Luke 2:11; 19:9) and the Scripture has been "fulfilled" (4:21). God has inaugurated the kingdom. The church lives according to

However we interpret the aorist tense in this passage, the result is the same.[23] Mary and/or the Lukan audience believed that what God had accomplished through the conception and life of Jesus had and would effect sociopolitical change. Christ-focused songs helped to inform church members how they should conduct their affairs amid an oppressive regime.[24]

Those old enough remember how "We Shall Overcome" encouraged those struggling for civil rights in the 1960s. The song represented their cause, aspirations, and determination to resist non-violently the system that held sway over human life. As they sang in unison, the lyrics proclaimed simply, but powerfully that one day oppressors would no longer rule and fortunes would be reversed.

Stanza:　　1. We shall overcome
　　　　　　2. We'll walk hand in hand (3x) + someday (at end)
　　　　　　3. We shall all be free
　　　　　　4. We are not afraid
　　　　　　5. We are not alone
　　　　　　6. The whole wide world around
　　　　　　7. We shall overcome

Chorus:　　Oh, deep in my heart
　　　　　　I do believe
　　　　　　We shall overcome
　　　　　　someday (sung after each stanza)[25]

The lyrics reminded the oppressed that universal freedom was on the horizon, but not yet achieved ("The whole wide world . . . *someday*"). Until

---

kingdom ethics.

23. Although not entirely connected with the interpretation of the aorist tense, a related issue is the origin of the hymn itself, i.e., where did Luke find this hymn? According to Farris, *Hymns*, 14, there are three options. First, Mary composed the lyrics. The words actually came from Mary's lips. Second, Luke composed the lyrics and placed them on Mary's lips. Third, they came from another source and Luke incorporated them into his narrative. Luke was not an eyewitness to these events (Luke 1:1-4). If Mary is the versifier, she likely sang the original version in Aramaic. Her song would have been passed down orally and translated into Greek by the time Luke penned his Gospel. One can imagine Christ followers in the nascent church singing the Magnificat during their symposium worship gatherings.

24. An idiomatic use of the aorist/Hebrew perfect can serve also as the basis of the already/not yet eschatological scheme, i.e., that which began in the past has present consequences; yet, it remains to be consummated at the Parousia. See Dunn, *Jesus and the Spirit*, 309.

25. Song in public domain.

that time, they kept the faith ("in my heart I believe") and remained united ("We'll walk hand in hand"), knowing that God was on their side ("We are not alone"). In a similar manner, through songs, the early church proclaimed its alternative vision of the world. Believers gathered weekly to encourage each other. Songs like the Magnificat stirred them to persevere.

4.3 Mary and Her Sisters

Mary was the latest in a long line of female prophets who raised their voices to God in song. After God's triumph over Egypt, the Hebrew masses crossed the Red Sea in jubilant celebration (Exod 15:1-18). A procession of dancing women—tambourines in hand—then followed "the prophet Miriam" who sang and exhorted them with these words: "Sing to the Lord, for he has triumphed gloriously; horse and rider he has thrown into the seas" (vv. 20-21).

Since both Miriam and Mary musically celebrate a change of fortunes because of God's intervention, does Luke's audience make a thematic connection between the two events? Some support this thesis because at this juncture in the narrative Luke chooses to designate Mary as Μαριάμ, the "undeclinable Hebrew form" of her name, rather than Μαρία, the more Hellenized version (Luke 1:46).[26]

Mary's song may also prompt Luke's readers to remember Deborah's paean of praise following God's triumph over the Canaanites, Israel's fierce foes (Judg 5:1-31). Despite being outnumbered and outflanked by their adversaries, Deborah and fellow judge Barak bravely led the Hebrew army into battle. When God threw the Canaanite troops into confusion, Israel took strategic advantage of the chaos and emerged victorious. At battle's end, Deborah and Barak lyrically memorialized the account in a new song that attributed battlefield success to divine intervention. They told how God used women, the mothers of the nation, to accomplish victory. As a result, the tables were turned as the high and mighty fell, and the Jewish peasants divided the spoils.

Mary's rhythmic librettos are also reminiscent of Hannah's song and may be modeled after it.[27] Upon receiving word that she is pregnant, Hannah, like Mary, forecasts the downfall of political powerbrokers and military chiefs, and prosperity for the formerly subjugated Jewish people: "The

---

26. Miller, *Rumors*, 96.
27. Buffa, "Magnificat," 377.

bows of the mighty are broken, but the feeble gird on strength. Those who were full hire themselves out for bread, but those who were hungry are fat with spoils" (1 Sam 2:4-5a). Hannah and Mary—two "young mothers whose sons are poised to do great things in . . . service to God"—sing of a reordering of society and a return of social justice.[28] Both Hannah's and Mary's song "take on tones of social hymns," i.e., songs that address "the abuse of power and injustice" and use "strong reversal imagery and socio-political language."[29]

The lyrics found in all three songs speak of Israel's disobedience to the covenant and the resultant outcome, but they also contain God's promise of restoration. Mary's song (ca. 6 BCE) was simply the latest musical iteration.

4.4 The Birth of Jesus

Luke gives little information regarding the actual birth of Jesus, other than placing Jesus' birth in its sociopolitical context: "In those days a decree went out from Emperor Augustus that all the world should be registered" (Luke 2:1). The census was a tool of oppression used to count the population and determine the amount of taxes that tributary nations owed Rome.

Luke adds, "This was the first registration [census] and was taken while Quirinius was governor of Syria" (v. 2). There is no reference outside the Gospel of Luke to a worldwide census taking place under Caesar Augustus and carried out in Syria in 6–4 BCE. Josephus dates Quirinius's governorship a decade later.[30] While many have sought to explain away the discrepancy, it may be that Luke is not concerned with specific dates but simply uses the taxation story as a literary device to get the couple to Bethlehem, Joseph's ancestral home (vv. 3–5), where Messiah must be born.[31]

> While they were there, the time came for her to deliver her child. And she gave birth to her firstborn son and wrapped him in bands of cloth, and laid him in a manger, because there was no place for them in the inn. (Luke 2:6-7)

"While" conveys the idea that Mary and Joseph were in Bethlehem for a period before the birth. With no lodgings available, a stable or possibly a

28. Miller, *Rumors*, 95.

29. Buffa, "Magnificat," 377.

30. Josephus, *Ant.* 18.1-4.

31. Fitzmyer, *Luke I-IX*, 393.

cave became the delivery room, and the animal trough served as a cradle. These circumstances speak to the lowly economic standing of the family and the Jewish Messiah's lack of status. Unlike Caesar, who was born in the lap of luxury, Jesus is born into poverty in a backwater town on the easternmost edge of the empire. That such a one is destined to rescue Israel from oppression challenges logic and must cause Joseph and Mary to wonder if their angelic visit was not a deceiving spirit.

4.4.1 A Birth Announcement

Luke tells how a group of shepherds learn of Jesus' birth and make a night trek to the manger, and thus become the first eyewitnesses of the event. Earlier that evening, as they guarded their flocks, possibly in the same fields as David a thousand years before, God's glory shone, turning night into day and an angel suddenly appeared (vv. 8-9). To console the shaken sheepherders, the angel announced, "Do not be afraid; for see—I am bringing you good news of great joy for all the people: to you is born this day in the city of David a Savior, who is the Messiah, the Lord" (vv. 10-11). This could mean only one thing—God was about to reestablish David's throne and set up his kingdom. The promises made centuries before were being fulfilled "this day."[32]

For the shepherds as well as for Luke's readers (ca. 85 CE) the term "good news" was familiar. Caesar Augustus was the originator of good news. He alone rescued the Republic and transformed it into a thriving and expanding empire. Caesar was Lord (*kyrios*) and Savior (*sōtēr*) as this well-known *Priene Calendar Inscription* confirms:

> Augustus, whom she [Providence] has filled with arete [i.e. virtue] for the benefit of humanity, and has in her beneficence granted us and those who will come after us a Saviour (σωτῆρα) who has made war to cease and who shall put everything [in peaceful] order; and whereas Caesar, having become [God] manifest, transcended the expectations of all who had anticipated the good news, not only by surpassing the benefits conferred by his predecessors but by leaving no expectation of surpassing him to those who would come after him, with the result that the birthday of our God (τοῦ θεοῦ) signalled the beginning of Good News for the world because of him; ..... Proconsul Paul Fabius [Maximus] has discovered a way to

---

32. Garland, *Luke*, 123.

honour Augustus that was hitherto unknown among the Greeks, namely to reckon time from the date of his nativity; therefore, with the blessings of Good Fortune and for their own welfare, the Greeks in Asia decreed that the New Year begin for all the cities on September 23, which is the birthday of Augustus; and, to ensure that the dates coincide in every city, all documents are to carry both the Roman and the Greek date, and the first month shall, in accordance with the decree, be observed as the Month of Caesar, beginning with 23 September, the birthday of Caesar.[33]

The inscription, carved in two stone tablets and discovered at Priene (an ancient Greek city situated in Western Turkey), uses "gospel" in reference to Augustus Caesar, showing it was a political term and was used prior to the Christian era but later borrowed and applied to Christ (Mark 1:1). Designated as the Priene *Calendar* Inscription, it proclaims that the city of Priene and sister cities (located in modern–day western Turkey) intend to change its calendar and begin its new year on the birthday of Emperor Augustus. The good news (gospel) of Caesar's birth inaugurated a new era of peace and deliverance for all peoples who surrendered and pledged allegiance to their new king, designated as a god manifested in the flesh.

The good news delivered by a heavenly messenger announcing the birth of a new "Savior" and "Lord"—shockingly identified as Christ the Jewish Messiah King—challenged an essential Roman belief.

The angel then reveals, "This will be a sign for you: you will find a child wrapped in bands of cloth [swaddling clothes] and lying in a manger" (v. 12).

Newborns were customarily wrapped tightly in swaths of cloth;[34] therefore, this alone cannot be the sign. But what if one found a baby nestling in a food trough for animals?

Fitzmyer observes that Luke's narrative brings to memory the saying of Isa 1:3 (LXX), "An ox knows its owner and an ass the manger of its lord, but Israel knows me not, and my people do not comprehend."[35] Israel's native elites will miss the birth of their Messiah, but humble shepherds and barn animals will witness the dawning of a new age, one that will replace the era instituted by Caesar.

---

33. Dio Cassius, *Hist.* 51.20.6–8; Suetonius, *Aug.* 52. Danker, *Benefactor*, 217, dates *The Priene Inscription* to 9 BCE.

34. Pliny, *Nat.* 7.2–3.

35. Fitzmyer, *Luke I–IX*, 394.

4.4.2 Angels We Have Heard on High

> And suddenly there was with the angel a multitude of the heavenly host, praising God and saying, "Glory to God in the highest heaven, and on earth peace among those whom he favors!" (Luke 2:13-14)

The angelic song, known as the *Gloria in Excelsis* became "the first Christmas cantata."[36]

The *Gloria* further challenged Caesar's imperial claims. Roman peace was considered Caesar's greatest gift to the world. It entailed a promise of peace and security for all living under the protection of Rome. But according to the angelic choir, *Pax Romana* was inadequate. *Pax Christi* would replace it.

On their travels to and from the site of discovery, the shepherds tell of their incredible encounter with the angels and the eschatological message they brought, "and all who heard it were amazed at what the shepherds told them" (vv. 15-18, 20). The shepherds become the first human heralds of the good news of Christ and his kingdom.

Everyone is ecstatic, including Mary, but at the same time she is also perplexed. Luke writes that she "treasured" and "pondered" the meaning of the events "in her heart" (v. 20). Mary kept her promise to God. Now she must wait for the future to unfold.

36. Powell, *Introduction*, 170.

CHAPTER 5

A Lyrical Prologue (John 1:1–18)

In the beginning was the Word, and the Word was with God, and the Word was God. He was in the beginning with God. All things came into being through him, and without him not one thing came into being. What has come into being in him was life, and the life was the light of all people. The light shines in the darkness, and the darkness did not overcome it.

There was a man sent from God, whose name was John. He came as a witness to testify to the light, so that all might believe through him. He himself was not the light, but he came to testify to the light. The true light, which enlightens everyone, was coming into the world.

He was in the world, and the world came into being through him; yet the world did not know him. He came to what was his own, and his own people did not accept him. But to all who received him, who believed in his name, he gave power to become children of God, who were born, not of blood or of the will of the flesh or of the will of man, but of God.

And the Word became flesh and lived among us, and we have seen his glory, the glory as of a father's only son, full of grace and truth. (John testified to him and cried out, "This was he of whom I said, 'He who comes after me ranks ahead of me because he was before me.'") From his fullness we have all received, grace upon grace.

The law indeed was given through Moses; grace and truth came through Jesus Christ. No one has ever seen God. It is God the only Son, who is close to the Father's heart, who has made him known. (JOHN 1:1–18)

5.1 Historical Context

No scholarly consensus exists regarding who wrote the Gospel of John. In the second century Irenaeus identified the "beloved disciple" as John, the son of Zebedee, based on the testimony of Polycarp, who personally knew John.[1] While internal evidence indicates the author is the "beloved disciple" (John 19:26; 21:7, 20), it never links him to a particular name or person.

The recipients of John's Gospel are both Jewish and gentile Christ followers, possibly living in Ephesus or some other city in western Asia Minor at the end of the first century CE.[2] If this time frame and location are correct, those who pledged their fidelity to Christ in baptism understood it to be a life and death decision.[3] Messianic Jews connected with synagogues in the region often faced persecution from their non-messianic counterparts; hence, the Gospel of John includes an account of a confrontation between the man born blind and his parents with angry synagogue officials over the identity of Jesus; "for the Jews had already agreed that anyone who confessed Jesus to be the Messiah would be put out of the synagogue" (John 9:22). While the parents escaped expulsion, their son did not: "And they drove him out" (v. 34). Many Pharisees who believed in Jesus were fearful of proclaiming him the Christ "for fear that they would be put out of the synagogue" (12:42–43).

Gentile Christ followers, on the other hand, faced opposition from pagan family, friends, neighbors, and fellow guild members who worshiped and sacrificed to Caesar and the gods. A pagan might face economic

1. Irenaeus, *Haer.* 3.1.1.

2. According to tradition, the Gospel of John is written to Ephesus, based on its likely association with Revelation. If true, the audiences might be the same. The dating is based on the discovery of the Rylands Papyrus (P52) containing John 18:31–33, 37–38, placing the Gospel of John at the end of the first century or the first part of the second century at the latest.

3. See Streett, *Caesar and the Sacrament*, for an in-depth treatment of the subject.

deprivation and loss of social identity if s/he abandoned idolatry and the imperial cult to worship Jesus exclusively.

In a note of consolation, the gospel promises "eternal life" to all Jewish and gentile believers in exchange for their faithfulness (John 3:16).

Unlike the Synoptics, the Gospel of John covers three years in the ministry of Jesus, starting in Galilee, but focuses mainly on Jesus' activities in and around Jerusalem (John 8-20). Much of the gospel is written in the form of a quest motif with either Jesus seeking followers or people seeking Jesus.[4] These encounters end in either acceptance or rejection of Jesus.

Other features of the gospel include: 1) mention of signs performed by Jesus that point to his identity and authority to grant eternal life for those who believe; 2) strategically placed accounts of Jesus' attendance at Jewish festivals, including Passover, Tabernacles, Dedication, and defining himself in light of these rituals; 3) the coming together of Jewish elites to oppose Jesus and his apocalyptic movement.

The prologue serves as the preface to John's Gospel and takes the form of a hymn.[5] It "introduces the audience to four major elements that will be elaborated subsequently in the gospel story."[6] They include, Jesus' origins (vv. 1-5), John the Baptizer's witness to Jesus (vv. 6-8), the people's response to Jesus (vv. 9-16), and Jesus' relation to Moses (vv. 17-18).[7]

This poetic foreword touches upon several themes, which will reappear in the gospel narrative, including the preexistence of the Word, light versus darkness, and Jesus as the Son of God, among others. It portrays Jesus as the human embodiment of God's glory in contrast to the tabernacle/temple, the traditional site of the Shekinah (John 1:14). Later in the first chapter, and after the prologue, Jesus is also identified as the "King of Israel" (1:50). These latter two themes are interconnected and run throughout the book. In Cana of Galilee, Jesus performs his first sign "and reveals his glory; and his disciples believe in him" (2:11).[8]

John's audience, many of whom are gentiles, have turned from emperor worship to Jesus worship. As a result, they have already faced or will face persecution. The emperor at the time is Domitian (81–96 CE),

4. Painter, "Inclined to God," 355.

5. Schnackenburg, Gospel, 224-25 reviews pro and con arguments whether John 1:1-18 is a hymn or poetic prose.

6. Carter, Telling Tales, 214.

7. Carter, Telling Tales, 214.

8. John 11:4, 40; 13:31-32; 17:1-5; 17:22.

characterized in Revelation as a "beast." He required his subjects to address him as "*Dominus et Deus noster*," i.e., "our Lord and god."[9] Most people in Asia Minor had no difficulty worshiping Caesar as a god. When Christ followers refused, he unleashed his wrath upon them.[10]

5.2 Structure of the Prologue

The prologue is written in poetic language and reflects how the Johannine community viewed Jesus Christ. Did the hymn preexist before the Gospel was written or did it come from the fertile mind of the Johannine composer? Unlike other hymns found in the NT letters, this song seems to be written in the style of the Gospel writer and is likely his original composition.

There are varied and creative ways to divide the song for analysis. Culpepper, for example, finds a chiastic structure:

A (1–5) The relationship of the Logos to God, creation, and humankind.

   B (6–8) The Witness of John the Baptist to the Light.

      C (9–11) The arrival of the Light/Logos and its rejection.

         D (12–13) Benefits of believing in the Light/Logos.

      C1 (14) The arrival of the Light/Logos and its reception.

   B1 (15) The witness of John the Baptist.

A1 The relationship of the Logos to humans, creation, and God.[11]

For Culpepper the pivot of the prologue is the central section (designated D), which focuses on the benefits of placing one's faith in Jesus.

C. K. Barrett offers a simpler four-part arrangement: 1) Verses 1–5, Christological Statement; 2) Verses 6–8, Witness of John the Baptist; 3) Verses 9–13, The Coming of the Light; 4) Verses 14–18, Attributes of Salvation.[12] Our analysis of the hymn will follow this structure.

9. Suetonius, *Dom.* 13.2. This is the same title ascribed to Jesus found in John 20:28 and Rev 4:11, showing Caesar has competition.

10. Eusebius, *Hist. eccl.* 3:19.

11. Culpepper, "Pivot," 1–31.

12. Barrett, *Gospel*, 149–50.

5.2.1 Stanza 1 (The Nature of the Word)

The hymn opens with a majestic acclamation: "In the beginning was the Word, the Word was with God, and the Word was God" (John 1:1).

The nature and identity of the "Word" (*logos*) has been a matter of theological conversation throughout the centuries. Stoic philosophers saw it as the divine principle that gave order or logic to the universe.[13]

Many first-century Jews equated the *logos* with the OT concept of Wisdom (*Sophia*), which was present with God at creation and God's agent to humankind (Prov 3:19; 8:22-31; Sir 1:4; 24:1-18; Wis 7:12—8:4). Following this line of thinking, Carter and Levine, see the Johannine Jesus as "Wisdom incarnate: the manifestation of God in human flesh."[14]

Philo of Alexandria combined Stoic and Wisdom theories. For him, the *logos* represented both the manifestation of God's presence and the mediator between God and the world.[15]

Possibly the Johannine author uses the term "Word" (*logos*) simply because words are vehicles of revelation. They are "the expression of what is in one's mind."[16]

We get to know each other through verbal communication. To use a contemporary example, think of a first date. You desire to know your date, so you ask all kinds of questions about family, hobbies, likes and dislikes, hopes, and dreams, career goals, favorite movies, etc. Your partner does the same. By the end of the evening, you both know each other better than when you first met. The more we speak the better we know each other.

God revealed himself through the Word. It was "God's utterance" about himself.[17] The Word conveyed God's nature and his will. Since the song later reveals Jesus as the human embodiment of the Word, the more one knows about Jesus, the more s/he knows about God.

---

13. Barrett, *Gospel*, 152.

14. Carter and Levine, *New Testament*, 75.

15. Philo, *QE* 2.68.

16. Bruce, *John*, 29.

17. Malina and Rohrbaugh, *Social Science*, 31. The authors note that in ancient society, illiterate persons (90 percent of the population) understood the term "word" to refer to a verbal utterance and not what they read. A word was not a single noun, or verb, but the totality of what was spoken. When asked to repeat a word, a person might repeat everything he or she had just said. In this sense, one might say the Logos was God's total utterance about himself (35).

Verse one provides three immediate facts about the Word. First, the Word is *eternal* ("In the beginning was the Word"). This links the *logos* to creation in Gen 1:1. "When creation occurred, the Word already existed."[18] Nothing preceded it. The Word was there at the beginning of creation.

Second, the Word is *equal* to God ("the Word was with God"). The Greek preposition πρὸς, translated "with" can also be rendered "toward" and refers to direction. The "Word" stood metaphorically face to face with God, literally "*the* God" (τὸν θεόν), a likely allusion to God as Father, which John develops later in the gospel. While the Word and God were separate, they were related as a Son to a Father.

Third, the Word is of the same *essence* as God ("and the Word *was* God"). In this instance, no definite article modifies God. The pre-existent *logos* possessed God's divine nature, but was not the Father. The Word was God but was not all of God.[19]

Verse 2 reiterates the second line: "He was in the beginning with [the, τὸν] God."

Next the lyrics declare that the entirety of creation, without exception, owes its existence to the *logos*: "All things came into being through him, and without him not one thing came into being" (3a). The Hebrew Bible also links God's Word to creation (Ps 33:6), providing a Jewish context for the claim.[20] The Word was "God's companion in creation."[21] The lyrics use both positive ("all things . . . came") and negative language ("not one thing came") to accentuate the inclusiveness of the Word's creative power. Additionally, the Word is personified by the use of the pronoun "his" (αὐτός), which will be identified later as incarnate in Jesus (v. 17).

The *logos* was not only an eternal being, but also a living being: "in him was life."[22] As possessor of eternal life, he was self-existent. He needed nothing outside of himself to survive. As possessor of life, he had the capacity to impart life to his creation without diminishing his own supply of life.

18. Bruce, *John*, 31; Harris, *John*, 18.

19. Carson, *John*, 117.

20. Philo, *Cher.* 125-27, depicted the Logos as the channel of creation.

21. Michaels, *John*, 49.

22. Later in the Gospel, Jesus claims he is "life" (John 11:25; 14:6).

The song continues "and the life was the light of all people" (v. 4b).[23] Life and light are used synonymously (life equals light).[24] They are "attributes of God."[25] The *logos* was not only the life giver but the light giver. It revealed for all to see what had been unseen or unknown previously, in this case about God.[26] It shone on all sentient beings.

To emphasize the ongoing aspect of revelation, the lyricist pens, "The light shines in the darkness" (v. 5a), i.e., it still shines and is available for all to see. The writer then adds a historical note about an attempt to snuff out the light: "the darkness did not overcome it" (v. 5b).

Darkness is the absence of light. When a match is struck even amidst pitch blackness, the light, however weak, prevails. It reveals what the darkness had hidden from view, in this case, the knowledge of God. As light shines, darkness dissipates. The brighter the light the more one can see clearly.

If "light" and "life" are equated, then one might assume the same is true of "darkness" and "death." The light and life of the *logos* prevailed over darkness and death. The Gospel of John records many unsuccessful attempts to stamp out Jesus and his life-giving mission, ending at the cross. When Jesus emerged from the tomb, the power of darkness and death, unable to overcome the *logos*, were defeated The light continued to shine, making knowledge of God available to all.

This verse may have been included to motivate John's readers to persevere amidst suffering, knowing that even if they are martyred by the powers of darkness, God will raise them from the dead just as he raised Jesus.

5.2.2 Stanza 2 (The Witness to the Word)

The composer introduces his audience to a divinely appointed emissary whose main mission was to testify that Jesus was the *logos*: "There was a man sent from God whose name was John" (v. 6).[27]

---

23. Jesus will also refer to himself as the "light" in the Gospel account (John 8:12; 9:5; 12:46).

24. Philo, *Opif.*, 24-31, associated the Logos to both life and light.

25. Michaels, *John*, 51.

26. Philo, *Leg.* 3.169-78, reveals God.

27. Michaels, *John*, 45, believes the gospel story actually begins with verse 6 and verses 1-5 serve as a preface to the story.

John is identified specifically as "a man" whereas the Word is described as "God" (v. 1). Unlike Luke, who elaborates on the messenger's identity, no such effort is made here, which indicates that the Johannine community is already familiar with John. If written to Ephesus and surrounding areas, a John the Baptist movement may still be active among Jews and competing for disciples (Acts 19:1–7). If so, this stanza serves a twofold purpose. First, it places John's human status below Jesus' divine status. Second, it places John in the role of an authoritative ambassador who verifies Jesus' identity: "He came as a witness to testify to the light" (v. 7a).

According to the gospel writer, the *logos* was the *light*.[28] God's purpose for commissioning John to be a witness to the light follows: "so that all might believe through him." John was God's prophetic mouthpiece calling the nation to repentance and pointing to Jesus (vv.19-28).

Stanza 2 reiterates, "He himself was not the light, but he came to testify to the light. The true light, which enlightens everyone, was coming into the world" (vv. 8-9). That these words need to be repeated supports the possibility of a burgeoning John the Baptist movement in the region that received the gospel. They need to abandon loyalty to John, since he was subordinate to Jesus. John was the forerunner, the messenger, commissioned to bear witness to the light that shines on every person without exception or distinction. The light of revelation was for all: Jews, gentiles, freed, enslaved, women, men, barbarians, and citizens alike. No one was excluded. Apart from the light of revelation no one can know God.

5.2.3 Stanza 3 (The World and the Word)

This stanza introduces how the world reacted both negatively and positively when the Word entered time and space: "He was in the world, and

---

28. Later in the chapter, the Baptist will use another metaphor to describe logos: "Here is the Lamb of God who takes away the sin of the world" (John 1:29). He will then go on to explain how he recognized the logos:

> I myself did not know him: but I came baptizing with water for this reason, that he might be revealed to Israel. And John testified, "I saw the Spirit descending from heaven like a dove and it remained on him. I myself did not know him, but the one who sent me to baptize with water said to me, 'He on whom you see the Spirit descend and remain is the one who baptizes with the Holy Spirit.' And I myself have seen and have testified that this is the Son of God." (vv. 31-34)

the world came into being through him; yet the world did not know him" (v. 10).

Unlike the birth narratives in Matthew or Luke, the lyricist offers no explanation how the eternal *logos* became a human. Neither does he mention Jesus by name; although the audience at the end of the first century already knows that Jesus is the *logos* made flesh. The verse simply says that humankind at the time of his arrival did not recognize its own creator.

In addition to not recognizing him, the world refused to acknowledge him even after John baptized him, the Spirit descended, and God verified Jesus' identity: "He came to what was his own, and his own people did not accept him" (v. 11). Does "his own people" refer to Jews only? Or was he was rejected by humankind in general and "his own people" in particular? If the gospel writer views *logos* and wisdom as interrelated, 1 Enoch may provide a context for understanding this rejection:

> Wisdom found not a place on earth where she could inhabit; her dwelling therefore is in heaven.
>
> Wisdom went forth to dwell among the sons of men, but she obtained not a habitation. Wisdom returned to her place, and seated herself in the midst of the angels. But iniquity went forth after her return, who unwillingly found a habitation, and resided among them, as rain in the desert, and as a dew in a thirsty land. (1 En. 42:1–2)

In the role of the *logos*, "Wisdom dwells among humans and so reveals God's presence and will."[29] Like Wisdom, the *logos* will return to heaven, but not until it is rejected and crucified.

Despite being rebuffed by the majority, a remnant responded positively to Christ and his message: "But to all who received (ἔλαβον) him, who believed (ἔδωκεν) in his name, he gave power to become children of God" (v. 12).[30] To receive someone conveys the idea of welcoming or embracing the person. To believe in his name means to commit or entrust oneself to the person and his cause. He gave those who sided with him the right or authority to enter God's family. The offer was made to them "who were born . . . of God" (v. 13 a, e).

This is a metaphorical allusion to the second or new birth, a theme John develops in chapter 3. All people enter a human family through physical birth. To some, however, Jesus granted the right to be "born again" into

---

29. Carter and Levine, *New Testament*, 75.

30. Philo, *Conf.* 1.146-47. The *logos* empowers humans to become children of God.

God's eternal family. This is comparable to Jesus' divine conception, only now God implants his seed into believers by his spirit and they become his children.

Verse 13 also includes three negatives: "who are *born not* of blood or of the will of the flesh or of the will of man, but of God" (v. 13). These three conditions are insufficient and do not qualify one to become a child of God. The first, "not of blood" (οὐκ ἐξ αἱμάτων), literally "bloods" (plural) is found in Ovid and used idiomatically to mean bloodshed (similarly in 2 Sam 16:8).[31] The Zealots wished to usher in the kingdom through use of violence.

In this context, however, it likely means the mingling of bloods, i.e., the blood of two parents in the normal process of human procreation.[32] One's ancestry or being born of Jewish parents does not qualify one to become a child of God. This theme will arise again when a group of Jews confront Jesus and claim they are children of God based on their relationship with Abraham. Jesus responds, "If God were your father, you would love me, for I came from God and now I am here." He then identifies the devil as "their father" (John 8:39-44). Even Jews must be born from above. As Jesus tells Nicodemus, one must be born a second time to enter the kingdom of God (John 3:3-8).

The second negative, "or of the will of the flesh" (οὐδὲ ἐκ θελήματος σαρκὸς), may refer to human nature but, more likely, points to the inability of carnal effort—keeping Jewish traditions, purification laws, festivals—to gain one's entrance into the family of God.

The third negative, "or of the will of *man*" (ἐκ θελήματος ἀνδρὸς), specifically refers to the "male" gender (ἀνδρὸς, *andros*) as opposed to the female. While difficult to understand the meaning of this statement, it may lean toward the idea that when a Jewish male reached adulthood and became a son of the law, he was accepted as a full member into God's kingdom. The lyrics say otherwise.

To receive the status as God's child, one must be "born of God." The song does not explain or elaborate on how one is born again. But it is a privilege granted to those who received and believed on Jesus. Later the Gospel will address the Spirit's role in the process.

---

31. Ovid, *Metam.* 1:151-76.

32. Barrett, *Gospel*, 164. Just as Jesus was conceived by the Holy Spirit, so his followers must be reborn by the Spirit.

5.2.4 Stanza 4 (The Incarnation of the Word)

"And the Word became flesh and lived among us" (v. 14 a). The eternal *logos* entered time and space and took on human form. The verb "lived" from the Greek ἐσκήνωσεν can be translated "encamped," in which case it means the *logos* pitched his tent and tabernacled in our midst.

The divine Word became something he previously was not—a human—in order to make God known. The verse continues, "and we have seen his glory" (v. 14 b). The "we" refers to those who received him over against those who rejected him.

After the exodus, God's glory—manifested as a cloud by day and a pillar of fire by night—guided his people across the wilderness. Whenever it stopped, the people halted and erected the portable tabernacle at that location. God's glory descended, entered the tabernacle, and rested between the wings of the cherubim in the holy of holies. The tribes pitched their tents, three tribes to the east of the tabernacle, three to the west, three to the north, and three to the south. God dwelt or encamped in the midst of his people.

At the dedication of the temple, after Solomon prayed and offered a sacrifice to God, "fire came down from heaven and consumed the burnt offering and the sacrifices; and the glory of the Lord filled the temple" (2 Chr 7:1).

After the fall of Babylon and the destruction of the temple, God's glory departed Israel. While there is no unambiguous scriptural evidence that the glory ever returned to fill the second temple, most Jews likely assumed it was present.[33] The Qumran community, however, disagreed and viewed the entire temple institution as corrupt.

Through the incarnation God chose to dwell once again among his people. Jesus served as the tabernacle for his glory. Occasionally Jesus' followers glimpsed the glory of God as Jesus taught, performed signs, and was transfigured before them.

The verse describes the glory as "the glory as of a father's only son, full of grace and truth" (v. 14 c). The unique son of God manifested his father's glory, initially at his baptism when the Spirit descended and remained on him and was witnessed by John the Baptizer, and then through his teaching and signs. God's glory in the son is characterized as "full of grace and truth."

33. Sanders, *Judaism*, 69–128. See (2 Macc 2:5–18; 14:35–36; Sir 50:1; 3 Macc 2:16). Josephus was one.

Nothing exceeds fullness. From a Jewish perspective, "grace and truth" are connected to God's covenant faithfulness toward his people. He provides for his people and keeps his promises (Exod 34:6-7).

In the context of Greco-Roman society, "grace" was associated with patronage and "truth" with revelation and knowledge of God.

The Roman social order was dependent on patronage, the giving and receiving of benefaction. According to Seneca, patronage was the "chief bond of human society."[34] Those with influence, authority, financial means, or property were under moral obligation to befriend and assist the needy. The Greek word *charis,* translated "grace," referred to the gift that the patron bestowed on the one seeking help. In return, the client pledged *pistis,* i.e., loyalty or faithfulness to the patron. This took the form of service to the benefactor and expression of public respect. A lifelong bond or friendship was formed.[35]

A broker or mediator often introduced the needy party to the patron and set up a relationship between the two. In Roman society, Jupiter, the highest god, was the ultimate benefactor whose benefits flowed through his son Caesar, the mediator, to all others.

When people became Christ followers, they often lost their former patronage. The Johannine hymn offers a new and infinitely better source of patronage. Jesus brokered a deal between God, whom Jesus revealed as a Father, and the born–again ones, whom the hymn calls God's children. Believers were assured all their needs would be met. In return they owed God their faithfulness (*pistis*).

The songwriter adds a parenthetical note in verse 15 that seems to confirm the above conclusion: (John testified to him and cried out, "This was he of whom I said, 'He who comes after me ranks ahead of me because he was before me'"). With unlimited resources at his disposal, the one greater than John, became the mediator between God and humankind: "From his fullness we have received grace upon grace" (v. 16). God's benefits through Christ were unlimited. This is a message that the recipients, having abandoned former means of patronage, needed to hear.

The song ends with a comparison and a proclamation aimed specifically at a Jewish audience: "The law indeed was given through Moses; grace

34. Seneca, *Ben.* 1.4.2.

35. DeSilva, *Introduction*, 100-107, from which this material was gleaned, provides an excellent overview of patronage in the Roman Empire. Also see deSilva, *Honor, Patronage*, 95-121, which expands on the topic.

and truth came through Jesus Christ" (v. 17). While the law was good, it was temporary. Moses was God's anointed leader but, like John, he pointed to the coming Messiah (Deut 18:15), here identified by name. This is the only mention of "Jesus" in the hymn. It seems the lyricist saved his name until the end to provide a fitting climax and crescendo. Jesus provided "grace" (divine benefits, especially eternal life) and "truth" (revelation of God).

The song concludes, "No one has ever seen God. It is God the only Son, who is close to the Father's heart, who has made him known" (v. 18). As the pre-incarnate *logos*, Jesus Christ is uniquely God's Son, and has had an intimate relationship "with" (*pros*) his Father. He "made him known" (ἐκεῖνος ἐξηγήσατο); or as Bruce observes, "The Son is the exegete of the Father."[36] He revealed and explained what God is like. Without revelation humankind remains in darkness.

The Synoptic Gospels recount the life and ministry of Jesus, the man, and by the end of each gospel, auditors feel they know *Jesus* better. The Gospel of John, on the other hand, tells the story of the *logos* "made flesh" and by the end the readers know *God* better. As Jesus said to his disciples, "If you have seen me you have seen the Father (John 14:9).

5.3 Conclusion

John 1:1–18 is one of the richest and most beloved of the christological hymns in the NT. Theologically packed, it sets the stage for the remainder of John's Gospel. Written in lyrical form, the prologue announces explicitly and unequivocally that the divine *logos* became the man Jesus. The future belongs to this exalted God-man. The song serves to inspire believers to remain faithful to Christ, despite challenges and threats, knowing that as God's children they will inherit the kingdom.

---

36. Bruce, *John*, 45.

CHAPTER 6

A Hymn of Christ (Philippians 2:6-11)

Who, though he was in the form of God,
did not regard equality with God
as something to be exploited [grasped],
but emptied himself,
taking the form of a slave,
being born in human likeness.
And being found in human form,
he humbled himself and became obedient
to the point of death—even death on a cross.
Therefore God also highly exalted him
and gave him the name
that is above every name,
so that at the name of Jesus
every knee should bend,
in heaven and on earth and under the earth,
and every tongue should confess
that Jesus Christ is Lord,
to the glory of God the Father.
(Phil 2:6-11)

THE PHILIPPIAN HYMN APPLIES titles and ascribes accolades to Jesus that normally were reserved for Caesar alone. In doing so, it presents Jesus as an imperial head of God's kingdom, a competitor to the Roman Empire. When outsiders heard Christ followers sing these lyrics, they must have been shocked. By honoring Christ, believers were shaming Caesar.[1]

6.1 Introduction

Paul writes this letter from prison (1:13) to console church members in Philippi who have supported his ministry even while facing their own suffering and difficulties.

Philip II, the father of Alexander the Great, changed the name of Krenidees (meaning "springs") to Philippi following his conquest of the region in the fourth century BCE. The city was located strategically in the rich valley along the Egnatian Way, the major trade route between east and west. Alexander the Great (356-323 BCE), king of Macedon, chose Philippi as the base from which he launched his invasion of Asia.

In time, Rome ascended in power, marched eastward, and gained control of Philippi in 168 BCE. The Hellenized city switched allegiance.

On March 15, 44 BCE in an attempt to topple the Roman government Brutus and Cassius murdered Julius Caesar and fled to Philippi, where Octavian and Antony pursued them. The assassins held the high ground. Octavian and Antony occupied the lower ground and were at a strategic disadvantage. With their supplies dwindling and food running out, morale ebbed, and defeat loomed. In a unified decision, the people of Philippi came to their aid and provided supplies and salt to pay their volunteer army.[2] With renewed enthusiasm, Antony and Octavian, along with 100,000 soldiers and 130 warships, launched a massive assault. Believing defeat was imminent; Cassius drew his sword and took his own life. A few days later, on another front, Brutus did the same.[3] The battle was over.

When Octavian was named *princeps* of the newly formed Roman Empire, he expressed his gratitude to the city that sided with him against

---

1. Martin, "*Philippians 2:6-11*," 93.

2. The English word "salary" is derived from the Latin *salarium* that, in turn, comes from *sal* (Latin for "salt"). *Salarium* and *sal* were often used as synonyms when referring to a soldier's pay.

3. Suetonius, *Jul.* 89.

the assassins and bestowed on Philippi the status of a colony.[4] He renamed Philippi, *Colonia Iulia Augusta Philippensis* and sent aristocrats to govern and Romanize the city. Many of its inhabitants were granted Roman citizenship and gained the same rights and privileges as citizens living in the capital city of Rome. They embodied Roman culture, used Roman coinage, accepted Latin as the official language, took Roman names and titles, dressed in Roman garb, followed Roman law (*ius Italicum*), and were exempt from paying imperial taxes. The Greek city was transformed into a miniature Rome with Roman architecture, forums, even bathhouses, toilets, amphitheaters, and temples dedicated to the Roman gods and Caesar.[5]

Philippi became a launching pad for exporting Roman customs throughout the region of Macedonia.[6]

In appreciation of its new status, Philippi honored the emperor by composing and displaying honorific inscriptions prominently throughout the city, promoted *Pax Romana*, and gave space and voice to the cult of the emperor. Many people in Greece worshiped Caesar as divine.[7] They offered libations to Caesar and the gods after every meal and symposium. Beautiful temples to Mercury, Zeus, Cybele, and Isis towered over the city.

The city was also populated with former soldiers who, after 20 years of faithful service, were retired to Philippi and given citizenship, a lifelong stipend, and land grants.

6.2 Paul's Arrival in Philippi

Paul's Macedonian call changed the geographical trajectory of his second missionary journey (51–54 CE). Led by the Spirit, he and his team moved westward, crossed the Adriatic into the region of modern-day Europe (Acts

---

4. Along with Thessalonica, Corinth, and Antioch Pisidia, Philippi was one of four Roman colonies mentioned in the NT where Paul visited and preached the gospel.

5. Hansen, *Philippians*, 2–3.

6. As a resident of Baltimore, Maryland for nearly four decades, I enjoyed visiting "Little Italy," an Italian neighborhood in the heart of Baltimore, where immigrants from the old country settled and never moved out. I was not required to travel to Rome to experience its traditions, architecture, music, or eat delicious pastas. Little Italy was a Rome away from Rome. In like manner Philippi was a taste of Rome on the eastern edge of the continent.

7. In 6 BCE Augustus Caesar granted Philippi permission to build the first temple in his honor as long as they also built a temple in honor of the goddess Roma, for whom Rome was named.

16:6-10). When Paul arrived in Philippi, he did not find a synagogue and very few, if any, Jews (vv. 11-13). His first gospel contact was Lydia, a transplanted businesswoman from Thyatira and likely a gentile God-fearer who worshiped Yahweh. Paul preached Christ, and Lydia and her family were baptized (vv. 14-15). Her home became the locus for the first church on European soil.

According to the Lukan account, Paul faced opposition when he invoked "the name of Jesus Christ" and successfully cast a demon spirit out of an enslaved female fortuneteller (Acts 16:16). By identifying the demon as πνεῦμα πύθωνα (a spirit of python), Luke links the seer to the oracle of Delphi who made predictions on behalf of the goddess Gaia and Python, her son. According to Greek mythology when Apollo, the son of Zeus, slew the pair, he became the new source of divine inspiration and prophecy.

After Paul exorcised the spirit, a mob brought him before the town magistrate and charged him with sedition, saying, "These men are disturbing our city; they are Jews and are advocating customs that are not lawful for us as Romans to adopt or observe" (Acts 16:21-22). Paul and Silas were stripped, "beaten with rods," shackled, and placed in the innermost chamber of the prison (vv. 23-24). Rather than fret they sang hymns to the exalted Christ as "the prisoners . . . listen[ed] to them" (v. 25).

After an earthquake opened the prison doors and the jailer and his family were converted, the magistrates discovered they had unlawfully beaten a Roman citizen. Fearful of the consequences, they groveled and apologized and requested that Paul and Silas depart the city (vv. 26-39). Before moving on to their next location, they stopped by Lydia's house to meet and instruct the new Christ followers (v. 40).

Paul left Philippi and continued to preach the gospel of the kingdom in other eastern European venues. While visiting Jerusalem he was arrested and eventually sent to Rome to appeal before Caesar. While incarcerated (62-64 CE), he wrote his letter to the Philippians. Six years had passed since he first visited Philippi.

6.3 The Letter to the Philippians

Paul addressed his letter, "To all the saints in Christ Jesus who are in Philippi, with the *bishops* and *deacons*" (v. 1a). Since the Philippian recipients of the correspondence were mainly, if not entirely gentiles, these designations for church officers should be interpreted in a gentile rather than Jewish context. The same nouns were used in the first century to describe leaders of Roman guilds, councils, and voluntary associations. Inscriptions uncovered at Rhodes indicate that the term *episkopos* (bishop) was used as a title for officials in the temple of Apollo.[8]

Likewise, wide attestation exists for the use of *diakonos* to describe guild and temple officers who oversaw a sundry practical activities ranging from maintaining order and handling finances. Growing evidence suggests the church at Philippi was structured like a voluntary association. Paul's admonition, "Let the elders who rule well be considered worthy of double honor" (1 Tim 5:17), supports this conclusion. As Kloppenborg points out, minutes have been discovered and translated from a first-century voluntary association that contain this same language and advice.[9]

The imperial cult existed side by side with various voluntary associations, all of whom honored the emperor and poured out libations to him along with those made to their patron gods.

From chapter 1 we learned that the churches of the first century functioned primarily as Christ associations with a weekly *deipnon* and *symposion*. Rome was supportive of sanctioned associations, but only tolerated unofficial ones and viewed them with suspicion, thinking they might engage in subversive activities that promoted practice contrary to recognized social standards. Churches fit into that category. Their meals, for instance would have been egalitarian in nature with people of all social classes reclining together, eating, worshiping Christ, and discussing kingdom affairs.

Paul's opening greeting mimics imperial language, but at the same time subverts it: "Grace (χάρις) to you and peace (εἰρήνη) from God our Father and the Lord Jesus Christ" (v. 2). Paul turns this motto on its head, holding that sufficiency and protection come from "our Father and the Lord Jesus Christ." He offers an alternative to the Roman gospel. Believing the gospel of Christ had exclusive claim on the lives of believers, Paul is concerned that some Christ followers in Philippi are continuing to depend on gentile benefactors, attending guild meetings where meals are served, and worshiping Caesar and the gods. Possibly, their status as citizens depends on it.

After general greetings, Paul addresses the congregation's concerns. He knows they are anxious over his imprisonment and possible upcoming

---

8. Dreissman, *Biblical Studies*, 230.

9. See chapter 7, "Meals" in Kloppenborg, *Christ's Associations*, 209-44.

execution. So, he writes to console them.[10] He also knows they face strong opposition and temptations, and therefore, advises them to stand firm in the faith: "Live your life in a manner (πολιτεύεσθε) worthy of the gospel of Christ" (1:27a). The play on words is not obvious in our English translation. But "it conveys the notion of citizenship (πολιτεία; cf. Phil 3:20) and the responsibilities that citizenship entails."[11] Hence, the approximate meaning is: "Behave like citizens of the gospel of Christ." This language clearly "would have struck a chord with the Philippians, whose social identity turned on being citizens of a Roman colony . . . and as such citizens of Rome."[12] The gospel of Christ and the gospel of Rome conflicted, each making exclusive demands. In a sense, Paul presents the church as "a political alternative" to the present political order and invites people to align with it.[13]

That Paul charges them to live like citizens of heaven possibly indicates he feels they are failing to meet the standard or at least in danger of doing so. He follows his command with a purpose statement:

> [S]o that, whether I come and see you or am absent and hear about you, I will know that you are standing firm in one spirit, striving side by side with one mind for the faith of the gospel, and are in no way intimidated by your opponents. For them this is evidence of their destruction, but of your salvation. And this is God's doing. For he has graciously granted you the privilege not only of believing in Christ, but of suffering for him as well—since you are having the same struggle that you saw I had and now hear that I still have. (27b-30)

The exhortation, then, is intended to spur them to faithfulness even when faced with persecution. They must unite ("side by side") and conduct their lives in accord with kingdom ethics. This entails being of "one spirit" and "one mind."

---

10. Holloway, *Philippians*, 33-35, identifies the entirety of Paul's correspondence as a "letter of consolation" designed to comfort a church, which is anxious over his imprisonment and safety. He even says he plans to send Timothy to assure them he is holding up (Phil 2:19).

11. Holloway notes that this reference "presumably would have struck a chord with the Philippians, whose social identity turned on being citizens of a Roman colony . . . ." He adds, "Paul's point is that, like Roman citizenship, the 'gospel' carries not only privileges but also duties that it would be shameful to neglect" (*Philippians*, 105).

12. Holloway, *Philippians*, 105.

13. Hauerwas, *Resident Aliens*, 41.

Success in following Paul's instruction will bring him great joy (Phil 2:1-2). So, he commands them, "Do nothing from selfish ambition or conceit, but in humility regard others as better than yourselves. Let each of you look not to your own interests, but to the interests of others. Let the same mind be in you that was in Christ Jesus" (vv. 3–5). The imperative in verse 5 sets the stage for what follows.

The phrase "same mind" speaks of an attitude or a certain way of thinking. Most people living in Philippi saw themselves as persons of status, deserving recipients of privilege. They were self-focused and proud. Paul offers a different way of thinking. Christ followers must be other-focused, i.e., selfless.

Paul presents Jesus as the supreme model of self-denial and self-effacement.[14] The pathway of humility—not pomposity—is the road that leads to exaltation. For many who held Roman citizenship and took great pride in their status as Philippians, humility may have been a struggle. Because of their elevated status over most others in the empire, they have received the beneficences of the empire's largesse.

To explain what he means by having the "same mind" as Christ and to make his case Paul quotes a well-known hymn.[15]

Who, though he was in the form of God,
    did not regard equality with God
    as something to be exploited [grasped],
but emptied himself,
    taking the form of a slave,
    being born in human likeness.
And being found in human form,
    he humbled himself and became obedient
    to the point of death—even death on a cross.
Therefore God also highly exalted him
    and gave him the name
    that is above every name,

---

14. Hawthorne, *Philippians*, 78.

15. Because Phil 2:6–11 does not invoke God directly, a minority of commentators such as Adela Collins does not view the section as a hymn, but prose only. See Collins, "Psalms, Philippians," 361–72. Also see Fee, *Philippians*, 191–97, who characterizes the paragraph as "exalted prose." On the other hand, Martin, *Hymn of Christ*, devotes an entire volume to exploring the nature and interpretation of this paragraph as a christological hymn. Martin, "Subversive Hymnos," 109, on the basis of rhetorical theory, judges the passage to be a hymn because it "displays all the characteristics" that are "essential to the genre."

so that at the name of Jesus
   every knee should bend,
     in heaven and on earth and under the earth,
  and every tongue should confess
   that Jesus Christ is Lord,
     to the glory of God the Father. (Phil 2:6-11)

No scholarly consensus exists regarding the origin of this hymn. Whether Paul wrote it or quoted an existing hymn, he used it to illustrate and support his argument.[16] If borrowed, Paul's readers likely knew the hymn and sang it during the symposium portion of the communal meal.[17] The song not only evokes memory of Christ, but also contains a subtext against Roman imperialism.

6.4 Traditional Interpretations of the Hymn

Gorman succinctly summarizes the eight most prominent interpretations of the hymn.[18] They include that the hymn:

1. offers a christological interpretation of the fourth Servant hymn of Isaiah,

2. speaks of Christ's pre-existence, incarnation, and glorification,[19]

3. compares and contrasts the humble Christ with Adam, who grasped for godhood,

4. presents a Christian reinterpretation of a Gnostic redeemer myth,

5. portrays Christ as emptying himself of deity and operating only as a human (kenosis),

6. represents Christ as the ultimate example of self-sacrifice and humility,[20]

7. depicts Christ as sovereign Lord who is worthy of worship,

---

16. Holloway, *Philippians*, 115, believes 2:6-11 is "a piece of encomiastic prose composed by Paul" and used to address a specific need of this congregation. Lohmeyer, *Der Brief an die Philipper*, 90–91, on the other hand, argues that Phil 2:6-11 is a hymn, but is non-Pauline in origin.

17. Martin, *Hymn of Christ*, 28, 94–95, supports Lohmeyer by placing the hymn in a "Eucharistic context."

18. Gorman, *Elements*, 130–31.

19. Fee, *Philippians*, 193-94.

20. O'Brien, *Philippians*, 262.

8. promises resurrection and eternal life to all based on Christ's resurrection.

All of these respected interpretations have one thing in common. They approach the hymn from a Jewish perspective but give little, if any, attention to the cultural context at the time of the writing. The Philippian Christ followers were mainly gentiles and lived in a highly Romanized city.[21] Therefore, a fresh look at the lyrics from a sociopolitical context is in order.

6.5 The Structure of the Hymn

In 1927 Ernst Lohmeyer published *Kyrios Jesus* (Lord Jesus), a breakthrough study of Phil 2:5-11, which changed the way many scholars understood the passage. He believed the hymn consisted of six, three-line strophes.[22] This opened the door for other new approaches. Jeremias divided the hymn into three strophes; while Ralph Martin arranged it into six stanzas that "could be chanted in an antiphonal manner."[23] Fee, Silva, and Hawthorne, however, divided the hymn into two stanzas: 1) Verses 6-8, and 2) Verses 9-11.[24] This is the approach we will take.

6.5.1 Stanza One (vv. 6-8)

Paul attaches the relative pronoun "who" to the hymn's opening words, which links it to Jesus, mentioned previously in verse 5. This is a characteristic of other hymns such as Col 1:15-20; 1 Tim 3:16; and Heb 1:1-4. The song declares that he "*was* in the form (μορφῇ) of God." The majority of scholars take this phrase as a reference to Christ's pre-incarnate state and status. However, the verb "was" is not always time specific and can refer to anything that happened in the past and does not necessarily harken back to Christ's pre-existence. Talbert, for instance, suggests it refers to the human existence as Jesus of Nazareth.[25] Such a position, while in the minority, does

---

21. The writer of Philippians makes no allusions in his letter to the Hebrew Scriptures and the lone reference to things Jewish is found in 3:2-6.

22. Lohmeyer, *Kyrios Jesus*, 193.

23. Martin, *Hymn of Christ*, 32–36.

24. Fee, *Philippians*, 195; Silva, *Philippians*, 94. Hawthorne, *Philippians*, 90–120.

25. Although this is a minority view, Talbert, "Problem," 141-43, makes a strong case that verse 6 is not about pre-existence.

not inevitably deny the reality of the pre-incarnation, but simply argues that this verse in the hymn speaks of Jesus' earthly existence.[26] Jesus was God in the flesh.

Verse 6 may imply that the man Jesus was God on earth in contradistinction to Augustus Caesar, the son of divine Julius Caesar and the legendary son of Apollo. Many citizens in Philippi highly honored him, especially because he granted the city the status of a colony.

Holloway notes, however, that Paul may have borrowed this phrase "form of God" from *Bacchae*, a popular story of metamorphosis written by Euripides and his most famous Greek tragedy.[27] Penned ca. 405 BCE in Macedonia and well known in Philippi, the play opens with the god Dionysus announcing, "Here I am having changed my form (morphēn) from that of a god to that of a man."[28]

The verse concludes, "Though . . . in the form of God, [he, Jesus] did not regard equality with God (ἴσος θεός) as something to be exploited (ἁρπαγμὸν)," i.e., grasped or clutched, or used for personal advantage.[29]

The lyrical phrase "equality with God" (ἴσος θεός) would be an insult to Jewish sensitivities, since no human had a right to claim equality with God.[30] But in a gentile context, the song opens on a politically controversial note, since it challenges the divine status of the emperor and his sovereignty over the world. Caesar had a rival.[31]

Augustus Caesar did not deem it robbery to claim equality with god or to use his power and authority for personal gain, adulation, and even worship. The imperial cult had gained universal acceptance. Temples in Philippi were dedicated to both Augustus and the goddess Roma.

Unlike the emperor, however, Jesus did not exploit or seek to hold tightly onto his divinity for personal advantage, "but emptied himself" (ἀλλὰ ἑαυτὸν ἐκένωσεν) (v. 7a). This is the main verbal clause in stanza

26. Howard, "Phil 2:6–11," 368–87, expands on this idea.

27. Holloway, *Philippians*, 121n49, "The Bacchae continued to be performed well into the first centuries CE."

28. Euripides, *Bacch.* 1.1–5; 53–54.

29. But what happens when a human, made in God's image, tries to be God, or possess what is not rightfully his? That's what Adam did. Being in the image of God was not enough. He wanted equality with God. Jesus did not consider it robbery to be equal with God but emptied himself of his divine prerogatives.

30. The Jews are enraged when Jesus forgives sin and charge that he makes himself equal with God (John 5:18).

31. Heen, "Phil 2:6–11," 125.

one and the point Paul wants to make. Human gods such as Caesar and the other emperors held tightly to their divine status and used it to enrich themselves.

Christ followed a different path. But what does "emptied himself" mean? Some suggest this self-emptying involved divesting himself of his divinity or relinquishing his prerogatives as God. But the text does not say Christ "emptied himself *of* anything."[32] It says he "emptied *himself.*" Rather than exploiting his divinity for personal gain as did Caesar, he voluntarily gave himself over to serving the needy. He "poured out himself, putting himself totally at the disposal of people."[33] This speaks of complete self-renunciation.[34] The two participles that follow explain how he accomplished this by "*taking* the form (μορφή) of a slave" and "*being* born in human likeness (ὁμοιώματι ἀνθρώπων)" (v. 7b).

First, his earthly life took on the quality of a slave/servant. This explains the nature of the self-emptying.[35] Whereas in verse 6 the noun μορφή ("form") describes Christ as being God, here it speaks of his role as a slave/servant. He actually took on the role of a slave.[36] He washed his disciples' feet.

Second, Christ became a human. This explains and expands on what it means to be a servant. The term "likeness" (ὁμοιώματι), just as "form," means more than outward appearance. In this context, it speaks of identity or reality.[37] Through the birth process Christ identified fully with humankind and took the form of a servant.

Stanza one builds on verse 7b and concludes with a statement of consequence: "Being found in human form, he humbled himself" (v. 8a). Rather than seek honor and praise, he chose a life of self-sacrifice and debasement. The extent of his willingness to follow this path of humility and serve others comes next: "and [he] became obedient to the point of death" (v. 8b). He "chose the path that led to death."[38] Like Isaiah's Suffering Servant, "he poured out himself to death" (Isa 53:12). Jesus could have fought with his

---

32. Fee, *Philippians*, 210.

33. Hawthorne, *Philippians*, 86. See Luke 22:20.

34. Silva, *Philippians*, 104.

35. This idea is similar to, "he was rich, yet for your sakes he became poor" (2 Cor 8:9).

36. Hawthorne, *Philippians*, 86.

37. Hawthorne, *Philippians*, 81–83. This verse does not suggest a Docetic Jesus.

38. Fee, *Philippians*, 216.

opponents or called down fire from heaven or negotiated a compromise; rather, he passively faced death.

The hymn does not interpret Christ's death theologically as atonement for sin or the means of salvation. In this instance death is simply the final disgrace and shame Jesus experienced. He trod the path of humility and servanthood all the way to the end. The lyrics call on believers—in this case Philippians—to follow in the steps of their master.

The song continues to say, Jesus suffered the most ignoble kind of death, "even death on a cross" (v. 8c). He died in a state of humiliation.[39]

Public crucifixion in the first century CE was "the ultimate in human degradation."[40] Cicero (106–44 BCE) described the horrors of crucifixion and urged his fellow Roman citizens never to think of, mention, or view a crucifixion.[41] It was reserved only for non-Roman citizens who committed the most heinous crimes and for insurrectionists, citizens or not, who sought to overthrow the government.

The thought of Jesus dying in this manner certainly would have been abhorrent to most colonial citizens living in Philippi. And yet Paul uses this image when asking them to follow in Christ's steps![42] Such an idea was almost scandalous. To transfer ultimate loyalty to Christ from Caesar is an act of betrayal which might lead to loss of citizenship and worse, possibly crucifixion itself.[43]

The point the hymn makes is that the Philippian believers must follow in Jesus' steps regardless of the price and embrace the role of servant (v. 5).

39. When facing crucifixion Jesus did not exercise his divine prerogative or resort to human violence to free himself from the executioner's stake, but entrusted the outcome to his Father and submitted to death as an act of obedience to God (v. 8). This is the apostolic understanding of the cross (Acts 4:25–29).

40. Hawthorne, *Philippians*, 90.

41. Cicero, *Pro Rabirio* 5.10, 16.

42. Some scholars believe "even the death of the cross" was added to the song.

43. Crucifixion, like public lynching in nineteenth and twentieth centuries in America, was meant to stifle further civil unrest and to drive fear into the hearts of the masses. A writhing and limp body hanging in plain view at a village crossroads dehumanized the victim, brought shame on his family, and served as a vivid warning to passersby. This is not the path any sane person would choose. Yet, to follow Jesus might lead to this end.

6.5.2 Stanza Two (vv. 9–11)

This stanza pivots from Christ's actions to God's actions. Whereas humility was the topic of stanza one, exaltation is the topic here.

> Therefore God also highly exalted him
> and gave him the name that is above every name. (v. 9)

Opening with "Therefore," v. 9 addresses the result of Jesus' obedience as a servant; God raised him from the dead (vv. 9–11). From the throes of death, God elevates him to new heights. Those "in Christ" at Philippi can expect eschatological vindication as well. A reversal is coming to those who follow in the steps of Jesus (Matt 23:12; Luke 14:11; 18:14).

God rewarded Jesus in two ways. First, he promoted him to a position of supreme authority or rank. To be "highly exalted" (ὑπερύψωσεν) implies that God raised him to superstar status, i.e., one far beyond that of any other human.

Second, God conferred on Jesus a new name, described here specifically as "the name" (v. 9a). The definite article links the appellation to a unique name. The lyrics describe it as the one "that is above every name" (v. 9b). For a Jew no one possessed a name higher than "Yahweh."[44] If this is the case, the God of Israel gave his own name to Jesus.[45] In the final verse, the name is specifically identified as *kurios*, the LXX equivalent of Yahweh. Such a claim was blasphemous. For the average gentile Philippian, no name was more sacred than Caesar. For Christ followers to sing of Jesus in these terms was perfidious and dangerous.

Ironically, the exalted Jesus receives a status he did not seek or exploit while on earth (v. 6). In reality it is Caesar who is the "pretender to a throne that rightfully belongs to Jesus."[46]

Paul made similar kinds of statements about Christ during his missionary endeavors in Philippi, which put him "on a collision course" with governmental authorities.[47] The gathering mob hauled Paul before the magistrate and accused him of "teach[ing] customs which are not lawful for us being Roman to receive or observe" (Acts 16:21).

---

44. Holloway, *Philippians*, 127. Phil 2:1, however, identifies the name as "Lord."
45. Silva, *Philippians*, 110.
46. Heen, "Phil 2:6–11," 150.
47. Borg, *Jesus: Uncovering the Life*, 279.

God's purpose for rewarding Jesus' obedience is found in the next line of the song:

> so that at the name of Jesus
>   every knee should bend,
>   in heaven and on earth and under the earth,
>   and every tongue should confess
>   that Jesus Christ is Lord,
>   to the glory of God the Father. (vv. 9–11)

God's intent ("so that," *hina*) for exalting and installing the crucified Jesus to a position of ultimate authority was eschatological in nature—that everyone will bow in obeisance to Jesus as Lord.[48] At the Parousia, the entire cosmos will yield to Christ's reign, including those presently "in heaven (angels, both elect and evil) and on earth (humans) and under the earth (the dead)" (v. 10b). This company is all inclusive—Christ followers and Christ haters.

Not only will they bow, but every tongue will "confess that Jesus Christ is Lord." Caesar, the Senate, Roman and native elites, and the demons behind them will acknowledge Jesus by his unique name, Lord, Yahweh (Isa 45:23). In the end it is all "to the glory of God the Father" (v. 11b).

6.6 Summary and Conclusion

The Philippian hymn contrasts Christ with Caesar. Augustus Caesar and his successors claimed divine status. Rome possessed a manifest destiny to rule the world. Paul challenged Rome's great tradition. He pictured the church as an alternative *polis* to the empire. As believers raised their voices in song at the communal meals, they were committing subversive acts against the empire. The Philippian songsters knew full well that the lyrics: 1) challenged Caesar's claims, 2) called on people, including Roman citizens, *liberteri*, and others in Philippi to switch allegiance to Christ and his kingdom and trust him and his heavenly Father to meet all their needs, 3) encouraged believers to pray for God's kingdom to arrive on earth, 4) declared Jesus to be the absolute ruler over heaven and earth.

---

48. According to Matt 28:18–20, God gave Jesus authority over heaven and earth at his resurrection. In Peter's Pentecost sermon, he equates or at least conflates resurrection and exaltation (Acts 2:22–36).

Philippians 2:6-11 contains some of the strongest anti-imperial lyrics possible.[49] For Christ followers to raise their voices in praise and declare Jesus, an executed messianic fraud, to be Lord of all bordered on rebellion. As the saints gathered and sang in upstairs tenements, their non-believing neighbors heard them and surely understood that the lyrics were dangerous and seditious.

Christ followers expected to suffer as a result. In the midst of persecution, they were to remain humble and emulate their Lord. Consider the price the Philippian jailer paid for switching his oath of allegiance from Caesar to Christ.[50] As a resident of a Roman colony and likely a retired soldier, he kept inviolate his loyalty to Caesar for years and was rewarded with citizenship and given a government job.

Since his conversion, however, the jailer and his family identified with the Christ movement. They gathered with believers in Lydia's home to worship. When they joined in singing to Jesus as the one with "a name that is above every name" they acted outside the law. As a result, the jailer possibly lost his source of income, patronage, and even his citizenship. Philippian gentiles paid a high price to follow Jesus.

49. Crossan and Reed, *In Search of Paul*, 289; Heen, "Phil 2:6-11," 125.

50. Bruce, *Acts*, 336, states that the jailer was likely a Roman soldier before his retirement. He knew the implications of saying Jesus, not Caesar, is Lord.

CHAPTER 7

Song of Supremacy (Colossians 1:15-20)

He is the image of the invisible God, the firstborn of all creation;
  for in him all things in heaven and on earth were created,
things visible and invisible, whether thrones or dominions or rulers
or powers—all things have been created through him and for him.
  He himself is before all things, and in him all things hold together.
He is the head of the body, the church. He is the beginning, the firstborn
  from the dead,
    so that he might come to have first place in everything.
    For in him all the fullness of God was pleased to dwell,
and through him God was pleased to reconcile to himself all things,
        whether on earth or in heaven,
      by making peace through the blood of his cross.
          (Col 1:15-20)

THROUGHOUT HISTORY GOVERNMENTS HAVE utilized songs to promote their own political agendas, inflame nationalism, and to bring the populace in line with accepted cultural mores. Recall John Philip Sousa's "Stars and Stripes Forever" and how it inspired Americans for over a century toward patriotism; or how singing "We're Marching to Pretoria" emboldened British troops to bravery during the Boer War; or even how rousing renditions of "Vorwarts! Vorwarts!" moved naive German youths to join Hitler's misguided quest for world domination. Music has been used to motivate masses and support their respective government's agenda or military efforts. No wonder Rome used hymns as an "imperial tool of indoctrination."[1] In like fashion, lyrical songs of the nascent Christ movement inspired and instructed believers to stand firm in their commitment to Christ and his kingdom. In doing so, they conversely, if not directly, implied that Christ followers must avoid participation in the imperial cult.

7.1 The Sociopolitical Setting for the Colossian Hymn

Colossae, a city in the province of Phrygia in Asia Minor (modern western Turkey), lay 12 miles southeast of Laodicea along the main road that ran through the Lycus Valley. Like the other cities in Asia Minor it was a hub of pagan cultic activity and worship of the emperor. Colossae was the home of Cybele, the mother goddess, the personification of fertility. Numismatic evidence also indicates that the cults of Isis, Sarapis, and Mithras were prominent in the region. Many worshiped astral bodies and the elemental spirits that ruled over them.

Besides the majority gentiles, a significant minority of Jews lived in the region and traced their ancestry back to Babylon (ca. 200 BCE), when Antiochus III deported them to the Lycus Valley.[2] Members of the Jewish communities worshiped in local synagogues. Being Hellenized they likely practiced their faith in an accommodating way. In his letter, the author addresses both gentiles and Jews who have become Christ followers (1:27; 3:11). They have been generous in their support of the gospel and as result the word of Christ has spread far and wide (Col 1:4–8).

7.1.1 Authorship and Date

Until the late-nineteenth century, Christians attributed the letter of Colossians to Paul, written during his first imprisonment in Rome (60–62 CE). Contemporary scholars are divided over the issue.[3] From the text we know Paul did not found the church (Col 1:4; 2:1). Epaphras, one of Paul's missionary team, is a more likely candidate (Col 1:7; 4:12; Acts 19:9–10).

---

1. Medley, "Subversive Song," 428.
2. Josephus, *Ant.* 12.147–53.
3. For simplicity, I will use the name Paul when speaking of the author.

The letter, while written to Colossae, was distributed to Laodicea as well (4:15-16) and likely had application for all the churches of Phrygia.

The dating of the letter is difficult to determine. A major earthquake hit the region in 61 CE, destroying both Hierapolis and Laodicea, and it is reasonable to assume Colossae was demolished as well, although no records exist. When comparing the dates of Paul's imprisonment and the earthquake, it is unlikely that he had time to pen the letter and for them to receive it before disaster struck. Travel over land from Rome to Colossae took more than 200 days.

7.1.2 The Problem Facing the Colossians

The writer identifies "philosophy" as the main problem that confronts the church (Col 2:8), but the nature of this particular philosophy "remains an unsolved puzzle."[4] The original audience, however, was cognizant of the situation. It concerned regulations about diet, observance of special days connected to new moons, festivals, and Sabbaths (Col 2:16, 21), along with the worshiping of angels, submitting to purification guidelines—"Do not handle, Do not taste, Do not touch"—(Col 2:21), and the practice of abstinence and self-denial (Col 3:5-11), all of which its advocates believed were an enhancement to spirituality. From the text it is difficult to determine whether the "philosophy" should be interpreted from a Jewish or gentile perspective or both.

7.1.3 Understanding the Philosophy from a Jewish Perspective

Special days and observances, visions of angels, and asceticism were all common to Judaism. In Colossae Judaizers may have been attempting to persuade gentile Christ followers to observe Jewish laws, very similar to what is found in Galatians. If this is the case, the author exhorts, "See to it that no one takes you captive through philosophy and empty deceit," which he adds is: 1) "according to human tradition," 2) "according to the elemental spirits of the universe," and 3) "not according to Christ." Through these deceitful means the opponents of Christ attempt to entrap and enslave believers (Col 2:8).

---

4. Barth and Blanke, *Colossians*, 39.

The first phrase, "human tradition" was a common way of speaking of Jewish customs and interpretative practices of the law. The second phrase "the elemental spirits of the universe" (στοιχεῖα τοῦ κόσμου) might be translated alternatively as "rudiments of the world" and can carry a Jewish connotation. The rudiments were the ABC's or elementary principles of a matter, in this case the law of Moses.[5] For the author, the law was not intended to be the end all in spiritual development, but more like an "elementary" education or schoolmaster to bring one to Christ.

The author then offers the reason one must avoid being lured by rudiments of the world: "For in him [Christ] the whole fullness (πλήρωμα, *pleroma*) of deity dwells bodily and you have come to fullness in him" (vv. 9-10a). Compared to Christ, everything else is lesser. God's *pleroma* is not found in the law (the A, B, Cs), but in Christ (the A to Z, i.e., the alpha and omega). Hence, the law adds nothing to Christ, or to a Christ follower. Speaking further he adds that Christ "is the head of every ruler and authority" (v. 10b), including Moses and the Mosaic law.

Next, the Pauline writer makes reference to another time-honored Jewish ritual—"circumcision"—and argues that gentiles need not submit to its demands because they have already received a superior circumcision: "In him also you were circumcised with a spiritual circumcision, by putting off the body of the flesh in the circumcision of Christ; when you were buried with him in baptism, you were also raised with him through faith in the power of God, who raised him from the dead" (vv. 11-12). Another circumcision with hands will not improve their status with God.

> And when you were dead in trespasses and the uncircumcision of your flesh, God made you alive together with him, when he forgave us all our trespasses, erasing the record that stood against us with its legal demands. He set this aside, nailing it to the cross (vv. 13-14).

The author pictures Christ's crucifixion as a circumcision in which all believers participated. Through his death and resurrection, Christ followers are raised to newness of life and experience the future kingdom in the present.

This was all God's doing. He forgave gentile believers who were dead 1) in trespasses, and 2) in the flesh, and wiped out the "legal demands" of the law that once stood "against" them. Christ paid the debt (the unlimited

---

5. In Gal 4:3 and Heb 5:12, *stoicheia* likely refers to the rudiments or teachings of the law.

I.O.U.) humankind owed God by nailing it "to the cross." Once a debt was paid, the charges applied no longer. The language is likely an allusion to the Roman practice of placing charges against a criminal on the crucifixion crossbar for all to see.

Finally, the writer comments that on the cross Christ "disarmed the rulers and authorities and made a public example of them, triumphing over them in it" (v. 15). Who are these rulers and authorities that Christ embarrassed? According to this view, they include Jewish synagogue authorities who made demands on the gentile believers.

"Therefore," Paul admonished the Colossians not to embrace Jewish laws (food, drink, Sabbaths, etc.) which "are only a shadow of what is to come, but the substance belongs to Christ" (v. 17). A shadow points to something greater than itself—to reality, and is only a vague reflection of the person or substance it represents. It would be foolish to concentrate on the shadow, if one can hug the actual person. The law pointed to Christ. Now that he has arrived, the shadow is insignificant. Christ's death nullified the law.

The church must abandon all forms of self-denial, angelic worship, and visions that puff up and instead hold "fast to the head [Christ], from whom the whole body, nourished and held together . . . grows with a growth that is from God" (vv. 16-19). Human effort, i.e., obeying the law does not lead to spiritual advancement. Full status is related to one's identification with Christ's death. In a series of probing questions, the author asks, "If with Christ you died to the rudiments of the world" why continue to "submit" to temporal rules that cannot tamp down "self-indulgence?" (vv. 20-23). The law does not take away one's desires or increase spirituality. Only death to the old nature through the cross can succeed at this task.

7.1.4 Understanding the Philosophy from a Gentile Perspective

In the main, commentators interpret the "philosophy" and "elemental spirits of the universe" from a gentile viewpoint, especially in light of the prevailing imperial cult and the Roman mystery religions linked to it.[6] Romans believed the sun, stars, and moon that resided in upper regions of the

6. Carter and Levine, *New Testament*, 209, mention both mystery cults and Hellenized churches offered the gift of life after death and competed with each other. "Colossians uses the language of 'mystery' (1:26-27; 2:2; 4:3) to explain why Jesus' followers need not be concerned with spirits" (214).

ether were astral deities that controlled human destiny.[7] Whereas, lesser spirit beings filled the lower atmosphere and served as mediators between the heavenly realms and earth. Upon death, the human soul gravitated toward heaven, but had to pass through the regions controlled by these spirits (στοιχεῖα τοῦ κόσμου) or ascended masters.[8] To prepare for their own ascent, people practiced ascetic disciplines (fasting, abstaining from sex, undergoing purification rites, etc.).[9]

Possibly some believers bought into this proto-Gnostic philosophy, even believing that God's fullness was mediated through a series of spirit beings, who had to be placated, if one were to be reconciled to God in the afterlife. In correcting them, Paul writes that Jesus is Lord not only over the church, but the entire universe, including astral spirits and ascended masters. If one has Christ s/he has access already to the fullness of God.

On the cross Christ "disarmed the rulers and authorities and made a public example of them, triumphing over them in it" (v. 15). According to this view, the rulers and authorities over whom Christ triumphed were the gods and the demonic forces behind the Roman authorities from Caesar to native elites that ruled on his behalf.

Paul pictures Christ's death, not in terms of a defeat at the hands of his enemies and the forces behind them, but as a victory. To do so, Paul borrows language associated with an established custom known as a Roman Triumph. The highest honor the Senate could bestow on a victorious emperor or respected general was to grant him permission to lead a triumph or victory march through Rome. It was a public spectacle that marked the honoree as a military hero of the highest order.

A triumph served two purposes. First, it publicly demonstrated Rome's superiority over its enemies. Second, it was the initial step toward deification. Without being granted a triumph, no emperor could attain apotheosis.

Paul pictures the cross as a decisive battlefield on which Christ emerged victorious. In death and resurrection, he exposed his enemies (rulers and

7. Heiser, *Unseen Realm*, devotes an entire volume to identifying and defining the unseen forces of the cosmos.

8. Eckankar is a modern example of a religion that holds a similar philosophy. It teaches that one's soul must pass through twelve spiritual planes of the cosmos; each controlled by a spiritual intermediary or ascended master, before it can reach Sugmad, the eternal source of all existence. One's journey may be shortened and even attained in this lifetime through the mastery of astral projection or soul travel, as taught by Eckankar.

9. Carter and Levine, *New Testament*, 209.

authorities) as defeated foes. They were unable to stop his movement. It continues years later and has spread empire wide.

Only his followers recognized the cross as Christ's Triumphal march. According to the gospel, it was central to his mission as Suffering Servant. Paul writes to the Romans, "Through the resurrection Christ was declared to be Son of God in power" (Rom 1:4). Baptized believers share in the status as sons of God.

Which interpretation—Jewish or gentile—is correct? Was Paul warning gentile believers not to be deceived by Jewish demands to keep the law or was he advising both Jewish and gentile Christ followers not to be drawn into pagan philosophy? Since Paul is speaking to both Jewish and gentile believers, he might also be using ambiguous terms, interpreted differently by each audience.[10] The Lycus Valley was a center of Roman and Jewish cultic activities. People were variously dedicated to the cult of the emperor, mystery religions, pagan temples, and synagogues. Jews in the region were Hellenized and lived amongst idolaters. Some worked in trades and jobs associated with guilds, received patronage, and went along to get along. Survival often involved a series of compromises and an ability to work the system. This was life as usual.

Whether one interprets philosophy as Jewish or gentile, or both, the author's point is clear: it cannot add to the fullness one finds in Christ. He is Lord of all and the fullness of God.

The author *closes* chapter 2 with the words, "If with Christ you *died* ... [all else adds] no value" (Col 2:20, 23). The author then *opens* the ethical section of his letter with, "If you have been *raised* with Christ ..." (3:1) and proceeds to give instructions on how to live as citizens in the kingdom of God (Col 3-4).

As we shall discover, when interpreted within the sociopolitical context, the Colossian hymn (Col 1:15-20) functions as the backbone for the entire letter, providing structure and support.[11]

7.2 Analysis of the Colossian Hymn

After opening his letter with a typical greeting and prayer, the author says of Christ: "He has rescued us from the power of darkness and transferred us into the kingdom of his beloved Son, in whom we have redemption, the

10. Heiser, *Unseen Realm*, 327n17.

11. One might say it serves as the spinal "chord" as well as the spinal cord.

forgiveness of sins" (Col 1:13-14). Paul recognizes two political kingdoms exist, one associated with darkness and the other with God. Although the Colossian believers live under Roman domination, they are now members of God's kingdom. A transfer has taken place. Therefore, their ultimate allegiance is no longer to Caesar or empire, which previously held them in bondage. They are in the world but not of it.

Paul did not compose the Colossian hymn. It was likely pre-Pauline in origin.[12] If so, Christ followers were familiar with it and sang it regularly at their suppers.[13] The author embeds the hymn in his letter for illustrative purposes and uses it to make key points.

When one reads the hymn in its historical setting, s/he discerns how each stanza actually challenges Rome's imperial claims of supremacy over the world.[14] In this context, Col 1:15-20 constitutes a hymn of resistance. This poem/hymn contains terms and titles usually associated with Caesar. Everyone in the empire was familiar with vocabulary used in the Colossian hymn.

Divided into two main stanzas, the hymn describes 1) Christ's relationship to *creation*, i.e., "all things" (vv. 15-17) and, 2) his relationship to the *new creation*, i.e., the redeemed church with Christ being the "head of the body" (vv. 18-20).[15]

When viewed in the framework of empire, it becomes apparent that the song's lyrics stir up in the singers images of living in a new world order. Just as Moses' song of victory on the heels of the Passover/Exodus aroused

---

12. Martin, "Early Christian Hymn," 199. Bruce, "'Christ Hymn,'" 100.

13. O'Brien notes that a majority of scholars consider Col 1:15-20 to be "a pre-Pauline 'hymn' inserted into the letter's train of thought by the author" (*Colossians, Philemon*, 32). The audience would have known it, sung it, or chanted it as a creed. Still, some scholars question the designation of "hymn" to describe the pericope. In his 2009 Greco-Roman Meals lecture entitled "Chances and Limitations of Ritual Analysis of Early Christian Meals" Mathias Klinghardt expresses his conviction that Col 1:15-20, Phil 2:6-11, and John 1:1-18 were "written text for readers, but were never sung." He does state, however, that songs were part of ritual meals and that a need exists for scholarly exploration of this much neglected topic. Lecture given at the Society for Biblical Literature (New Orleans, LA: November 11, 2009). On the other hand, Dunn, *Colossians and Philemon*, 86, sees Col 1:15-20 as a performed hymn and voices the opinion of most scholars. This chapter assumes the performance of the hymn occurred in a Christian meal setting and proclaimed that "Jesus is Lord" and thus undermined Roman ideology.

14. For an excellent comparison between the Colossian hymn and imperial ideology, referencing primary sources, see Gordley, *Christological Hymns*, 134 (Table 4.2).

15. Martin, *Colossians*, 44-49, among others believes the hymn contains three strophes.

in Israel a new social imagination to function as an alternative society under the reign of God, the Colossian hymn does the same.

7.2.1 Strophe One

> He [lit., "who"] is the image of the invisible God, the firstborn of all creation; for in him all things in heaven and on earth were created, things visible and invisible, whether thrones or dominions or rulers or powers—all things have been created through him and for him. He himself is before all things, and in him all things hold together. He is the head of the body, the church. (vv. 1:15–18a)

The song opens with the relative pronoun "who" (ὅς, *hos*), not the normal way to begin a song. This suggests that Paul inserted an existing song in the letter at this point and replaced the original subject with a relative pronoun.[16] Thus, he is able to identify the subject with the antecedent, "his beloved son" (1:13), i.e., Jesus Christ. Other writers use the same technique when introducing a song (1 Tim 3:16; Heb 1:3; 1 Pet 2:2).

If one removes the hymn (vv. 15–20) from the letter, verses 13–14 and 21–22 will fit together flawlessly without violence to the text as seen below:

> He has rescued *us* from the power of darkness and transferred us into the kingdom of his beloved Son, in whom we have redemption, the forgiveness of sins (vv. 13–14). . . . And *you* who were once estranged and hostile in mind, doing evil deeds, he has now reconciled in his fleshly body through death, so as to present you holy and blameless and irreproachable before him. (vv. 21–22)

The pronoun "who" followed by the verb "is" describes Christ in two ways. Line 1 denotes his connection to God. Christ is "the image (εἰκών, *eikōn*) of the invisible God" (v. 15a). An image can refer to the outward representation of a person as depicted on a painting, statue, or coin. But it can also speak of the embodiment and manifestation of the innermost essence of the being.[17]

For Bruce and Dunn this affirmation reflects a "Wisdom Christology."[18] Just as wisdom (*sophia*) in the Hebrew Bible is representative of the image of God, so is Christ in the NT. Dunn draws a parallel between Wis 7:25 and

16. Moo, *Letters*, 116–17.
17. Barth and Blanke, *Colossians*, 195.
18. Bruce, "Christ Hymn," 100; Dunn, *Theology*, 269.

Col 1:15, Prov 8:22 and Col 1:15, Prov 3:19 and Col 1:16, Wis 7:14 and Col 1:18, 20.[19]

Fee, however, links Jesus to Adam, the first man to bare the image of God (Gen 1:26; Col 1:15). In Jesus' role as the eschatological Adam, he reveals what God is like to humankind. This is the weaker position of the two, since Adam is part of creation, while Christ stands as creator and essentially bears God's image.[20]

While these "theological" explanations are plausible, and even helpful, they can be short-sighted if they fail to consider the sociopolitical context of the first century. Rather than comparing Christ to Wisdom or Adam, it might be advantageous to compare him to Caesar, since images of Caesar permeated the entire empire. The divine image of Caesar, as Jupiter's representative, was plastered everywhere. It appeared on coins, statuary, frescoes, jewelry, in the marketplace, city square, public baths, gymnasia, palaces, and temples, to name a few.[21] That's what dictators do.[22] His all-pervading image made it seem as if Caesar were omnipresent. According to the hymn, Jesus, not Caesar, reveals what God is like.

But does *eikōn* (Col 1:15) describe Christ in his pre-incarnate, earthly, or his post-resurrection state? The answer is debatable.

The next phrase of the hymn speaks of Christ's status as "the firstborn of creation" (v. 15b). This does not mean that God created Christ before he created the rest of creation. It has nothing to do with Christ's origin, but with his "position of preference and dominance."[23] The patriarch Joseph

---

19. Dunn, *Theology*, 269. Likewise, Witherington, *Letters*, 130, believes the song is indebted to Jewish wisdom literature, particularly to various passages in the Wisdom of Solomon. He includes a helpful chart to make his case.

20. Lohse, *Colossians and Philemon*, 48.

21. Lohse, *Colossians and Philemon*, 48.

22. Pyke, "Red Redeemer," 5-7, a former Methodist missionary to China, recalls how Maoism became the new religion in China after World War II. Maoism was essentially a personality cult with Mao as redeemer. His picture was found everywhere from billboards to buildings, even in every home. Families were required to bow each morning in front of Mao's portrait and then stand quietly for five minutes, "Asking for Instructions." Pyke writes, "In hotel rooms Mao's picture, painted on the transom, glows at night when the light is switched off. Even in sleep the weary traveler takes China's haloed presence with him into his dreams to be refreshed by China's new 'god' during the night's unconscious hours." Mao was neither the first nor the last dictator to receive adulation normally reserved for a deity. In the first century CE, Caesar was the Mao of his day.

23. Barth and Blanke, *Colossians*, 195.

had two sons. In order of birth Manasseh was eldest (Exod 41:51-52), but in importance, God calls Ephraim "my firstborn" (Jer 31:9).

As God's firstborn, Jesus is superior to all others. The psalmist tells how God anointed King David (Ps 89:20) and declared, "I will make him the firstborn, the highest of the kings of the earth" (v. 27), despite David being Jesse's seventh and lastborn son. In like fashion, as reigning Lord, Jesus is supreme over all.

Paul gives his reason for the designation: "[F]or in him all things in heaven and on earth were created" (v. 16a). He was the agent of creation. The words "all things" are inclusive. Everything owes its existence to Christ, including "things visible and invisible, whether thrones or dominions or rulers or powers—all things have been created through him" (16b). The designation of "thrones," "dominions," "rulers," and "powers" likely should "be understood as political titles, whose bearers control and exert . . . dominion" over the masses.[24] Some of these "invisible" beings may refer to angelic or demonic principalities that exercise authority over nations and regions for good or ill (Dan 10:13-20; Eph 3:10; 6:12; 1 Cor 15:24; 1 Pet 3:22), and serve as the powers behind the earthly thrones.[25] The main point the lyric makes is that the most powerful political rulers, human or angelic, "like the rest of creation, are subject to Christ."[26] By virtue of being creator, Christ exercises universal dominion over all.

These entities were not only created "through him," but "for him" (16c). They exist to serve him and they owe their allegiance to him.[27] While Caesar and his cohorts are oblivious to this fact, the singing church is well aware of it. This *inside* information means that Christ's peasant-disciples understand the nature of reality better than the Roman and Jewish elites.

Notice the progression: 1) "In him" (16a). As divine architect he first conceived of creation. It existed as an idea in his mind—he is its source; 2) "Through him" (16b). Christ was the agent of creation; 3) "For him" (16c). This is the rationale for creation. It was created to serve him. "He is the *telos* of creation."[28]

---

24. Barth and Blanke, *Colossians*, 201.

25. Barth and Blanke, *Colossians*, 201.

26. Bruce, "'Christ Hymn,'" 103.

27. Gordley, *Christological Hymns*, 140, notes that rather than serving, "they are at war with the Creator and his agent."

28. McKnight, *Colossians*, 152.

Thus, Christ was: 1) the primary cause of creation, 2) the instrumental cause of creation, and 3) the final cause for creation. He planned it, produced it, and gave it purpose for existence.

All of creation is meant to serve and be subservient to Jesus as the "firstborn." According to Martin, these verses "show that Christ is Lord of creation and has no rival in the created order."[29] He is supreme over all.

The closing words of stanza one ring out loud and clear: "He himself is before all things, and in him all things hold together" (v. 17). As the "preexistent one Jesus is Lord over the universe."[30] This means he is superior to all. He, not Caesar or the gods, brings order to the world. In other words, Jesus is the bringer of peace. "What Christ has created he maintains" and prevents it from falling into absolute chaos.[31]

These christological affirmations challenge the idea that Caesar is the agent of the gods and that Roman peace (*Pax Romana*) is the divine plan for the nations.[32] Borrowing from Roman imperial language and applying it to Christ and kingdom ethics, the Colossian hymn offers a superior cosmic vision and universal peace plan under the sovereignty of King Jesus. The recipients of the letter, who regularly sang this hymn, lived as outliers in direct defiance of the established social order. It reminded them where their allegiance lay.

7.2.2 Strophe Two

> He is the head of the body, the church; He is the beginning, the firstborn from the dead, so that he might come to have first place in everything. For in him all the fullness of God was pleased to dwell, and through him God was pleased to reconcile to himself all things, whether on earth or in heaven, by making peace through the blood of his cross. (vv. 18b–20)

Strophe two makes four key points regarding Christ and his redemptive relationship to the new creation. First, Christ is "head of the body, the church," i.e., the ruler of a new social order. The hymn uses a triad of political words: "head" (κεφαλή, *kephalē*), "body" (σώματος, *sōmatos*), and

---

29. Martin, *Colossians*, 45.
30. Lohse, *Colossians and Philemon*, 53.
31. Harris, *Prepositions and Theology*, 47.
32. Carter and Levine, *New Testament*, 215.

"church" (ἐκκλησίας, *ekklēsias*).[33] Jupiter was the head over the universe, which was metaphorically viewed as a "body." In modern times the leader of a country is a "*head* of State." S/he controls the "body politic," defined as "a group of persons politically organized under a single governmental authority."[34] The church, therefore, is more than a religious institution; it is a political entity as well, over which Christ is head. He is not only the rightful ruler over earth, (which Caesar claims for himself), but he also rules over a completely new creation, i.e., the church.[35] Walsh and Keesmaat conclude that Christ dislodges Caesar as supreme, and the church replaces empire as the authorized divine institution.[36] Rome's claim of supreme power is illegitimate. While the letter's recipients should not rebel against the empire, they must recognize that Rome's claims are unfounded and adjust their own ethics in accord with God's kingdom.

Second, "He is the beginning *(ἀρχή, archē),* the firstborn from the dead."[37] Resurrection is the basis of Christ's political headship. As the first to be raised, he is the fountainhead of a new humanity. What the Jews expected to happen in the future—resurrection and kingdom rule—has already occurred through the resurrection of Jesus.

Third, a purpose statement follows: "so that he might come to have first place in everything." In a world where "divine" Caesar is head of the body politic and claims supremacy over all political structures and social institutions, those hearing this song are keen to recognize that Paul is "contrasting Jesus with Caesar."[38] To those other than Christ followers the song must have sounded "treasonous."[39]

33. Paul borrowed *ekklēsia*, a word already used and connected with voluntary association and town councils, to describe the church. From Paul's perspective, the church is a sociopolitical entity.

34. https://www.merriam-webster.com/dictionary/body%20politic.

35. Moses, *Practices of Power*, 177, believes that by introducing "the church" into a hymn that focuses on Christ's cosmic rule, Paul brings "the cosmic drama" down to the local level. This redaction might be feasible, if one does not view the church as the new creation.

36. Walsh and Keesmaat, *Colossians Remixed*, 153.

37. The author of Revelation uses the same designation (Rev 1:5), possibly pointing to its common usage by Christ followers in the Lycus Valley.

38. Walsh and Keesmaat, *Colossians Remixed*, 89.

39. Walsh and Keesmaat, *Colossians Remixed*, 89, make a compelling case throughout their book that Colossians is a subversive text that calls for its readers to embrace an alternative kingdom vision for living that liberates rather than to accept the empire's vision that enslaves (11). Like other commentators, however, they do not connect Col

The lyrics provide a twofold *reason* why Christ is preeminent, connecting it to God's good pleasure: 1) "For in him all the fullness of God was pleased to dwell" (v. 19). Contrary to Jewish and pagan thinking, God's fullness resides in Christ not the temple or mediated through a plethora of intermediary spirit beings; 2) "and through him God was pleased to reconcile to himself all things, whether on earth or in heaven" (v. 20). This means that Christ is God's only authorized and divinely empowered representative who brings peace to the world.

"[A]ll things" of creation (the visible and invisible including thrones, dominions, rulers, and powers), which owed their existence and continuance to Christ, also needed to be reconciled to God. This assumes that Rome and its rulers (earthly and heavenly) were out of sync with God's will and incapable of restoring harmony to the universe. God accomplished through Christ that of which Caesar was incapable.

Fourth, reconciliation was achieved "by making peace through the blood of his cross" (20b). The hymn challenges Rome's contention that universal peace can be accomplished by use of violence and military manpower. Rome wielded force to bring people to their knees and submit to its rule. But brutal and aggressive measures never end in lasting peace, only a lull before the next outbreak of rebellion occurs. By contrast, the lyrics declare genuine peace is achieved ironically through Christ's humiliating death.

If Christ establishes peace by becoming the victim of violence, then Rome's method falls short of the mark. The Colossian hymn perceives "the cross as the place where the reconciliation occurred."[40]

According to the song, God transformed the ultimate symbol of Roman oppression—"the imperial instrument of terror"[41]—and turned it into the symbol of hope and reconciliation for all people, including those beaten down by the empire. In viewing the cross of Christ as a triumph, the song reverses honor/shame language, and reimagines the cross as the instrument by which Christ shamed and exposed Rome and its divinities as weak and defenseless against the power of God.[42]

The resurrection of Christ likewise revealed Rome's inability to maintain peace through use of brute force, all in the name of "law and order."

1:15–20 to its possible use as a symposium song.

40. Lohse, *Colossians and Philemon*, 60.

41. Neil Elliott, "Anti-Imperial Message," 167.

42. Medley, "Subversive Song," 431.

Thinking it could quash the nascent Jesus movement, Rome moved with vengeance and killed its messianic leader, hoping to drive fear into the hearts of Jesus' followers. The resurrection not only exposed the limitations of Roman power to accomplish its desired goal but galvanized the disciples into a faithful company who trusted God to overturn Roman tyranny. The one who was the passive victim of Roman violence, God raised up and placed in the highest position in the cosmos, installing him as head over his universal kingdom.

Although the hymn never mentions the emperor by name, the original hearers and singers understood that the lyrics existentially contrasted Christ with Caesar. The references to the "image of God," "firstborn," and "first place" were all monikers that Roman society attributed to Caesar alone.[43]

In relationship to Christ, Paul uses the comprehensive phrase "all things" four times in the song, plus the phrases "all creation" and "all the fullness of God." The "thrones or dominions or rulers or powers" (v. 16), which modify "things visible and invisible" (v. 15), are also all inclusive.[44] When Christ's rule is placed in the context of "heaven and earth," nothing exists over which he does not have authority.[45]

In comparison to God's ultimate plan in Christ, Caesar's efforts must have seemed miniscule and insignificant. No empire holds more power than Christ and none is a threat to his sovereignty.

After receiving Paul's correspondence, Colossian believers must have sung their symposium hymn with new vigor and understanding. They saw themselves as participants in events of historic proportions. As baptized believers, they had been transferred into Christ's kingdom, infused with his resurrection life, and empowered to serve Christ under difficult circumstances.[46] They had no guarantee that their lives would improve economi-

43. Medley, "Subversive Song," 89–90.

44. For purposes of this essay, the exact identity of these powers is not essential to the argument that Christ and God rule the world, not Caesar and the Roman deities. Many scholars have sought to identify these categories, among them Caird, *Principalities and Powers*; Berkhof, *Christ and the Powers*; Wink, *Naming the Powers*; Yoder, *Politics of Jesus*; Boyd, *God at War*.

45. Walsh and Keesmaat, *Colossians Remixed*, 91.

46. Medley, "Subversive Song," 435n95, drawing on Maier, *Picturing Paul*, 65, offers the following insight: "In a manner similar to Paul's understanding of baptism in Rom 6:3-11, Colossians identifies baptism as a ritual extraction (from the rule of and devotion to principalities and power—'the powers of darkness' [Col 1:13]) and of incorporation into God's beloved Son."

cally or socially in the near future, but they were promised positions in God's future kingdom, if they remained faithful to Christ.

7.3 Relationship to Philippians 2

There is a similarity between the christological hymns in Colossians and Philippians. One difference, however, is the Colossian hymn lacks any servant language. While Philippians speaks of Christ's resurrection as divine vindication, Colossians speaks of it as a "cosmic victory."[47] The cross in Colossians is the means of redemption and Jesus is the agent of reconciliation.[48]

7.4 Conclusion

The Colossian hymn serves as the spinal column supporting the entire letter. It announces lyrically that Christ reigns supreme over all creation; thus, the emperor's claim was blatantly false. Colossian believers are called to remain faithful to their baptismal vows, renounce participation in the emperor cult, mystery religions, worship of Roman gods, and instead embrace the ethics of God's kingdom under Christ (Col 3-4).

Christ's kingdom, of which the Colossian believers were part, welcomed everybody—"Greek and Jew, circumcised and uncircumcised, barbarian, Scythian, slave and free" (Col 3:11)—groups that typically did not get along with each other, but in Christ they became one.

Based on this agenda for the world the author advises, "And let the peace of Christ rule in your hearts, to which indeed you were called in the one body. And be thankful. Let the word of Christ dwell in you richly; teach and admonish one another in all wisdom; and with gratitude in your hearts *sing psalms, hymns, and spiritual songs to God*" (Col 3:15-16).

---

47. Witherington, *Letters*, 131.

48. Gordley, *Christological Hymns*, 111.

CHAPTER 8

The Mystery of Godliness (1 Timothy 3:16)

Without any doubt, the mystery of our religion is great:
He was revealed in flesh,
vindicated in spirit,
seen by angels,
proclaimed among Gentiles,
believed in throughout the world,
taken up in glory. (1 Tim 3:16)

8.1 Introduction

FIRST TIMOTHY 3:16 IS a song that challenged the acclamation, "Great is Artemis of the Ephesians!"

Written under the name of "Paul, an apostle of Christ" and addressed "to Timothy" (1 Tim 1:1-2), this epistle "presupposes that Timothy was left in Ephesus by Paul while the latter made a brief visit to Macedonia" (Acts 20:1-3).[1] It is one of three letters popularly called Pastoral Epistles and attributed to the apostle Paul.[2]

---

1. DeSilva, *Introduction*, 650.

2. Some scholars believe The Pastorals are *pseudepigraphal* writings that carry on the Pauline tradition. For a discussion of this issue see Raymond Collins, "Pastoral Epistles," 88–131; Carter and Levine, *New Testament*, 238-40, note that while scholars debate whether or not Paul is the author, the focus is clear: guarding correct doctrine, maintaining church order, complying with social norms, and living piously within the household

Timothy, the son of a Jewish mother and Greek father, lived in Lystra in southern Asia Minor, a region known for the worship of divine Caesar and a host of Greco-Roman deities. Joining Paul on his second missionary journey, he submitted to circumcision in order to participate in Jewish evangelism (Acts 16:1-3). He traveled with Paul in Macedonia, strengthening the believers in Thessalonica and later joined Paul in Corinth (Acts 18:5; 1 Thess 3:6). Timothy also accompanied Paul on his third missionary journey, which included spending time in Ephesus (Acts 19).

A major city in the Lycus Valley (modern-day Turkey), Ephesus became part of the Roman Republic in 129 BCE. Known for its world-class library and later for its 25,000-seat open-air amphitheater, it was a center of culture and commerce. It attained honored status in 6 BCE when Augustus granted permission to build temples dedicated to Roma and himself. The imperial cult and the Artemis religion were intricately related, and Ephesians worshiped both the emperor and Artemis as gods.

8.2 The Cult of Artemis

The cult of Artemis (Diana to the Romans) was a celebrated Greek mystery religion that traced its origins back to the sixth century BCE. It's second temple, built in Ephesus (356 BCE), was one of the seven wonders of the ancient world and drew visitors from all over the Mediterranean.[3] The poet Antipater of Sidon describes his reaction when seeing the temple for the first time:

> I have set eyes on the wall of lofty Babylon on which is a road for chariots, and the statue of Zeus by the Alpheus, and the hanging gardens, and the Colossus of the Sun, and the huge labour of the high pyramids, and the vast tomb of Mausolus; but when I saw the house of Artemis that mounted to the clouds, those other marvels lost their brilliancy, and I said, "Lo, apart from Olympus, the Sun never looked on aught so grand."[4]

The massive structure, measuring 239 feet wide and 418 feet long, supported by 127 giant marble pillars towering 56 feet into the air, each a gift from a king and bedecked with jewels was overlaid with gold.

---

of God.

3. Along with the temple of Herod, Hanging Gardens of Babylon, and the Great Pyramids.

4. Antipater, *Greek Anthology* IX.58.

Artemis was identified loosely with Cybele (aka, The Great Mother), the focus of a well-known mystery religion, whose origin could be traced back ten centuries. The Apocalypse refers to "Mystery Babylon, the Great Mother of Harlots" (Rev 17:5), a possible allusion to the cult. The Ephesians believed a statue of Artemis, which fell from heaven, landed in their city (Act 19:35). They displayed it prominently in their temple.

According to myth, Artemis was the twin sister of Apollo and became the goddess of reproduction and midwifery, although she remained a virgin. Artemis was associated mainly with salvation. Over the years the cult went through many iterations.

People far and wide sought membership in the mysteries of Artemis, which included going through an elaborate initiation process. With each step the initiate became privy to knowledge and beliefs that had been hidden for the ages that were symbolized by the cycle of death and rebirth. Just as the earth passed through seasons of summer, autumn, winter, and spring, so must the soul. Initiation rites included magical incantations, undergoing secret rituals in sacred groves, eating meals dedicated to Artemis, washings, and taking blood oaths never to reveal the secrets.

Some elites sought membership for personal advantage, hoping it would open economic opportunities or advance their political careers.

During the age of the empire, the cult was placed under the control of Ephesian town officials loyal to Rome who were charged with protecting its teachings and making certain it supported the social and political agenda of the empire.[5] The religion of Artemis and the imperial cult existed side by side. Despite the temple of Artemis being world famous, the enormous temple of Augustus Caesar stood at a higher elevation, lest there be any doubt which one Rome considered more important.[6]

Music formed an important part of Artemis worship. Hymn writers were paid to compose songs to the goddess and boys' choirs performed at public feasts, festivities, and processions that were sponsored by the cult.[7]

5. Tactitus, *Ann.* 3.61.1–2, mentions that debtors escaping their creditors and even criminals often sought asylum in the temple. This caused some concern in Rome and a Senate investigation was launched.

6. Rogers, *Mysteries*, 121.

7. Gritz, *Paul, Women Teachers*, 40.

The embedded christological hymn found in 1 Tim 3:16 includes lyrics that imitated language associated with the cult of Artemis but challenged its most sacred beliefs.[8]

8.3 Historical Context for the Hymn

According to the book of Acts, Paul traveled to Ephesus to preach the gospel of the kingdom. For the first three months he expounded from the Scriptures that Jesus is the Christ. When faced with overwhelming opposition, he moved his base of operation to the school of Tryrannus (Acts 19:9). In all he spent three years in the city (19:8-11).

Ephesus was also a destination for itinerant Jewish exorcists and a stronghold for a group of John the Baptist followers (19:1-7; 11-17). In recounting his time in the city, Paul tells how he preached faithfully the gospel, despite continuous Jewish efforts to hinder him (Acts 20:18-20). Jews were not Paul's only detractors. He made great inroads into the gentile community, especially among the worshipers of Artemis who practiced hidden arts. As a result, many of his pagan converts "confessed and disclosed their practices," tossing their occult manuals into a bonfire (Acts 19:18-20).[9] This raised the ire of the town's business community who profited from the cult. Demetrius, a silversmith who made statuettes (i.e., idols) of Artemis, gathered guild members and charged Paul with teaching "that gods made with hands are not gods." He then warned that "there is danger not only that this trade of ours may come into disrepute but also that the temple of the great goddess Artemis will be scorned, and she will be deprived of all her majesty that brought all Asia and the world to worship her" (Acts 19:23-27). When

8. Quinn and Wacker, *Timothy*, 323, view 1 Tim 3:16 only as a portion of a stanza. Since it contains key christological elements (incarnation in flesh, vindicated in spirit, taken up to glory) found in other hymns as Hebrews 4:1-2; Col 1:15-20, Phil 2:6-11, this text fits into the category of a single verse hymn, functioning as a doxology or liturgical confession.

9. Practitioners of the Artemis cult ritually uttered an incoherent incantation, or magical formula, known as *Ephesia Grammata* (i. e. "Ephesian words"), which they believed divinely protected them from evil. According to tradition the words were inscribed into the pedestal dedicated to Artemis, which sat in the center of the temple of Artemis. Plutarch (46-119 CE), *Quaest. conv.* 706D, writes that magicians often encouraged demon possessed people to recite the *Ephesia Grammata* during exorcisms. This may have a link to the exorcisms in Acts 19:13-16 when a group of superstitious Hellenistic Jewish exorcists attempted unsuccessfully to use a more effective formula ("in the name of Jesus").

they realized that both their religion and their livelihood were endangered, the angry artisans shouted repeatedly, "Great is Artemis of the Ephesians!" (v. 28).

The chants caused a ruckus and word spread quickly throughout the city that Artemis was being maligned. Thousands flocked into the amphitheater and forcibly dragged two of Paul's companions with them. As the crowd became enraged, they "shouted in unison" for two continuous hours, "Great (*mega*) is Artemis of the Ephesians" (vv. 29–35).

This type of chant, known as an "acclamation," is a "rhythmically-formulated, sing-song-like or recited cry, with which the crowd expresses approval, praise, and congratulations . . . ."[10] As oral performances, acclamations allow even the marginalized to find their voice. In the Lukan account, the Ephesians chanted publicly, and acclaimed that Artemis was the superior to all other deities, including Paul's Jewish god. Rome encouraged devotion to Artemis and sanctioned the cult as one of the religions that supported Roman ideology. Paul's strange Jesus cult was not sanctioned! Hence, the acclamation "Great is Artemis" served a sociopolitical purpose and brought pressure on the local government to act against Paul.[11]

City officials were concerned over the public uproar as events reeled out of control. The town clerk arose, quieted the throng, and asked rhetorically if there was anyone on earth who did not know "that the city of the Ephesians is the temple keeper of the great Artemis" and the statue "that fell from heaven?" (v. 36). He then encouraged Demetrius and his guild members to take proper legal steps if they wished to file a complaint against Paul and his band of men (vv. 37–39), and then added, "For we are in danger of being charged with rioting today" (v. 40).

Rome did not tolerate riots and punished cities, disbanded guilds, and removed civil servants from office if they failed to maintain law and order.[12] While Artemis worship had prominence in Ephesus, it would lose all status if Rome cited the city for failure to keep peace. The idol makers would find themselves without an income and the tourist trade would dwindle to nothing. The importance of the cult of Artemis to the city cannot be over emphasized.

10. Bitner, "Acclaiming Artemis," 133.

11. Bitner, "Acclaiming Artemis," 127–41.

12. Dio Chrysostom, *Nicom. Or.* 38.33–37; Plutarch, *Praec. ger. rei. Publ.* 813 F, 825 C; Cassius Dio, *Rom. Hist.* 54.7.6; Suetonius, *Aug.* 47; Tacitus, *Ann.* 12.58.

When seeking to understand the hymn in 1 Tim 3:16, one must consider the sociopolitical atmosphere in which it was written.[13] In light of Roman imperialism and the Artemis cult, the six-strophe hymn can be seen as a song of resistance.

8.4 The Literary Context of the Hymn

At the start of his letter Paul charges Timothy to confront false teachers in the church who are disseminating "different doctrine" and wasting time on "myths and endless genealogies that promote speculation" rather than devoting themselves to God's revealed plan, which they originally accepted "by faith" (1 Tim 1:3-4). From verses 8-11 we learn that some Jewish Christ followers are trying to get gentile believers to keep the law of Moses.

Paul then offers a word about his former life as an obedient law keeper, even while he ignorantly and violently persecuted Christ followers and blasphemed the name of Christ (vv. 12-13). Yet, God in his mercy spared Paul and called him to serve Christ. Paul now declares, "The saying is sure and worthy of full acceptance, that Christ Jesus came into the world to save sinners—of whom I am the foremost" (vv. 14-17). Paul knows the purpose and function of both the law and the gospel in saving Jewish sinners.[14] Timothy must now follow Paul's instructions in good conscience and stand firm against false teachers, lest he end up shipwrecked like Hymenaeus and Alexander (vv. 18-20).

Paul offers Timothy specific directives on how to carry out his assignment among the Ephesians. These include praying for all people in authority, including "kings" and those "in high positions" in order that believers may live peaceably, and the gospel may advance unhindered (1 Tim 2:1-3). This advice is based on the proposition that God wishes for "everyone to be saved and come to the knowledge of the truth" (v. 4). Then he explains: "For there is one God; there is one mediator between God and humankind, Christ Jesus, himself human, who gave himself a ransom for all" (v. 5). God chose Paul at this time in history to reveal the message of redemption,

13. For a summary and evaluation of several traditional interpretations, see Gundry, "Form," 203-22. Gundry, however, gives no consideration to Roman religious ideology when seeking to understand the text, and thus in this writer's opinion, misses the hymn's political significance and anti-imperial nature.

14. The law, when understood correctly, served an interim purpose, and was intended to lead one to Christ. It was not intended to be added to Christ.

especially to gentiles (vv. 6-7). In the remainder of chapter 2, Paul gives instructions with regard to proper dress, the need for good works, and the limited role of women as teachers in Ephesus (vv. 8-15). The latter suggests that female Christ followers as well as men were responsible for the false teaching spreading throughout the congregation.

Paul follows these admonitions with guidelines on how to appoint "bishops" and "deacons" in the congregation, giving particular attention to the ethical qualifications (1 Tim 3:1-13).[15] Next, Paul reveals for the first time his specific purpose for writing to Timothy: "I hope to come to you soon, but I am writing these instructions to you so that if I am delayed, you may know how one ought to behave in the household of God, which is the church of the living God, the pillar and bulwark of the truth" (v. 15). Everything is about rules of conduct, i.e., how-to live in accordance with the principles of Christ regardless of the price or consequences. The locus of conduct is the Christ community, described as the support column ("pillar") and the fortification ("bulwark") for the gospel ("the truth").[16]

Most likely, Timothy is having difficulty maintaining order in the church. Because of his youth, his parishioners may not be responding positively to his instruction. A letter from Paul, in which he transfers his authority to Timothy, might carry weight. These authorized instructions will be read aloud in front of the church when it meets to eat the Lord's Supper. Paul plans to visit in the near future; so, Timothy and the church will have to face Paul when he arrives. This should be an incentive for them to get their house in order.

To make his point about living in accord with the "the truth" of the gospel (v. 15), Paul quotes a familiar hymn that shows Christ is worthy of devotion and obedience. His life, death and resurrection serve as the foundation and motivation for godliness.

Without any doubt, the mystery of our religion is great:

> He [Who] was revealed in flesh,
>   vindicated in spirit,
>   seen by angels,
>   proclaimed among Gentiles,
>   believed in throughout the world,

15. Long, "Ἐκκλεσία on Ephesians," 193-234, examines how the term ἐκκλεσία was used in pagan settings in the first century CE to depict a genuine earthly and heavenly relationship with Caesar and the gods.

16. Paul may be using language associated with the temple of Diana to describe the church as a pillar of truth, which by implication means the cult of Diana is not.

taken up in glory (1 Tim 3:16).

One can almost hear him sing it aloud as he transcribes the words onto the parchment. This is likely a hymn the church sang regularly; so, the people were familiar with it.

8.5 Structure of the Hymn

Quinn and Wacker believe 1 Tim 3:16 is only a portion of a larger hymn.[17] However, when compared to other fully developed christological hymns (John 1:14; Phil 2:6-11; Col 1:15-18), it contains all the features of an entire hymn. This is how we will approach the text.

Commentators have divided the hymn variously and imaginatively. Marshall, like Lenski before him, sees it as a unique, self-contained, one stanza song or poem that makes six statements about Christ.[18] It starts with his earthly ministry and concludes with his heavenly triumph.

Gordley, taking his cue from Ralph Martin, holds that the hymn should be divided into two equal strophes. Strophe 1 deals with the life of Christ: "[Who] was revealed in flesh, vindicated in spirit, seen by angels" (vv. 1-3). Strophe 2 deals with the life of the church: "proclaimed among Gentiles, believed in throughout the world, taken up in glory" (vv. 4-6).[19] In this scenario, "taken up to glory" refers not to Jesus' exaltation, but the church's eschatological ascent at the *parousia*.[20]

Other scholars favor dividing the hymn into three couplets.[21]

1. was revealed in flesh; vindicated in spirit,

2. seen by angels; proclaimed among Gentiles,

3. believed in throughout the world; taken up in glory.

If this structure is adopted, does the first couplet ("was revealed in flesh") speak of Christ's incarnation and ("vindicated [or justified] in spirit") of his resurrection? Or, does it mean God vindicated Jesus' claims as messiah while he was on earth through Spirit-produced signs and miracles?

17. Quinn and Wacker, *Timothy*, 323.

18. Marshall, *Pastoral Epistles*, 497; Lenski, *Paul's Epistles*, 607-9.

19. Gordley, *Christological Hymns*, 187; Ralph Martin, *Worship*, 48-49.

20. Gordley, *Christological Hymns*, 187.

21. Fee, *Timothy*, 54-58; Knight, *Pastoral Epistles*, 183-4, offers a survey of these structures and interpretations.

What about the second couplet? How does it progressively advance the story? Does "seen by angels" refer to angelic witness to the resurrection and "proclaimed among the Gentiles" refer to Paul's unique apostolic mission? If so, then the third couplet ("believed in throughout the world" and "taken up in glory") seems to break the pattern, since Christ's ascension actually *preceded* the worldwide mission.

On the other hand, did the lyricist intend for each couplet to stand alone with an emphasis on the contrast between the nouns?

1. was revealed *in flesh*; vindicated in *spirit*,

2. seen by *angels* (spirit beings); proclaimed among *gentiles* (human beings),

3. believed in throughout the *world* (earth); taken up in *glory* (heaven).

As Knight points out, "if this analysis is correct, the six lines present also a chiastic pattern of a-b, b-a, a-b. The first couplet presents Christ's work accomplished, the second, his work made known, and the third, his work acknowledged."[22]

8.6 The Preface of the Hymn

"Without any doubt" (καὶ ὁμολογουμένως) carries the idea of a premise or statement that is beyond question on which all can agree by unanimous consent. The preface calls on Christ followers to attest to the following proposition: "The Mystery of our religion is great" (μέγα ἐστὶν τὸ τῆς εὐσεβείας μυστήριον), i.e., magnificent, or grand. The NRSV translation of εὐσεβείας as "religion" has been a cause for much confusion and likely refers to the foundation of all Christian beliefs, i.e., the gospel of Christ. The idea not only speaks of gospel truths, but also includes Christ-honoring behavior and duty (e.g., piety and godliness) toward God that is associated with the truth. Right belief produces right living.[23] The term "religion" is used this way later in 1 Tim 4:7–8 and 6:3, signifying that conversion and conduct go hand in hand.

The mystery (μυστήριον, *mystērion*) i.e., a grand secret that cannot be known unless it is revealed, is called great (μέγα, *mega*). In Ephesus the

22. Knight, *Pastoral Epistles*, 183.

23. Fee, *Timothy*, 56, associates the mystery with Christ's humiliation and exaltation and the church's witness to him.

word was commonly associated with the cult of Artemis or one of the other great mystery religions, whose mysteries or secrets were hidden from view of all except the initiated.[24]

Paul's use of *mega* and *mystērion* likely brought back memories for Timothy. With the cult of Artemis still entrenched in the city, Paul's use of the terms places the gospel in opposition to Artemis worship.[25] Many of the Christ followers in Ephesus were likely former participants of the cult. Possibly, they are being lured back into the cult by family, friends, and colleagues.

First Timothy 3:16 may have become a weekly doxology sung in the church at Ephesus as a counter-acclamation to the shout, "Great is Artemis!"

When examined in its literary context, we discover that Paul used the term "mystery" seven verses earlier when he advises that deacons must "hold fast to the mystery of faith" (1 Tim 3:9), a certain reference to the gospel. Paul uses the phrases "mystery of faith" and the "mystery of godliness (religion)" synonymously. The essence of this mystery is contained in the embedded hymn, which Paul will explicate in six distinct sentences that follow. Part of the mystery includes God's revelation to Paul that gentiles can enter the kingdom apart from keeping the law.

8.7 General Observations

By adding the relative pronoun "Who" (ὅς) to the opening lines, Paul takes an existing hymn and applies it to Christ (cf. Phil 2:6; Col 1:15; Heb 1:4). This identifies the lyrics as a hymn and not simply a first-century creedal statement, although it may serve that purpose as well. In describing the mystery, the song uses six passive voice verbs that relate to Christ and the Christian mission.

Rather than divide the hymn into artificial stanzas that tend to color one's interpretation, we will examine this single verse hymn one line at a time and make a few observations.

---

24. Rogers, "Ephesian Tale," 71, lists Demeter, Dionysus, and Aphrodite as the other mystery cults.

25. Witherington, *Letters*, 215. Hurtado, *Lord Jesus*, 517, on the other hand, links *mega* to the cult of the emperor, placing the Christ movement in opposition to it. However, as previously mentioned, both the imperial cult and the religion of Artemis were so closely related that to oppose one was to oppose both.

First, each passive verb ends in θη, providing an observable rhythm, making the song easy to remember and sing.

Second, Christ is the object of the passive verbs.

Third, the gospel of Christ is the subject of the hymn.

Fourth, the three pairs of propositional phrases: 1) "in flesh" (material) and "in spirit" (immaterial); 2) "by angels" (super humans) and "among gentiles" (humans); 3)"in . . . world" (earth) and "in glory" (heaven) are grouped as opposites. This pattern allows the hymn to be sung antiphonally.

8.8 Exegesis

The song contains six certainties, one for each line.

Line 1: "He was revealed in flesh" (ἐφανερώθη ἐν σαρκί). Most commentators link these words to Christ's incarnation, meaning he took on human flesh. The God who concealed himself, disclosed himself. He became God with us. While this theological interpretation might hit the mark, Paul may have another or an additional thought in mind. The language was also used in connection with the imperial cult to designate the emperor as an epiphany of God, at least for the audience in Ephesus and throughout Asia Minor.[26] From a Roman perspective, Line 1 sent a message that Caesar had a challenger.

Line 2: Christ was "vindicated in spirit" (ἐδικαιώθη ἐν πνεύματι). God declared Jesus innocent, even though Jewish temple authorities condemned him as a false messiah and the Romans convicted him as a revolutionary.[27] In executing Jesus, the authorities doomed God's chosen spokesperson and thus opposed God's will. But God had the last word. He reversed their verdict and declared Jesus "not guilty" by raising him from the dead and exalting him to a position of authority.

The preposition ἐν can be translated variously as "in, by, or with." If the former, Paul is likely contrasting "spirit" to "flesh" in Line 1. Jesus ministered in the realm of the flesh and was raised in the realm of the spirit or as a spirit being. If we translate ἐν as "by or with" then it speaks of the instrumentality of the Spirit in raising Jesus from the dead (similar to Rom 1:4; 8:11). The choice is difficult because both options are feasible.

26. Going back in time Greeks, including Ephesians, thought of Alexander the Great as a god.

27. Wright, *Resurrection*, 270.

Line 3: Jesus was "seen by angels" (ὤφθη ἀγγέλοις). The mention of angelic witnesses to the resurrection is unique to Timothy.[28] This has led some to seek an alternative meaning. Micou makes a less than convincing argument that "angels" refers to human messengers.[29] As Knight notes, the NT nearly always uses ἄγγελοι when speaking of supernatural powers.[30] This understanding makes sense when contrasted with ἔθνεσιν ("Gentiles" = humans) in Line 4. The angels witnessed the actual resurrection and according to the gospel accounts informed Christ's closest followers (Matt 28:5-7; Mark 16:5-7; Luke 24:4-7; John 20:11–13). They had eyes to see and attested that God brought Jesus back from the death. Others could not see the resurrected Jesus unless God opened their eyes.

Line 4: Christ was "proclaimed among the Gentiles." Apostles and others spread the good news of Christ's death-defeating resurrection to gentiles who lived beyond the boundaries of Palestine, deep into the Roman Empire (Matt 28:18; Luke 21:24; Acts 8-28). This takes the reader back to another aspect of the "mystery" mentioned in the hymn's preface, i.e., that gentiles are accepted into God's family apart from the law. Paul's main mission was making the gospel known to the gentiles. Ephesus is a prime example. The gospel is universal in scope.

Line 5: Jesus was "believed in throughout the world." Many received the gospel with gladness. At the time of the writing, many throughout the Roman Empire who once gave their allegiance to Caesar had now submitted to Christ as Lord. As the gospel made inroads, onlookers proclaimed, "These men are changing the world" or "turning the world upside down" (Acts 17:6; John 1:12; 3:16).

Line 6: Jesus was "taken into glory." This stands in juxtaposition to "throughout the world." But as Knight observes, if Line 1 refers to the incarnation, Line 6 might reference his enthronement and serve as bookends around the short hymn. Christ entered into the presence of God where he obtained a place of ultimate authority from which he rules creation.[31]

This revolutionary mealtime song would strengthen the disciples in their faith and motivate them to live for Christ in front of a watching world.

28. Wright, *Resurrection*, 271.

29. Micou, "On ὤφθη ἀγγέλοις," 201-5.

30. Knight, *Pastoral Epistles*, 185.

31. According to Knight, "The first couplet speaks of the accomplishment of Christ's work, the second of the accomplishment made known, and the third of the response of the accomplishment. It is this great mystery of godliness that the church confesses . . . and that shapes the church's conduct before the living God" (*Pastoral Epistles*, 186).

The very essence of the song contradicts Roman ideology and offers its own counter-narrative. Could anything be more subversive than such lyrics?

8.9 Practical Implications for Paul's Audience

The church is entrusted with the mystery of the gospel. It raises its voice in song weekly, but it must also conduct its ethical affairs in accord with the gospel. Godliness is related to the revelation that Jesus reigns on the throne of God. All his followers must live faithfully and serve the exalted Lord.[32] Christ himself, the epitome of piety, demonstrated obedience unto death. Timothy and the church must follow the example.

Immediately following the hymn, Paul warns that "some will renounce the faith" (i.e., the "mystery of our religion"). They will give heed to deceitful spirits and teachings of demons propagated by hypocrites and liars whose consciences have been seared (4:1-2). Paul also urges believers not to embrace asceticism, follow myths and old wives' tales, seek riches, or be drawn into disputes, but engage in good works and exercise charity toward others. He addresses the church's pastoral responsibilities with regard to youths, the elderly, widows, and the proper use of finances (1Tim 4-6). Timothy and the church must maintain a "good conscience" and "keep the commandment[s] without spot or blame" (6:13-14).

This magnificent christological hymn will serve as an ever-constant reminder to church members of their responsibility to live for Christ and his kingdom, and to avoid participation in Artemis worship, emperor worship, and mystery religions. Instead, they should continuously offer praises to God. Their alternative and counter-acclamation must forever be: "Great is the mystery of *our* religion: God was manifested in the flesh."

32. Towner, *Letters*, 278-9.

CHAPTER 9

Hymn Fragments

HEBREWS 1:3–4 AND 1 Peter 3:18b, 22 each contains a fragment of a hymn that the writer quotes to accentuate some key aspect of Jesus' mission.

We will briefly examine these fragments to discover how each of the writers embedded a portion of a popular song into his letter to grab the readers' attention and motivate them to act on the truth.

Part 1

The Glory Song (Hebrews 1:1–4)

Long ago God spoke to our ancestors
in many and various ways by the prophets,
but in these last days he has spoken to us
by a Son, whom he appointed heir of all things,
through whom he also created the worlds.
He [Who]is the reflection of God's glory and
the exact imprint of God's very being,
and he sustains all things by his powerful word.
When he had made purification for sins,
he sat down at the right hand of the Majesty on high,
having become as much superior to angels
as the name he has inherited is more excellent than theirs (Heb 1:1–4).

9.1 Introduction

Written anonymously during the closing decades of the first century CE, Hebrews addresses a local congregation of Christ followers (Heb 13:17, 24), facing persecution and a crisis of faith.[1] The letter hints that it is destined for Rome, the capital of the empire. The words "Those from Italy send you greetings" (13:26b) seem to come from companions of the writer who wish to say "Hello" to friends and family back home.[2] No consensus exists as to whether the recipients are Jews or gentiles.[3]

Some scholars believe the text offers a theological justification for the destruction of the temple,[4] since the Aaronic priesthood and sacrificial system have come to an end and have been supplanted by Christ's ultimate sacrifice and eternal priesthood. However, the author never mentions the temple, only the tabernacle. He compares the church to the OT saints and Christ to the glory that appeared in the tabernacle.

The letter lacks a typical salutation like most others found in the NT, but launches into a prologue, similar to the Gospel of John. This foreword to the letter of Hebrews contains a short hymn fragment that begins in verse 3 with "He" (ὅς, *hos*), a relative pronoun normally translated "who" as in Phil 2 and 1 Tim 3, and points back to God's son (v. 2). Though consisting of only two verses, the lyrics touch on key truths found in several other hymns we have examined thus far.

9.2 Analysis

As the writer begins his epistle, he wants to convey a single point: "God spoke" (v. 1b). This "affirmation is basic to the whole argument of the epistle."[5] Had God remained silent, humankind would have wandered

---

1. The dating of Hebrews ranges from the late reign of Nero to the late reign of Domitian. Both emperors persecuted Christians.

2. Hebrews, just as well, may have been penned in Rome and sent to believers living in some distant city. In this case, Christ followers in Italy were sending greetings to the latter.

3. Attridge, *Hebrews*, 9–11, suggests the letter is written to Hellenized Jewish Christ followers. Others, like Ehrman, *New Testament*, 418–20, and Geerhardus Vos, *Hebrews*, 16–18, opt for an entirely gentile audience. As with most letters, however, the congregation might consist of both Jews and gentiles.

4. Carter and Levine, *New Testament*, 267.

5. Bruce, *Hebrews*, 45.

without divine direction or purpose. God, therefore, took the initiative to reveal himself and his will. He first spoke "to our ancestors," i.e., the forefathers (v. 1c) and lastly "to us," i.e., the recipients of the letter (v. 1d).

The time when God first spoke is described as "Long ago" (v. 1a), tracing his communication with humankind to ancient Jewish history.

9.2.1 God Spoke in Antiquity

In antiquity God spoke "in many and various ways by (ἐν, *en*) the prophets," i.e., spirit-inspired persons. King David disclosed, "The spirit of the Lord speaks through me, his word is upon my tongue. The God of Israel has spoken" (2 Sam 23:2–3a).

God's diverse means of communicating included dreams, visions, lightnings and earthquakes, miracles, a still small voice, angels, the law, Urim and Thummim, and a burning bush, among others. The prophets, in turn, revealed God's will to the people.

To Abraham, Isaac, and Jacob, the fathers of Israel, God spoke of choosing a people for his name, through whom the nations would come to know him. Through Moses he established people into a kingdom of priests to represent him and gave them a law to follow. When Israel fell short and abandoned faithfulness to God, they found themselves enslaved to foreigners. Through Isaiah, Ezekiel, Daniel, and others God promised to restore the kingdom to Israel and carry out his plan to reach the world.

But God was not finished speaking. His revelation was progressive and moved beyond promise to fulfillment.

9.2.2 God's Final Revelation

"But in these last days (in contrast to the past) he has spoken to us." The entirety of what God said to the ancients did not convey the totality of God's message. He had more to say, which he did "by his son" (ἐν υἱῷ). Divine revelation was meted out piecemeal and progressed until the time of Christ (ca. 30 CE). He brought "together all God's former partial revelations."[6] The promises God gave to the prophets found their fulfillment in Christ. The author will quote texts from Psalms or Isaiah as if they speak *to* Jesus (e.g.,

---

6. DeSilva, *Introduction*, 713.

Heb 1:5a, 13; 5:5–6), speak *about* Jesus (e.g., Heb 1:5b, 6), or even are spoken *by* Jesus (e.g., Heb 2:12–13; 10:5–8).[7]

"Last days" reflects a semitic understanding of time and signifies the era prior to the restoration of God's universal kingdom. Since the recipients still live in the "last days," the new day has not yet fully arrived (1 Cor 10:11). The message that God spoke through Christ is for the last days and speaks of things "not yet seen" (Heb 11) or actualized.

Once God spoke in Christ, there was nothing more to say. All he wished to convey about himself and the future had been revealed. This final revelation in Christ took place at least a generation before the letter was written, but it had application for the readers. To see Jesus was to see the Father. He was the full revelation of God to humankind.

These opening verses set the stage for the remainder of Hebrews.[8] The author will explain that Christ is superior to all other revelators: prophets (1:1–3), angels (1:4–2:18), Moses (3:1–19), and Joshua (4:1–13). The writer further establishes Christ's priesthood as superior to Aaron's (4:14—10:18) and shows that it is based on a better covenant, tabernacle, sacrifice, and completed work. Unlike Aaron, the exalted Jesus' priesthood, according to the order of Melchizedek, is without end. Therefore, the readers of Hebrews are warned against abandoning Christ and reverting to a lesser revelation.

> Since, then, we have a great high priest who has passed through the heavens, Jesus, the Son of God, let us hold fast to our confession. (Heb 4:14)

> Now the main point in what we are saying is this: we have such a high priest, one who is seated at the right hand of the throne of the Majesty in the heavens. (8:1)

> And since we have a great priest over the house of God, let us approach with a true heart in full assurance of faith, with our hearts sprinkled clean from an evil conscience and our bodies washed with pure water. Let us hold fast to the confession of our hope without wavering. (10:21–23a)

In the final section of his letter the author speaks of the superiority of Christ's threefold provision for the church. They have:

7. DeSilva, *Introduction*, 713.

8. Buchanan, *Hebrews*, 3. Laansma, "Hebrews," notes the use of Pss 2, 8, and 110; the wisdom Christology of 1:1–3 and the descent-ascent pattern parallels of John 1:1–18, Phil 2:5–11, and Col 1:15–20.

1. *Faith* to enter boldly into God's presence (10:19–22) and stand fast in their confession (10:23–39). Examples of OT faithfulness are given for them to follow (11:1—12:2).

2. *Hope* in a future resurrection (12:3–39).

3. *Love*, which enables them to support one another and their church leaders (13:1–17).

9.2.3 Verses 3–4

Bruce detects that the writer offers seven truths about the Son found in verse 3 which "show why the revelation given in him is the highest which God can give."[9] First, the son is "heir of all things." There is nothing that exists of which he will not possess. "Heritage is closely related to sonship."[10] This resonates with Ps 2:8, when God says to King David, his son and anointed one: "Ask of me, and I will make the nations your heritage. And the ends of the earth your possession."

Second, through the son God "created the worlds (Gk, *aions*)." This echoes the words of Col 1:16. Years later John will emphasize the same truth (John 1:3). "God brought the universe into being by the agency of his Son."[11]

Third, the son "is the reflection of God's glory." In the past, God's glory or presence was manifested in a physical way in the cloud and fire that led the Israelites in the wilderness and descended and rested between the wings of the cherubim over the ark of the covenant in the tabernacle.[12] God was among his people whenever they stopped and pitched their tents around the tabernacle. After the Philistines defeated Israel and captured the Ark, Eli's daughter-in-law named her new baby Ichabod, meaning the "glory of the Lord has departed" (1 Sam 4:21–22). With the coming of his Son, God's glory returned. He radiated God's light in the world (John 1:4).[13]

---

9. Bruce, *Hebrews*, 46.

10. Buchanan, *Hebrews*, 4.

11. Bruce, *Hebrews*, 47.

12. Hebrews mentions "tabernacle" in 101 of its 303 verses, which may reinforce the premise the audience was Jewish.

13. Like Wisdom of old, Christ is a perfect reflection of divine light (Wis 7:26).

As the eternal "effulgence of God's glory and the image of his substance [he] is alone the adequate revealer and content of revelation."[14]

Fourth, the son is "the exact imprint of God's very being." Christ "is the paradigm *imago Dei*."[15] Like father, like son (John 14:9). Yet, the son is not the father (John 14:28). As God's authorized representative, he spoke for God. To reject Jesus was to reject God.

Fifth, "he sustains all things by his powerful word." Christ's word carries creation toward its appointed goal, namely the kingdom of God on earth (e.g., Col 1:17). His word accomplishes what it set out to do. Building something is one thing. Maintaining it is another matter.

Sixth, "he . . . made purification for sins." Christ's words (v. 3b) are accompanied by Christ's work. Old Testament priests were responsible for purification of sins. The role was transferred to Christ. As Gordley notes, "the agent of creation is also the agent of God in redemption."[16] Christ took on a body to offer it as a sacrifice (Heb 10:5–7); therefore, the writer of Hebrews says, "we have been sanctified through the offering of the body of Jesus Christ once for all" (vv. 10, 14). The royal priest became the sacrifice.

Seventh, "he sat down at the right hand of the Majesty on high." His redemptive responsibilities with regard to sins were now finished. This speaks of his exaltation to the ultimate position of authority and finds a counterpart in the Philippian song (Phil 2:9), a concept borrowed originally from Ps 110:1, 4 and interpreted from a midrash and christological perspective.

His position at God's right hand (no literal location is intended) denotes he is "much superior to angels."[17] As such, the name he inherited "is more excellent than theirs" (v. 4; cf. Phil 2:10). This may be a veiled warning against the worship of angels. To be superior to the angels means Christ is also superior to the law, which was mediated by angels (2:2–3).

9.3 The Hymn and Roman Rule

According to the song, God's story is a single narrative of which Christ has always been a part.[18] He was present and active in the creation of the world,

14. Meier, *Symmetry and Theology*, 316, as quoted by Gordley, *New Testament*, 193.

15. Middleton, *New Heaven*, 166.

16. Gordley, *New Testament*, 193.

17. Bruce, *Hebrews*, 50.

18. Marohl, "Hebrews," 491.

became part of the world, redeemed the world, and has been made ruler over the cosmos. He is moving the world toward its ultimate goal—the kingdom of God, described in the letter as "rest" (Heb 4:9), a metaphorical image of salvation or deliverance. Buchanan believes the writer of Hebrews portrays rest as "deliverance from Rome's rule." It carries political connotations.[19] When God restores his kingdom, Israel will rule the world under the messiah. Although the kingdom had not yet arrived in its fulness, Christ has already been placed on his heavenly throne. As the heralds of the gospel announce the present reign of Christ, people can enter a proleptic rest as they wait for the eternal rest to come.

The letter to the Hebrews presents Christ as the final prophet who speaks for God, the ultimate priest, who purifies God's people once and for all from all sins, and the eternal king, who sits on his throne next to God.[20]

Part 2

A Baptismal Song (1 Peter 3:18–22)

For Christ also suffered for sins once for all,
the righteous for the unrighteous, in order to bring you to God.
He was put to death in the flesh, but made alive in the spirit,
in which also he went and made a proclamation to the spirits in prison,
who in former times did not obey, when God waited patiently in the days of
Noah, during the building of the ark, in which a few, that is, eight persons,
were saved through water.
And baptism, which this prefigured, now saves you—not as a removal of dirt
from the body, but as an appeal to God for a good conscience,
through the resurrection of Jesus Christ,
who has gone into heaven and is at the right hand of God, with angels, au-
thorities, and powers made subject to him. (1 Pet 3:18–22)

9.4 Introduction

First Peter 3:18-22 is a difficult-to-interpret text on baptism and contains a fragment of a song, one the early church might have sung during the rite of

19. Buchanan, *Hebrews*, 9.

20. Bruce, *Hebrews*, 50.

baptism. In order to make sense of the passage and song, we must examine them within the larger context of First Peter.

From Tertullian onward, the church has traditionally attributed First Peter to the apostle bearing the same name, but recent scholars believe it to be the work of a pseudonymous author, perhaps a Roman believer and an advocate of Petrine teaching.[21] Scholarly consensus places the date of the letter between 80 and 90 CE, during the reign of Domitian.[22] The author desires to help a small group of Jewish Christ followers and a growing number of gentile believers navigate the hostile sociopolitical world in which they live without compromising their faith.

First Peter is written to "resident aliens" who have been dispersed throughout "Pontus, Galatia, Cappadocia, Asia, and Bithynia" (1 Pet 1:1), five Roman provinces located in northern Asia Minor. The author identifies these scattered ones as those: 1) "who have been chosen . . . by God the Father," i.e., selected from among the peoples of the world; and 2) "who have been . . . sanctified by the Spirit" (v. 2a), the latter which likely took place at baptism and set them apart for life in God's kingdom. As a result, they are empowered to live in obedience to Christ and receive continuous cleansing of their sins (v. 2b). A doxology follows that describes God as a Father who "has given us a new birth into a living hope through the resurrection of Jesus Christ from the dead" (v. 3). By definition, rebirth "implies a preceding death and termination of old associations and alliances," including allegiance to the empire's gods and agenda.[23] Christ's victory over death makes the separation from the world and inclusion into God's family possible.

Some scholars have suggested that First Peter is either a baptismal oration or instructions given to newly baptized believers at the time of their baptism and entrance into church membership.[24] Others see it as an epistle of hope and encouragement.[25] At the least, the letter is addressed to baptized believers, who after pledging their fidelity to the exalted Lord

21. Wright and Bird, *New Testament*, 758–60, however lean toward Petrine authorship.

22. Achtemeier, *1 Peter*, 39–50, provides an excellent discussion of the theories surrounding both authorship and date. For the sake of simplicity, this writer will refer to Peter as the author without regard to his identity.

23. Cross, *1 Peter*, 29, explicitly links this new birth to baptism. They cannot be separated.

24. This might account for the declarative statement, "Baptism . . . now saves" (1 Pet 3:21), which Brooks, *Drama*, 139, says is the controlling idea of First Peter.

25. For a helpful discussion of the options, see Achtemeier, *1 Peter*, 59–60 and Beasley-Murray, *Baptism*, 251–58.

Jesus, have faced persecution and possibly even death (3:13-17; 4:12-19). For a gentile to turn away from worshiping local and national deities and to align with a religion that had no visible gods was an egregious offense and the equivalent to becoming an atheist. The writer warns the readers not to abandon their faith when persecuted or rely on inappropriate means to resist satanic attacks. Instead, they are to follow the example of Christ who suffered and died (1:19; 2:21-25; 3:18). As they embrace and follow the alternative ethics of God's kingdom, they will fulfill their baptismal vows.

Among NT documents First Peter is one of the few that speaks of new birth and traces it back to God who implants the gospel seed in the hearts of the elect (v. 24).

First Peter connects baptism and salvation in a section that deals with Christ's suffering and vindication (3:18–22), and includes the embedded hymn fragment.[26]

> For Christ also suffered once for all, the righteous for the unrighteous, in order to bring you to God. He was put to death in the flesh, but made alive in the spirit, in which also he went and made a proclamation to the spirits in prison, who in former times did not obey, when God waited patiently in the days of Noah, during the building of the ark, in which a few, that is, eight people, were saved through water. And baptism, which this prefigured, now saves you—not as a removal of dirt from the body, but as an appeal to God for a good conscience, through the resurrection of Jesus Christ, who has gone into heaven and is at the right hand of God, with angels, authorities, and powers made subject to him. (1 Pet 3:18–22)

As Gordley rightly points out, only verses 18b and 22 constitute the actual hymn-portion of the pericope.[27]

> He was put to death in the flesh, but made alive in the spirit. (3:18b)

> who has gone into heaven and is at the right hand of God, with angels, authorities, and powers made subject to him. (3:22)

Everything "between these hymnic lines" elaborates on the phrase "made alive in the spirit."[28]

---

26. For an in-depth study of baptism as it relates to salvation, see Streett, *Caesar and the Sacrament*.

27. Gordley, *New Testament*, 197–99.

28. Gordley, *New Testament*, 197.

Issues discussed in this passage also can be found in other embedded NT songs.[29] For example, "death in the flesh" and "alive in the spirit" corresponds to 1 Tim 3:16, where "flesh" and "spirit" are contrasted. Christ's suffering is found in both 1 Pet 3:18 and Phil 2:8. Christ's exaltation to "the right hand of God" is found in both 1 Pet 3:18a and Heb 1:3b. His victory over "angels, authorities, and powers" (1 Pet 3:22b) is essentially the same as Phil 2:4b. Colossians 1:16 additionally identifies Christ as creator of angels and 1 Tim 3:16 notes he was seen by angels.

These connections seem to indicate that the author of 1 Peter was familiar with other songs that were circulating among first-century congregations.

9.5 Analysis

In verse 18, the author gives a theological explanation for Christ's death. First, his death was universal in scope: he "suffered once for all." Second, his death was vicarious: he "suffered *for* . . . all." Third, in his innocence, he died for the guilty: "the righteous for the unrighteous." Fourth, the reason for his death was reconciliation: he died "in order to bring you to God." Fifth, he was executed by the authorities: he was "put to death in the flesh." Sixth, God vindicated him by raising him from the dead: he was "made alive in [or by] the spirit." This litany is intended to encourage the readers to live righteously and to suffer for Christ, knowing that one day they too will be vindicated. Seventh, by means of the Spirit ("in which,"), he visited and preached to "the spirits in prison." These were likely the disobedient spirits ("sons of God") who in "the days of Noah" cohabitated with women (Gen 6:1–4).[30] This implies that Christ is Lord over all beings—angels as well as humans (see v. 22). While some commentators believe Christ descended into Hades to deliver his message to the imprisoned spirits,[31] 1 Pet 3:18a, 22 seems to link Christ's visitation to his exaltation to "the right hand of God, with angels, authorities, and powers made subject to him."

Achtemeier observes that verses 19 and 22 form an inclusion and that both verses speak of the resurrected Jesus' interaction with defeated

29. Gordley, *New Testament*, 198–99, insightfully observes how 1 Pet 3:18–22 is connected to other christological songs, some which I have used here.

30. Dalton, *Christ's Proclamations*, 32–36; Webb, "Intertexture and Rhetorical Strategy," 96. 1 En. 6:2; 12:2–4; Jude 6; 2 Pet 2:4.

31. This theory is based on 2 Pet 2:4.

spiritual beings. In verse 19 they are characterized as "spirits in prison." In verse 22, they are "subject to him" (i.e., to Christ). The course of Christ's movement in verse 22 is heavenward and likely is the same in verse 19.[32] Michaels comes to the same conclusion. He recognizes a sequential pattern: "put to death in the flesh" (v. 18b), "made alive in the spirit" (v. 18b), "gone to heaven" (v. 22).[33] There is no indication from the text that Christ ever descended and preached to the spirits in prison. More likely, the spirits he confronted were The Watchers mentioned in 1 Enoch who look from above.[34]

Into this context the writer introduces baptism. He mentions the great flood because he sees a corresponding relationship between the "former times" of Noah's day and the "now" of his audience, and compares "the few" righteous souls saved then with the miniscule number of Christ's followers living among the pagan masses in the Roman Empire.[35] Just as "the few were saved (i.e., delivered) through water" back then, the writer assures this faithful minority (the "chosen" of 1:2) that "baptism . . . now saves you" (σώζει βάπτισμα, sōzei baptisma).

This is the only verse in the NT where baptism serves "as the subject of an action verb."[36] The author, thus, conveys the impression that baptism actually accomplishes something—human salvation or deliverance.

The word "now" (νῦν, nun) should be viewed eschatologically (1:5) since Peter's audience and their experience of baptism are part of God's end-time plan of deliverance. Käsemann calls baptism "the seal of membership in the eschatological people of God."[37] The flood was a type that foreshadowed eschatological salvation. Baptism is the antitype (ἀντίτυπον) or fulfillment to which the flood pointed (3:21).

This leads to the question, "From what does baptism deliver?" Like the flood, baptism represents a "break with the old world"[38] and a fresh start in the new kingdom. Above all, it has a political connotation and speaks of a judgment to come.[39] The political systems of the ages, including the empire,

---

32. Achtemeier, *1 Peter*, 240–41.

33. Michaels, *1 Peter*, 197.

34. Achtemeier, *1 Peter*, 240–41.

35. Boring, *1 Peter*, 141.

36. Brooks, *Drama*, 139.

37. Cited in Bosch, *Transforming Mission*, 167.

38. Brooks, *Drama*, 139.

39. Noah's baptism in the flood waters included deliverance from an oppressive

will face adjudication at the consummation of the age. Those on Christ's side will escape such a fate.

Peter then explains what baptism is and is not, only in reverse order. He says it is "not (οὐ) . . . a removal of dirt from the body" like a Roman bath or Jewish ceremonial washing, but (ἀλλὰ) something of a completely different nature.[40] Rather, baptism is "an appeal (ἐπερώτημα, eperōtōma) to God for a good conscience," or as the NIV translates, "a pledge to God of [or "from"] a good conscience," thus placing it in the category of a *sacramentum* or vow.[41] It is more like a soldier's oath to serve Lord Caesar and the empire even to the point of death. The word *eperōtōma* speaks of commitment to keep one's end of a contract. It is a promise of fidelity.[42]

As Ananias instructed Paul, "Get up, be baptized, and have your sins washed away, calling on the name of the Lord" (Acts 22:16).

Qumran required all candidates seeking admission into membership to undergo a ritual bath and pledge their obedience to God and community.[43]

According to 1 Peter, baptism saves in a similar way as the flood saved. The water itself was not efficacious, but God used the rising flood waters to convey Noah and his sons to safety. In like manner, baptismal waters have no intrinsic saving powers, but deliver the believer from judgment "through the resurrection of Jesus Christ," linking baptism to the "new birth" (1:3).[44] According to Michaels, "The resurrection of Jesus Christ is what makes an appeal or pledge to God . . . efficacious and guarantees eternal life to the one baptized."[45] Apart from Christ's resurrection, baptism has no power to save.

---

political system and evil social order. His deliverance by water brought judgment upon the world.

40. This was possibly an erroneous belief among some Christ followers. Hence the author feels the necessity to make this point. Kelly, *Epistles of Peter*, 161-62, believes the "removal of dirt from the body" refers to circumcision, a position held by very few scholars.

41. Reicke, *Epistles of James*, 106-7, 139, translates the phrase as "a pledge of good will toward God." Also see Reicke, *Disobedient Spirits*, 182-86. This thought was possibly the basis for Pliny's report to Trajan that Christians "bound themselves by an oath (*sacramentum*)." Pliny, *Ep.* 10.96.

42. Ferguson, *Baptism*, 367.

43. 1QS 1.16; 5.7-8.

44. Gorman, *Inhabiting*, 59-60, 73-79 makes a strong case that the apostle Paul also identifies baptism with justification.

45. Michaels, *1 Peter*, 218.

9.6 Implications

The song's lyrics conclude on a positive note. Although executed by the power of the State, Jesus emerged from death, went "into heaven and is at the right hand of God, with angels, authorities, and powers made subject to him" (1 Pet 3: 22). The implications are several. First, Jesus now reigns over all living beings, both good and evil, earthly and heavenly. While not apparent, except through eyes of faith, the empire and the powers behind it have been conquered and stripped of their authority over Spirit-energized believers.[46] Second, Jesus, not Caesar, has received a manifest destiny to rule the world. Third, following Christ in baptism and worshiping him as Lord will not sit well with Caesar, the chief priest of the imperial cult. Suffering will follow. Hence Peter's words, "Dear friends, do not be surprised at the fiery ordeal that has come on you to test you, as though something strange were happening to you" (4:12).[47] Fourth, even if some are martyred, they are assured to be raised on the last day when evil is eradicated.

The letter's recipients are included in God's redemptive plan that he set in motion "before the foundation of the world," and unfurled at the "end of the ages for your sake," and accomplished by Christ (1:20). Just as Peter opened his letter, so he closes, reminding his readers that the present age is winding down and "the end of all things is near" (4:7). Therefore, he concludes by instructing them how to conduct their daily lives while living in enemy territory as they wait for the Lord's arrival from heaven (4:12—5:11).

Songs of Consequence

Negro spirituals date back to slave days in America. After long hours of laboring in the cotton fields, the transported and enslaved African workers gathered under the stars to sing away their blues. They dreamt of salvation, both earthly and heavenly. "Down By the Riverside"[48] is an example of a spiritual that carried a double meaning.

---

46. According to Jewish thought these defeated spirit beings were the powers behind human governments, hostile to God and the perpetrators of idolatry: 1 En. 99.7; Jub. 1.1; 22.17. Some NT writers seem to agree (1 Cor 10:19-21; Rev 9:20).

47. For those who support an early date for 1 Peter, such as Wright and Bird, *New Testament*, 760, "the fiery ordeal" is a veiled reference to persecution at the hands of Nero.

48. Public Domain.

Gonna lay down my burden . . .
Down by the riverside (3×)
Gonna lay down my burden
Down by the riverside
Chorus:
I ain't gonna study war no more
Study war no more
Ain't gonna study war no more

At face value, the lyrics speak of finding deliverance from worldly woes and conflicts ("Gonna lay down my burden") through Christian baptism ("down by the riverside"), which was prefigured by the Hebrew children crossing the Jordan River and finding rest in the Promised Land. On another level, however, the lyrics were hidden transcripts.[49] The riverside was a metaphor for the Ohio River. If the slaves could somehow reach and cross the waters of the Ohio, they would gain freedom.

As the slave masters sat on their plantation verandas in the cool of the evening, sipping their mint juleps and listening to the slaves sing their spirituals, they must have felt self-satisfied that they had trained their charges to be passive and content. They were unaware the slave songs actually defied the oppressive owners and the culture of the South.

Many slave songs were prayers put to music. What could be more subversive than to ask God to work on your behalf against the master, who believed god was on his side?

New Testament songs served a similar purpose. As Christ followers sang their own tunes of resistance, they resolved to live for Christ and dreamt of a future free from Roman domination.

49. "Follow the Drinking Gourd" is another popular Negro Spiritual with a hidden transcript. The drinking gourd was a veiled reference to the Big Dipper, whose two outermost stars point to the North Star. The lyrics called for slaves to follow the star northward to freedom.

CHAPTER 10

The Songs of Revelation

*You are worthy to take the scroll
and to open its seals,
for you were slaughtered and by your blood you ransomed for God
saints from every tribe and language and people and nation;
you have made them to be a kingdom and priests serving our God,
and they will reign on earth.*
(Rev 5:9–10)

THE BOOK OF REVELATION places songs at strategic locations in its visionary narrative and gives its earthly readers a glimpse of heavenly worship. The lyrical messages are intended to encourage suffering believers to worship Christ like their heavenly counterparts despite pressures to bow in obeisance to Caesar and the Roman gods, even under the threat of punishment and death.

10.1 Genre

Revelation falls under the category of apocalyptic literature with a narrative structure by which the author reveals hidden or concealed information normally inaccessible to the public. The revelation often deals with events and activities that take place in heaven and/or hell to which the author has become privy through a series of dreams and/or visions.[1] An other-worldly guide, oftentimes an angel, takes the visionary on a tour of the afterlife.[2] In John's celestial travels he witnesses events in the heavenly sphere that occur during the same time frame as different events take place below. In the modern media age, this scenario might be portrayed on a split screen to show both things happening at the same time. In the book of Revelation, those in heaven can be found rejoicing and worshiping while on earth Christ followers are suffering for their faith.

Ancient apocalyptic literature is intended to offer hope to people in crisis. In the case of John's Apocalypse, he encourages church members in Roman Asia to remain faithful despite persecution and to warn them of the consequences if they fail. Because Revelation deals in part with the future, it also serves a prophetic function (Rev 1:3) that focuses on things to come including judgment of evil and vindication of the righteous.

From the viewpoint of the Christ Movement, Jesus' death and subsequent resurrection inaugurated the eschatological age.[3] His resurrection was the first act of deliverance that guarantees the same for all believers (Matt 27:52–53).

Within the pages of Revelation, the phrase "new song" is used to describe two of the musical compositions that celebrate a "new" exodus for God's people and connect Jesus with Moses (Rev 9–10; 15:2–4). Both exoduses—one led by Moses and the other by Jesus—are associated with the slaughter of a Passover lamb. The second, like the first, commences a journey to a promised destination but is fraught with difficulty and danger along the way.

In this chapter we will examine several Revelation songs to discover their meaning and how they offered solace to the suffering churches of Asia Minor. This will not be an easy task since apocalyptic writing, by its very nature, is figurative and not to be taken literally. John's vision is filled with symbols, including numbers, colors, beasts, falling stars, candles, swords, among others. Without the angelic guide interpreting the symbols and events, they will remain a mystery.

---

1. Dante's *Inferno* is an apocalyptic example of a tour of hell. Woodchuck, "Images of Hell," 11–42, looks at several apocalyptic writings in pre- and post-apostolic times.

2. Collins, *Apocalyptic Imagination*, 5–6.

3. Collins, *Apocalyptic Imagination*, 271.

10.2 Historical Context

Written to seven churches located in the far eastern reaches of the empire (Rev 2–3) during the mid-90s CE at the time of Emperor Domitian's reign, Revelation contains several songs of resistance. Christ followers lived in a region influenced strongly by the Roman imperial cult and among pagan neighbors who paid homage to Caesar as a god, offering him sacrifices and paeans of musical praise at their association meals. Since many gentile believers had once been members of these groups, it was no easy task to worship Christ while occupying the same space as idolatrous family and neighbors.

Jewish believers faced a different set of difficulties than their gentile counterparts. As long as they were members of a synagogue, they had some protection from threats. But things had changed. Excommunicated from their synagogues, they became targets of persecution. This was the sociopolitical reality in which Christ followers found themselves in Asia Minor at the end of the first century CE.

The musical lyrics found in Revelation, which churches likely sang during worship, reveal a strong attitude of resistance to the cult of the emperor and to pharisaical Judaism. As members of God's kingdom, Christ followers worshiped a different Lord.

The revelator provides a glimpse of heaven to encourage faithfulness. Things were bad, but not hopeless.

10.3 John's Vision of Reality

John describes a series of visions he experienced while exiled on the isle of Patmos. According to his narrative, he fell into an altered state of consciousness and suddenly found himself on a guided tour of heaven. On his journey he learns that all beings in heaven praise the eternal creator, and that God has a redemptive plan for the cosmos. John's angelic chaperone shows him the true character of the emperor, the imperial cult, and the capital city of Rome. As the scenes unfold, the empire's self-promoting propaganda is exposed as a lie. In line with the popular idea of an angelic rebellion against God (1 En. 6–13), John sees Satan and his minions launching a final "desperate attempt to deceive people and lead them astray from God's truth."[4] John describes the emperor as a "beast" (Rev 13:2); the empire as a

4. DeSilva, Introduction, 815.

great whore (Rev 17:1, 4); Satan as a "great dragon" who deludes the whole world (12:9; 20:3, 10); and Rome as "Babylon the Great" (18:23). In the end, Rome's illegitimate reign over earth comes to naught and all supporting participants face judgment. As John writes, "After this I saw another angel coming down from heaven, having great authority; and the earth was made bright with his splendor. He called out with a mighty voice,

> 'Fallen, fallen is Babylon the great!
>> It has become a dwelling place of demons,
>> a haunt of every foul spirit,
>> a haunt of every foul bird,
>> a haunt of every foul and hateful beast.
> For all the nations have drunk
>> of the wine of the wrath of her fornication,
>> and the kings of the earth have committed fornication with her,
>> and the merchants of the earth have grown rich
>> from the power of her luxury.'
> Then I heard another voice from heaven saying,
>> 'Come out of her, my people,
>> so that you do not take part in her sins.'" (Rev 18:2–3)

Using the most graphic and risqué language, John likens participation with the empire ("Babylon") to an illicit act of sexually penetrating a prostitute ("the great whore") and commands the church metaphorically to "come out of her" or withdraw. The purpose for obeying is "that you will not take part in her sins," which ultimately leads to judgment (vv. 5–8).

As the curtain of heaven is pulled back his readers see that God has not left them to fend for themselves. He plans to judge the beast and restore his own rule over earth. The world will come to recognize its rightful king and worship God. Christ followers in Asia Minor must not forfeit their place in God's eternal kingdom in order to survive in the present. Instead, they must bear the strain of persecution, refuse to compromise with idolatry, remain loyal to the Lord Jesus Christ, and worship him in full-throated song just as their heavenly counterparts in the apocalyptic vision (Rev 4:1–8; 5:1–14; 7:12–17; 14:1–11; 15:1–4; 19:1–8). As they live in light of the eschaton God assures them that their future is sealed.

10.4 The Seven Churches in Their Sociopolitical Context

At their baptism, believers took an oath to serve Christ as Lord regardless of the cost.[5] One problem they faced was that Domitian (81-96 CE) (as mentioned in chapter 5,) demanded his subjects address him as "Our Lord and our God."[6] According to Eusebius, based on information he gleaned from the writings of Hegesippus (ca. 110-180 CE), Domitian released his wrath on believers.[7] Rev 2–3 paints a picture of persecution against the churches of the Lycus Valley. To those who overcome, i.e., turn their backs on the empire and reorient their lives in line with God's kingdom, Christ promised eternal life.

10.4.1 The Church in Ephesus

Ephesus was the unofficial political capital of Asia Minor.[8] Sitting at the intersection of three trade routes and on the mouth of a major harbor, it was a strategic center of commerce. Besides loyalty to Artemis/Diana many people were also devoted to the worship of Dionysus/Bacchus, the god of wine. This might explain the admonition, "Be not drunk with wine" (Eph 5:19). Plutarch tells how the townspeople responded when Marc Antony entered the city: "Women arrayed like Bacchanals, and men and boys like Satyrs and Pans, led the way before . . . the people hailing him as Dionysus . . . ."[9] Tacitus mentions that Messalina, wife of Emperor Claudius, threw her support behind wild Bacchic celebrations.[10] The cult, with its sensuous initiation rites, was still vibrant in Ephesus at the turn of the second century CE.[11]

5. See Streett, *Caesar and the Sacrament*, for an in-depth study of baptism as a rite of resistance in its first-century CE context.

6. Suetonius, *Dom.* 13.2. This title is nearly identical to how Thomas addresses Jesus in John 20:28. If written at the same time as the *Apocalypse*, the author may be showing that Caesar has a competitor. In Rev 4:11, the writer warns his readers, "There is no rest day or night for those who worship the beast and its image and for anyone who receives the mark of its name."

7. Eusebius, *Hist. eccl.* 3:19.

8. Pate, "Revelation 2–19," 68.

9. Plutarch, *Ant.* 24.3.

10. Tacitus, *Ann.* 11.31.

11. Justin, *Dial.* 69.

Domitian built a temple to honor Emperors Vespasian and Titus, and erected a magnificent colossus to himself. While the church at Ephesus did not succumb to idolatry, it failed to be a bold witness to Christ and forsook its "first love" (Rev 2:4), a reference arguably to the love feast, the Christian version of the Roman banquet.[12] John commands them to repent (v. 5).

10.4.2 The Church in Smyrna

Smyrna was located 40 miles north of Ephesus. Alexander the Great designed and built the city on four tiers starting at sea level and reaching a 500-foot plateau. The main thoroughfare was called the "Street of God," and curved around Mount Pagus as it wound its way upward to the acropolis and the temple of Zeus, the crown jewel of Smyrna. The city also erected a temple "to the goddess Roma, the personified and deified representation of Rome."[13] In 26/27 CE, Smyrna was granted the privilege to build a temple in honor of Tiberius.[14]

Jewish and gentile Christ followers suffered financial hardships, punishment, and even martyrdom because they refused to participate in idolatry (Rev 2:9–11).

10.4.3 The Church in Pergamum

Pergamum was the regional capital of Asia Minor and possessed the "right of the sword," i.e., the authority to execute criminals at will. The regional Roman proconsul lived in Pergamum and likely adjudicated the trials of Christians.

Like Ephesus, Pergamum was a center of the imperial cult in Asia Minor, and was the home of two temples, one dedicated to Caesar Augustus

---

12. Streett, *Subversive Meals*, 37–38; 283–84.

13. DeSilva, *Introduction*, 800.

14. Pate, "Revelation 2–19," 69.

(built in 29 BCE) and the other to *Dea Roma* (built ca. 20 BCE).[15] Cities of Asia Minor often competed for imperial honors.[16]

Other temples were dedicated to Asclepius, the god of healing symbolized by a snake on a pole, Dionysus/Bacchus, and Zeus/Jupiter, the father of all Roman gods. Jesus commends the faithful: "I know where you are living, where Satan's throne is. Yet you are holding fast to my name, and you did not deny your faith in me even in the days of Antipas my witness, my faithful one, who was killed among you, where Satan lives" (Rev 2:13). While commending the valiant ones, there were others who followed a different path. Jesus scolds, "But I have a few things against you: you have some there who hold to the teaching of Balaam, who taught Balak to put a stumbling block before the people of Israel, so that they would eat food sacrificed to idols and practice fornication" (v. 14). This is a reference to Num 25:1-2, which relates how Jewish men of old had physical relationships with Moabite women and ate cultic meals to their gods. Something similar may have been occurring in Pergamum with Christ followers eating cultic meals at pagan temples, and on Sunday eating the Lord's Supper and singing songs to Jesus. The author calls on his readers to "repent" or face the consequences (v. 16).

10.4.4 The Church in Thyatira

Thyatira was located 40 miles southeast of Pergamum and the least significant city in the Lycus Valley. Known for its garment industry and the manufacture of deep purple dyes (Acts 16:14), it was the home of several guilds whose members included weavers, tailors, dye makers, shoemakers, and tanners who gathered for association banquets and made sacrifices to their patron gods. This was a place where Christianity and paganism clashed. If a believer wished to work in one of these trades, he was expected to support the guild and attend its banquets. Compromise was always a temptation.

---

15. DeSilva, *Introduction*, 801-2, Pergamum and Ephesus each claimed to be the preeminent city of emperor worship and adopted for itself the title *neokoros* or "temple warden." Pergamum was the first to erect a temple to Augustus and Roma. Later Ephesus was granted the right to build a temple to Domitian that included a twenty-foot statue of the emperor. As a result, Ephesus also took the honorific moniker *neokoros*. The two cities competed with each other for the next 50 years, each trying to outdo the other in its promotion of the imperial cult.

16. Maier, *Picturing Paul*, 186-87.

After commending them for their "love, faith, service, and patient endurance," Jesus adds, "But I have this against you: you tolerate that woman Jezebel, who calls herself a prophet and is teaching and beguiling my servants to practice fornication and to eat food sacrificed to idols" (Rev 2:19-20). Most likely this is not referring to a church member named Jezebel, but one who acted like her. Jezebel of old, wife of King Ahab, brought Baal worship to Israel and killed the prophets of God. This local version of Jezebel, a self-identified prophetess, pressured church members to participate in cultic meals, which John labeled as "fornication." Libations, sacrifices and singing paeans to the gods fell into this category.

Jesus threatens, "I will strike her children dead. And all the churches will know that I am the one who searches minds and hearts, and I will give to each of you as your works deserve" (v. 23). But to those who remain loyal, even in the face of persecution or death, Christ applies Ps 2:8-9: "I will give authority over the nations; to rule them with an iron rod" (see Rev 2:27), which implies rule over the nations will be taken away from Rome and transferred to the people of God. Believers will rule with Christ when he sets up his kingdom on earth.

10.4.5 The Church in Sardis

Sardis, 40 miles southeast of Thyatira, was capital of the ancient Lydian Empire. Situated on a high cliff that jutted out from a mountain range with a 1500-foot abyss below, the city was protected on three sides from invaders. An earthquake in 17 CE destroyed Sardis. Emperor Augustus Caesar came to their rescue and rebuilt the city. At the time of Revelation, Sardis was known as a cultural center with gymnasia, stadiums, amphitheaters, bathhouses, and temples. The temple of Cybele (Sybil), the mother of Zeus, who supposedly had power to restore life, sat at the apex of the city.

To these church members, the Lord says, "I know your works; you have a name of being alive, but you are dead" (Rev 3:1). Looks can deceive. Reputation and reality do not necessarily correspond. Their "works" betrayed them, a likely reference to eating cultic meals and attending cultural events that honor the gods. From a human perspective they were "alive," but not from a divine one. Could Cybele raise them from the dead?

Jesus notices that among the Sardis congregation, only "a few" remain faithful and "have not soiled their clothes" (v. 4). Therefore, he calls for them to "repent" (v. 3) or else have their names blotted out of "the book of life" (v. 5).

10.4.6 The Church in Philadelphia

The same earthquake that destroyed Sardis also devastated Philadelphia thirty miles to the southeast. Tiberius Caesar rebuilt the city and issued a five-year tax moratorium. In his honor, the city took a new name, Neo-Caesarea.[17] The region was known for wool, leather, and textiles, and its rich vineyards, dedicated to Bacchus. It was the Napa Valley of Asia Minor and a center of many trade guilds.

Around 92 CE Philadelphia experienced a financial downturn when Emperor Domitian ordered vineyard owners to cut grape production by 50 percent and grow corn to feed Roman troops. In addition, he imposed heavy taxes on the people.

At Philadelphia, Christ followers strove to remain true to their Lord and he commended them: "you have kept my word and have not denied my name" (v. 8). Jewish believers in the city faced persecution from the synagogue, and Jesus labels it a "synagogue of Satan" (v. 9). Because of their faithfulness Jesus promised, "I will write on you the name of my God, and the name of the city of my God, the new Jerusalem that comes down from my God out of heaven, and my own new name" (v. 12).

10.4.7 The Church in Laodicea

Laodicea was located 40 miles southeast of Philadelphia and was a prosperous city. It was the banking center of Asia Minor, and people of means parked their money there. Laodicea was famous for breeding black sheep from which expensive shiny woolen garments were made and for manufacturing an expensive eye salve used for medicinal purposes. The church, like the city, had a reputation for being "rich" and self-sufficient. Like other cities in the valley, Laodicea was the home of temples to Zeus and Apollo, as well as an imperial temple honoring Caesar.

Jesus calls them "wretched, pitiable, poor, blind, and naked," several descriptive words associated with banking, eye-health, and clothing (v.17). After rebuking them, he offers a solution to their spiritual condition:

17. Pate, "Revelation 2–19," 71.

"Therefore I counsel you to buy from me gold refined by fire so that you may be rich; and white robes to clothe you and to keep the shame of your nakedness from being seen; and salve to anoint your eyes so that you may see" (v. 18). He calls for them to "repent" (v. 19), and offers help: "Listen! I am standing at the door, knocking; if you hear my voice and open the door, I will come in to you and eat with you, and you with me" (v. 20). This is banqueting language and a likely reference to the weekly Lord's Supper. The church has locked Jesus out of the communal meal. This may be metaphorical language used to describe how the rich have excluded the marginalized and poor, reminiscent of Matt 25:

> I was hungry and you gave me no food, I was thirsty and you gave me nothing to drink, I was a stranger and you did not welcome me, naked and you did not give me clothing, sick and in prison and you did not visit me. Then they also will answer, "Lord, when was it that we saw you hungry or thirsty or a stranger or naked or sick or in prison, and did not take care of you?" Then he will answer them, "Truly I tell you, just as you did not do it to one of the least of these, you did not do it to me." (Matt 25:42–46)

To exclude the poor, naked, and blind was to exclude Jesus. Those who ate rightly at the Lord's Supper, were promised to sit with Jesus on his throne in the kingdom (v. 21).

10.5 Anti-Imperial Songs

After delivering Christ's messages to the seven churches, John unveils a series of visions that span chapters 4–19. This section opens (Rev 4:1) and closes (Rev 19:10) with a song. Others are found in between. They all contain a single lyrical theme: God and the Lamb alone are worthy of honor and worship. All other worship is satanically misdirected.

10.5.1 Song One (4:1–8)

Chapter 4 begins with Christ issuing a summons to John. He instantly finds himself in heaven where he sees a throne and the king who occupies it (Rev 4:2). As he surveys the scene his eyes fall on a group of "twenty-four elders dressed in white robes with golden crowns on their heads, who sit on twenty-four thrones surrounding the central throne worshipping God"

(vv. 3–4). While it is impossible to identify precisely the 24 enthroned elders, deSilva ventures that they correspond "to the angelic order known as 'thrones' in Col 1:16" and in the T. Levi 3.[18]

John also sees four living creatures protecting the throne and singing ceaselessly to the one seated on the main throne:

> Holy, holy, holy,
> the Lord God the Almighty,
> who was and is and is to come. (v. 8)[19]

The visionary elaborates: "whenever the living creatures give glory and honor and thanks to the one who is seated on the throne" (v. 9) the twenty-four elders fall to their knees and worship God as they "cast their crowns before the throne" and sing,

> You are worthy, our Lord and God,
>   to receive glory and honor and power,
> for you created all things,
>   and by your will they existed and were created. (vv. 10–11)

This is the first song in Revelation. Analyzing the scene, Aune views the golden crowns as a parody of the golden crowns worn by priests of the imperial cult throughout Asia Minor.[20] But Stevenson views this action coupled with the elders' prostration before the throne (v. 10) as a ritualistic act and a "sign of vassalage" required of conquered rulers.[21] Defeated kings were forced to bend the knee in subordination to the victor. In this vision the elders, representing vassal kings, Stevenson believes, are expressing submission to the king of the universe. Neither analogy fully satisfies. Equally plausible, the elders represent the faithful people of God throughout the ages, who reign with Christ in God's kingdom, but acknowledge they do so under his authority.[22]

The heavenly hymn denies Caesar his due. Only one is worthy to receive "glory," "honor," and "power," all terms normally ascribed to the

18. DeSilva, *Introduction*, 813.

19. One also recalls Isaiah's vision of seraphim surrounding the throne of God who cry out holy to the Lord (Isa 6:1–3).

20. Aune, *Revelation*, 293.

21. Stevenson, "Conceptual Background," 268–69.

22. Josephus, *J.W.* 1: 393–94, chronicles the meeting between King Herod and Caesar Augustus at Rhodes, when the former laid his crown at the emperor's feet and asked for the emperor's protection. Caesar replied, "No, you shall not only be safe from danger, but you shall also be a king, . . . for you are worthy to reign over a great many subjects."

emperor or pagan deities. They were also associated with the patronage system and reserved for benefactors. Because a client was not able to repay his benefactor, he owed public praise as a substitute, so that all within earshot knew of the patron's worthiness. One practice known as the *salutatio* involved clients gathering outside the patron's home every morning to offer him acclaim when he emerged and then to follow him around during the morning hours to praise his acts of kindness and public speeches.[23]

The hymn's lyrics include the reason that God deserves continuous worshipful praises: "for you created all things, and by your will they existed and were created." As the ultimate patron, God provides all things necessary for life. Since his benefaction is ongoing, so are the praises. The readers learn from the song they no longer need patronage from Caesar and his surrogates but can trust God to meet their needs.

At the same time these paeans of praise are being sung in heaven, persecution is taking place below. "On earth, in the world organized and controlled by the Roman Empire, the emperor's throne holds sway. . . . The great hope that the apocalyptic vision transmits is that in heaven God's power holds sway. That is the basis for Christian hope and what makes it possible to resist the empire."[24] No matter how things appear in Asia Minor, the transcendent God is "the Almighty who was and is and is to come" (v. 8).[25] He, not Jupiter, controls history, and will have the final word.

This opening scene of praise features anti-imperial overtones. The praise that had been reserved for Emperor Domitian and the pantheon of gods behind his throne was now given to Yahweh alone.

10.5.2 Song Two (5:1–14)

Chapter five opens with a vision of "the one seated on the throne" holding in his right hand "a scroll written on the inside and on the back, sealed with seven seals" (v. 1).[26] Ezekiel had a comparable vision. He was handed a two-

---

23. Howard-Brook and Gwyther, *Unveiling Empire*, 205.

24. Richard, *Apocalypse*, 66.

25. According to deSilva, *Introduction*, 815n22, Roman citizens lauded Zeus "with the formula 'Zeus was, Zeus is, Zeus will be, O great Zeus!'" Christ followers borrowed and applied the formula to God.

26. Emperors sealed their documents for security reasons; especially those that contained secret plans or imperial edicts that they wanted to remain hidden. Also, last will and testaments were sealed seven times.

sided scroll that contained God's will for Israel (Ezek 2:10). The Revelation scroll contains God's end-time plans for the world. When an angel inquires, "Who is worthy to open the scroll and break its seals?" his question is met with silence. After a search, "no one" is found in the cosmos to open and read the divinely sealed scroll. By implication, the readers are reminded that even the emperor, the most powerful man on earth, is not worthy to break the seals.[27]

Unless the scroll is opened, God's plan for the ages will remain hidden to John's readers. The answers to their most profound questions (e.g., "why do the righteous suffer?") are locked in the scroll. Saddened by the silence, the anguished revelator begins to "break down and weep bitterly" (vv. 2–4). In the midst of his despair, an elder draws the visionary's attention to a standing figure: "See, the Lion of the tribe of Judah, the Root of David, has conquered, so that he can open the scroll and its seven seals" (v. 5).[28] The metaphor carries the mental picture of a mighty king, the messianic successor of King David. On the basis of his victory ("the Lion . . . has conquered") he alone can open the scroll.

Expecting to see a strong royal figure, John turns and discovers "a Lamb standing as if it had been slaughtered" (v. 6). The surprise must have been breathtaking. The conquering lion is transformed into a lamb, mortally wounded but now alive and standing erect next to God's throne and encircled by elders and living beings (v. 7). The one Rome shamefully crucified as expendable and relegated to the dust heap of history, God raised from the dead and reckoned to be of infinite worth. The lamb's victory over the empire was accomplished through nonviolence. Without lifting a finger or taking up arms, he exposed Rome's ultimate solution—death itself—as impotent against the power of the God of Israel. Jesus took all that Rome could throw at him and yet emerged unscathed. Just as Christ "conquered" (νικάω), so he calls the church to do the same (Rev 2–3).

John describes the lamb as "having seven horns and seven eyes, which are the seven spirits of God sent out into all the earth" (v. 6b). Seven, the number of completeness or perfection, likely speaks of the totality of Christ's authority ("seven horns") and his omnipresence ("seven eyes"), also

27. Boesak, *Comfort and Protest*, 53. The emperor's power could only affect the course of events on earth.

28. Jesus is described to the revelator as the mighty Lion of Judah and David's eschatological offspring—both messianic images borrowed from Gen 49: 9–10 and Isa 11:10, respectively, which Israel associated with an end-time military leader who would destroy her oppressors.

identified as "the seven spirits," a possible allusion to the fullness of the Spirit, that permeates "all the earth."

As John watches the conquering lamb acts: "He went and took the scroll from the right hand of the one who was seated on the throne" (v. 7). Like the transfer of a baton in a relay race, God hands the scroll to the living Christ. That move alone—even before he opens the scroll—causes a heavenly reaction. The elders and four living beings "fell before the Lamb, each holding a harp" (v. 8a). The harp was the preferred musical instrument used in the cult of the emperor. In 95 CE Domitian had a harp stamped on the back of all newly minted denarii.[29] Hence, the harp was associated with the worship of Caesar, but now it was being used to worship the lamb.

John notices that the worshipers also hold in their hands "golden bowls full of incense," representing the prayers of the saints that have risen to heaven (v. 8b). This scene assures church members that their endless prayers have reached the ears of God, and he will respond.

Throne attendants act next: "They sing a new song" (v. 9a). The label "new song" is associated with the acts of deliverance in Israel's past. It is a victory song.

During their exodus march, the Hebrew children sang a "song of salvation" (Exod 15:1-18). The title "new song" is also found in the Psalms, particularly Pss 33, 40, 96, 98 and 144, where it is connected to a "ritual of divine enthronement."[30] The same theme is repeated in liturgies found in Rev 11:15-18; 12:10-12; and 14:3.[31] It is both a song of deliverance and jubilation. Jesus reigns from above.

The Content of the Song

You are worthy to take the scroll
and to open its seals,
for you were slaughtered and by your

29. Kraybill, *Apocalypse*, 99.

30. Thompson, *Revelation*, 96. Thompson also notes that a "new name" is promised to the overcomers at Pergamum (2:17) and to those at Philadelphia, the risen Christ promises to inscribe on them the name of his city, the "New Jerusalem" (3:12). These promises and the subsequent vision which confirms their fulfillment are the impetus for singing the "new song" in Rev 5:19.

31. See Rev 11:15-18 and Rev 12:10-12, which speak of Messiah's throne, God's power, salvation (deliverance from imperial rule) for the saints, judgment for the rebellious nations and their rulers.

> blood you ransomed for God
> saints from every tribe and
> language and people and nation;
> you have made them to be a kingdom
> and priests serving our God,
> and they will reign on earth. (Rev 5:9b–10)

The "new song" contains three key verbs that provide clues as to why the lamb alone is worthy to break the seal. First, he was *slaughtered*, which pictures his death as an animal-like butchering. Second, he *ransomed* or liberated people from bondage, i.e., he set the captives free.[32] The price of ransom was the lamb's death. The scope was limitless and without boundaries, sociologically, ethnically, nationally. Third, he "*made* them to be a kingdom and priests." This is the same language first used in Exod 19:5–6 when God formed the Hebrew children into a holy nation that stood in contradistinction to the authoritarian regime of pharaoh's Egypt. This song portrays God's kingdom as an alternative government to empire and nullifies its plans for the world.

The church, here described as "a kingdom," will "reign on earth" in the age to come.

The implications are significant. God has instituted a new political entity. Christ's church, the locus of God's present kingdom and composed of priestly kings, is charged with calling people to switch allegiance from earthly rulers to the exalted Lord Jesus. It is God's instrument for reclaiming the world. The church possesses divine authority when it speaks and acts.

The lyrics (Rev 5:9b–10) imply, "Caesar's reign on earth is coming to an end. His oppression is limited."[33] The future belonged to Christ and his church. Imagine the members of the seven churches adopting this song and singing it during their worship services. What must Jewish and pagan neighbors have thought when they heard the melodic words wafting from the windows of the house churches?

---

32. Similar language is used by Jesus in Luke 4:18. The verb "ransomed" carries an economic connotation, and it signifies freedom purchased at a high price.

33. Boesak, *Comfort and Protest*, 60.

A Heavenly Host Joins the Choir

When news spreads throughout heaven that one has been found with the authority and ability to open the seven-sealed scroll, excitement fills the air and an innumerable host of angels join the others in exuberant praise. Heaven comes alive! John's attention is captured by the sounds and sights: "Then I looked, and I heard the voice of many angels surrounding the throne and the living creatures and the elders; they numbered myriads of myriads and thousands of thousands" (v. 11).

A multitude of heavenly hosts form innumerable concentric circles surrounding the throne that extend outward beyond John's sight. Then he hears them "singing with full voice" (v. 12a):

> Worthy is the Lamb that was
> slaughtered
> to receive power and wealth and
> wisdom and might
> and honor and glory and blessing! (v 12b)

The lyrics include a sevenfold praise. Each key word—worthy, power, wealth, wisdom, might, honor, glory, and blessing—is language drawn from the political realm and associated with accolades pronounced on kings and emperors.[34] In heaven they are heaped upon the lamb who refused to cave to imperial threats or beg for his life, but unequivocally trusted God as he faced death. Acting on the authority of Caesar himself, Pilate executed Jesus. The risen lamb is worshiped alongside Yahweh.

As the scene shifts the revelator is catapulted into the future where he sees the entirety of the cosmos singing the same song to the lamb:

> To the one seated on the throne and
> to the Lamb
> be blessing and honor and glory and
> might
> for ever and ever! (v. 13)

This scene closes out the first part of John's heavenly journey.

34. Thompson, *Revelation*, 97–98.

10.5.3 Song Three (7:12–17)

The next liturgical scene is preceded by a vision of the scroll's sixth seal being broken and followed by God's wrath being poured out on the earth. The revelator watches in horror as the "kings of the earth and the magnates and the generals and the rich and the powerful, and everyone, slave and free" hide from the presence of "the one seated on the throne and from the wrath of the Lamb" (Rev 6:15–16). Judgment has arrived. When the question is asked, "Who is able to stand?" (v. 17). The scene shifts in Rev 7 and the answer is given: "A great multitude that no one could count, from every nation, from all tribes and people and languages, *standing* before the throne and before the Lamb, robed in white, with palm branches in their hands" (Rev 7:9).

John sees an international gathering of people dressed in white togas. The reference to "white robes" was first used in Rev 3:4–5, 18 to describe the "overcomers" who were not seduced by idolatry. As a result, their names are found in "the book of life" and they are worthy to stand before the lamb. As recipients of grace, they have been spared wrath, and can stand in his presence. They wave "palm branches" in celebration of the lamb's victory.[35]

On the Sunday before his death Jesus rode into Jerusalem, the crowds waved palm branches and cried out to their hero, "Hosanna," i.e., "Save us now." They expected Jesus to overthrow the established authorities through the use of the sword and set up God's kingdom (Matt 21:9; Mark 11:9–10; John 12:13). God had other plans. Victory over evil was accomplished through Messiah's death.

The ones waving palms in Rev 7 are those who chose to follow the crucified lamb. They break into song: "Salvation belongs to our God who is seated on the throne, and to the Lamb! (Rev 7:10).

The empire, on the other hand, offered "salvation" to those who submitted to Roman rule. According to the Apocalypse, salvation belongs to God and the Lamb. This leads those closest to the throne to join with the multitude:

> And all the angels stood around the throne and around the elders
> and the four living creatures, and they fell on their faces before the
> throne and worshiped God, singing,
> > Amen! Blessing and glory and wisdom
> > and thanksgiving and honor

35. Plutarch, *Quaest. conv.* viii. 4, writes that palm branches were awarded to victors at the Delian Games.

and power and might
be to our God forever and ever! Amen. (vv. 11–12)

The content of this song is thematically identical to the "new song" in Rev 5.

With no clue as to the multitude's identity except that they came from all points on the compass, the revelator asks, "Who are these, robed in white and where have they come from?" (v. 13). An elder informs him, "These are they who have come out of the great ordeal [tribulation]; they have washed their robes and made them white in the blood of the Lamb" (vv.14).

In context of the opening chapters (2 and 3), "The great ordeal" refers to the trials that the believers in the seven churches of Asia Minor are undergoing at the time of the vision. Projected into the future, John sees these same believers standing before the throne. Their faithfulness unto death is rewarded. He describes their robes as "washed" and cleansed "in the blood of the Lamb." Normally, when clothes are washed in blood, they turn red, not white. So, what does this imagery signify?

Howard-Brook and Gwyther believe the imagery "mocks the priestly initiation of the cult Cybele, in which white robed candidates were dripped with bull's blood in order to 'purify' them."[36] The imagery may also refer to Hebrew soldiers after a battle who washed the enemy's blood off their bodies in order to be ritually cleansed. However, in this case, it is the lamb's blood that purifies.[37] If purification comes through the blood of the lamb, Rome killed the legitimate savior of the world.

> For this reason they are before the
>   throne of God,
> and worship him day and night
>   within his temple,
> and the one who is seated on the
>   throne will shelter them. (v. 15)

The blood-washed saints standing in the presence of God will never again experience persecution, harm, or deprivation for saying "no" to Caesar and "yes" to Jesus! (v. 16). Their fortunes will be reversed as previously prophesied in Mary's song (Luke 1:52–53). The reason follows: "For the Lamb at the center of the throne will be their shepherd, and he will guide them to springs of the water of life, and God will wipe away every tear from their eyes (v. 17).

---

36. Howard-Brook and Gwyther, *Unveiling Revelation*, 210.
37. Howard-Brook and Gwyther, *Unveiling Revelation*, 210.

The song's lyrics help John's audience to interpret history from a different vantage point. Reality cannot be judged by what is happening on earth alone. John wants his audience to know that God is working behind the scenes on their behalf. One can only imagine how the seven churches responded when they received and read the letter from Patmos.

10.5.4 Songs Four and Five (14:1–11/15:1–4)

After getting a glimpse of the scarlet woman and the beast she rides, the revelator looks and sees "the Lamb standing on Mount Zion!" (Rev 14:1). The martyred messiah, now alive, is surrounded by faithful followers.

> And I heard a voice from heaven like the sound of many waters and like the sound of loud thunder; the voice I heard was like the sound of harpists playing on their harps, and they sing a new song before the throne and before the four living creatures and before the elders. No one could learn that song except the one hundred forty-four thousand who have been redeemed from the earth. It is these who have not defiled themselves with women, for they are virgins; these follow the Lamb wherever he goes. They have been redeemed from humankind as first fruits for God and the Lamb. (Rev 14:2–4)

The vision has now shifted from heaven to earth and John discovers why everybody in heaven is singing the new song: the gospel has reached "every nation and tribe and language and people" (Rev 14:6). The mission has been completed. An angel announces, "Fallen, fallen is Babylon the great!" (v. 8) followed by another angel declaring that those aligned with Babylon will face God's wrath (vv. 9–11).

The "new song" that opens the chapter provides the members of the seven churches with incentive to persevere in faith in the midst of many hardships at the hands of Rome (v. 12). The chapter concludes with a vision of the "Son of Man" conquering the nations (vv. 14–20), a likely allusion to Dan 7, where "one like the son of man" comes before God, who gives him "dominion and glory and a kingship that all people, nations, and languages should serve him." His rule and kingdom are everlasting and "shall never be destroyed" (Dan 7:13–14).

As the vision fades and another unfolds, the Patmos seer observes seven angels ready to pour out God's last "seven plagues" on the earth and on the Beast. He also sees "those who had conquered the beast" standing by the "sea of glass mixed with fire" (vv. 1–2), evocative of the children of Israel before the Red Sea. The "new song" of Rev 14:12, gives way to a victory song (Rev 15:1–4) as the masses "sing the song of Moses, the servant of God, and the song of the Lamb" (v. 3):

> Great and amazing are your deeds,
>   Lord God the Almighty!
> Just and true are your ways,
>   King of the nations!
> Lord, who will not fear
>   and glorify your name?
> For you alone are holy.
>   All nations will come
>   and worship before you,
> for your judgments have been revealed. (Rev 15:3b–4)

The singers are the martyred saints! Their defeat—death at the hands of the beast—ironically leads to their victory over the beast, the same way as their Lord's victory. This song conveys the same message in lyrical form as the seven letters in chapters 2 and 3 express in prose (cf. Rev 12:11).

The "song of Moses" (Exod 15:1–18; Deut 31:30–44) and "the song of the Lamb" (v. 3a) are virtually the same song. As Yahweh used Moses to deliver his people out of a tyrannical and idolatrous empire, so God used Jesus, another Moses (Acts 3:22–23), to lead a new exodus. Moses was associated with Mount Sinai and Jesus with Mount Zion (14:1). In both cases, the salvation is wrought by God, who is identified as the "King of the nations!" (v. 3b). Neither Moses nor Jesus resorted to violence to free God's people but placed their faith in Yahweh to accomplish his salvific purposes, who manifested his power and glory in opening the Red Sea and raising Jesus from the dead. Likewise, the churches are now called to trust God and not the arm of flesh to conquer their imperial enemy. Whether the kingdom arrives in its fullness in their lifetime does not matter. Throughout the ages many have died in the faith, but the promise stands sure. The victory belongs to God, not the nations.

If early *ekklēssiai* adopted and sang the "song of Moses" at mealtime, they would not have been unique. The *Therapeutai*, the Hellenized Jewish sect from Alexandria, Egypt, sang the same victory song at their Passover feasts[38] to commemorate the exodus. John sees a parallel between God's

---

38. Philo, *Contempl.* 84–88.

victory over Egypt and over Babylon the Great. The latter constitutes a new exodus. That is something to sing about!

10.5.5 Song Six (19:1–8)

The final liturgical scene, which offers heaven's perspective of the last days is divided into two sections. The first takes place in heaven. The revelator writes, "After this I heard what seemed to be the loud voice of a great multitude in heaven, saying, "Hallelujah! Salvation (σωτηρία, *sotēria*) and glory and power to our God, for his judgments are true and just" (vv. 1–2a).

For readers of the Apocalypse, "salvation" had a political connotation. The empire used the term to speak of deliverance and protection of its people from their enemies. In reality, the people's enemy was the empire itself! The song posits salvation with God (v. 1) and assures the readers that deliverance shall be theirs. Rome will fall and its glory and power will disappear. Those who have drunk deeply at the wells of Roman idolatry in order to survive—including lapsed Christ followers—will face judgment while the saints will feast and drink at the Lamb's banquet.

The last song in Revelation takes place when God judges the great whore and avenges the blood of his servants. A series of four hallelujahs is lifted to God who sits on the throne followed by explanations for the praise (vv. 1–8).

John hears a final hallelujah and motive for praise.

> Hallelujah!
> For the Lord our God
>   the Almighty reigns.
> Let us rejoice and exult
>   and give him the glory,
> for the marriage of the Lamb has come,
>   and his bride has made herself ready;
> to her it has been granted to be clothed
>   with fine linen, bright and pure. (vv. 6–8a)

As John describes the closing scenes of his vision, he recalls, "And the angel said to me, 'Write this: Blessed are those who are invited to the marriage supper of the Lamb'" (v. 9a).

The revelator gets to listen to the joyous wedding song and is reminded of the words ascribed to Isaiah, which speak of an eschatological feast where the faithful of the ages will recline and be satisfied, and have their tears wiped away while the unrighteous face judgment (Isa 25:6–8; Isa 61:10).

A modern-day follower of Jesus who happens to live in a democratic country may have difficulty relating to what it was like for first-century believers to receive this correspondence. Filled with words of hope and encouragement, the songs of the Apocalypse were a balm for the soul, particularly for the writer himself, who also was suffering for the faith.

It is not difficult to understand why the suffering churches in the first century adopted these songs and sang them whenever they gathered. The songs offered a divine perspective of the world, provided hope that the kingdom would soon arrive, and helped the church discover its identity as an alternative society.

Each time they sang the embedded lyrics of the Revelation hymns, which extolled the one on the throne and the lamb, the churches stood against the empire and proclaimed their political allegiance to another empire, the kingdom of God.

CHAPTER 11

Conclusion

11.1 Summary

JESUS' DISCIPLES SPREAD THE story of his death and resurrection appearances throughout the empire. The various accounts had a common thread: 1) Jesus, an itinerant preacher from a small Galilean village, traveled through Palestine preaching the imminent arrival of God's kingdom; 2) he called on Israel and its leaders to return to the covenant faith of their forefathers; 3) he healed the sick and performed miracles through the power of God's spirit; 4) as his popularity grew, many believed him to be the messiah who would deliver God's people from Roman bondage and restore the kingdom to Israel; 5) Jewish and Roman authorities considered him a threat to political order and had him arrested, tried, and executed as a self-proclaimed king and an insurrectionist and; 6) the god of Israel raised him from the dead and exalted him to a heavenly position from which he reigns over the cosmos.

Heralds urged their hearers to believe the story and submit to a water ritual as a pledge of allegiance to Jesus as Lord. A paltry number responded. They gathered in small groups to receive instruction, live by kingdom of God principles, and worship.

Their songs of praise followed traditional Jewish and gentile models, except their lyrics focused on Jesus; hence, they were mainly christological in nature. By definition these songs were anti-imperial and challenged the claims of Caesar and empire. Their political content extolled Jesus above Caesar and God's kingdom above Rome's. They proclaimed in rhythmic style that the kingdom of this world operated under the authority of Satan and the Greco-Roman gods were demons. Through his death and resurrection, Christ defeated the powers and now reigned over them.

Many christological songs existed long before the Gospels and Epistles were written and delivered (48–86 CE). When examined in their historical context, these songs reflected the beliefs of a minority in contrast to the majority of people in the empire. They resisted social stratification, the imperial cult, ethics based on honor and shame, and Rome's divine right to rule the world.

Christological hymns did not call for violent revolution or attempt to overthrow the government. Instead, they rejected Rome's illusionary version of reality, i.e., its worldview.

11.2 Reflections

A pivotal scene in the movie *The Matrix*[1] takes place when Morpheus, a Christ figure, offers Neo, a searcher of truth, the choice between ingesting a blue pill or a red pill. If he swallows the blue one, his memory will be erased, he will forget this meeting, awaken in his own bed, and continue believing the lie generated by the Matrix. If, however, he swallows the red pill, his eyes will be opened and he will see the world as it really is—despite how dreadful and troubling that may be for him.

Christ followers in the first century accepted the red pill. Through the gospel story they glimpsed the reality of the world. Rome's glowing worldview was an illusion and nothing more than propaganda. The masses, however, swallowed the blue pill and were deceived.

With eyes wide open the believers sang songs that resisted the lie and countered with truth as they perceived it: a regime change had taken place and Christ was Lord of all. But it took a revelation to grasp it (1 Cor 2:10–16). As a result, they reoriented their lives according to the socio-political objectives of God's kingdom and divested themselves of societal expectations.

Ernst Käsemann (1906–1998), the well-known NT scholar, relates that from 1930–1933 he, like most other Germans, believed Hitler's promise that Germany was destined for greatness; unfortunately, it had been short-changed and humiliated by the signing of the Treaty of Versailles at the end of WWI. As a result, Germany was stripped of many former

1. The Wachowskis, dirs. Burbank, Warner Bros., 1999.

Conclusion

territories, neutered militarily, and forced to pay reparations. It now faced high unemployment and inflation. Hitler promised to restore national pride, invigorate the economy, and make Germany great again. In 1934, Käsemann voted for Hitler, but later regretted it when he witnessed Hitler's henchmen commit acts of violence in the streets only to be exonerated of all criminal charges. Some clergy began to speak out. In an attempt to get them on board, Hitler called on pastors and churches to stand with him in common cause and pledge their allegiance to him as he sought to fulfill his vision for Germany. Many acquiesced. Käsemann's eyes were not opened until 1937, when the Gestapo arrested 700 German Evangelical pastors and sent them to concentration camps.[2] Martin Niemöller, an outspoken critic of Nazism and its Aryan beliefs, was one of them.[3]

The following Sunday Käsemann mounted the pulpit and bravely preached on Isa 26:13, "Oh Lord our God, other Lords besides you have ruled over us, but we acknowledge your name alone." He writes that God's work cannot "be accomplished by compromising with our enemies. In the church the obverse side of freedom is and remains resistance to idolators."[4] The next day the Gestapo arrested Käsemann for being a subversive.

While incarcerated he penned, *The Wandering People of God*, a critical assessment of Nazism from a biblical and theological perspective. He concluded that the church is a pilgrim people with no earthly home. Its allegiance is to Christ and his kingdom alone and it must always stand in opposition to the kingdoms of this world, which are all based on an illusion.[5]

After years of reflection, Käsemann gave his final bit of advice and marching orders to the church: "As my last word and bequest, let me call to you in Huguenot style: 'Résistez!'"[6]

The surviving christological songs found embedded in the NT were songs of resistance and written by people with their eyes opened by the red pill of the gospel. They understood Rome's version of reality was an illusion.

First-century songsters variously wrote and sang that: 1) fortunes soon would be reversed and the last would be first in God's kingdom (The Magnificat); 2) the church was the colony of heaven under the Lord Jesus in

2. Käsemann, *On Being a Disciple*, xvii.

3. Schmidt, *Pastor Niemöller*, 102. Locke, *Exile*, 10–11, notes Niemöller spent the remainder of the war imprisoned in three facilities, including Dachau.

4. Käsemann, *On Being a Disciple*, xx.

5. Käsemann, *Wandering People of God*.

6. Käsemann, *On Being a Disciple*, xxi.

contrast to the earthly colonies under Caesar (Philippian Song); 3) Christ reigned supreme over all governments (Colossians Song); 4) the resurrected Christ announced his victory to the spirits in prison as he ascended into heaven, (1 Peter); and that 5) he was metaphorically both a lion and a lamb, and defeated Rome without lifting a finger (Revelation songs).

When Christ followers came together, they worshiped a king who ruled a kingdom. Their songs, which took many forms—psalms, paeans of praise, odes—were thus essentially political in nature.

Songs kept the story of Christ alive in the community and were a means of peaceful noncompliance with the demands of the empire.

Sacred songs with subversive lyrics, comforted the discouraged, emboldened the fearful, reinforced the gospel narrative, re-envisioned society, and provided an emotional outlet.

While this study of NT songs has been mainly descriptive and not prescriptive, it raises several important questions.

Where are the churches of resistance today? Where are the lyricists who see things clearly? How many new songs of resistance have been written in the twenty-first century? It seems churches—whether conservative, moderate, or liberal—especially those located in the West, would rather lobby those in political power, promising to deliver large blocks of votes, in exchange for political favors, support for their parochial causes, and a seat at the table.

This is a far cry from Christ's mission and the one he passed on to his disciples. When the church colludes with empire, it loses its way. The modern church must stop singing caesar's praises and start composing and singing songs of resistance.

The gospel of Christ and his kingdom was and still is the only antidote for the poisonous gospel of the empire.

Bibliography

Achtemeier, Paul J. *1 Peter*. Hermeneia. Minneapolis: Fortress, 1996.

Anderson, Bernhard W. *Out of the Depths: The Psalms Speak for us Today*. Louisville: Westminster John Knox, 2000.

Andrie, Leonard W. *The Christ Hymn of Colossians 1.15-20: Drawing from the Wisdom Tradition in Hellenistic Judaism*. Master's thesis. School of Divinity, University of St. Thomas: Saint Paul, MN, 2013.

Arnold, Clinton E. *Ephesians*. Grand Rapids: Zondervan, 2010.

Ascough, Richard S. *Paul's Macedonian Associations: The Social Context of Philippians and 1 Thessalonians*. Tübingen: Mohr Siebeck, 2003.

———. "What Are They Saying about Christ Groups and Associations?" *Currents in Biblical Research* 13 (2015) 207-44.

Ascough, Richard S., et al. *Associations in the Greco-Roman World: A Sourcebook*. Waco, TX: Baylor University Press, 2012.

Attridge, Harold W. *Hebrews: A Commentary on the Epistle to the Hebrews*. Hermeneia. Minneapolis: Fortress, 1989.

Aune, David E., ed. *The Gospel of Matthew in Current Study*. Grand Rapids: Eerdmans, 2001.

———. "The Influence of Roman Imperial Court Ceremonial on the Apocalypse of John." *Biblical Research* 18 (1983) 5-26.

———. *Revelation 1-5*. Word Biblical Commentary 52a. Dallas: Word, 1997.

Baker, Lawrence Henry. "Some Aspects of Pindar's Style." *The Sewanee Review* 3 (2012) 100-110.

Barrett, C. K. *The Gospel According to Saint John*. 2nd ed. Philadelphia: Westminster, 1978.

Barth, Marcus, and Helmut Blanke. *Colossians*. Anchor Yale Bible. Translated by Astrid B. Beck. New Haven, CT: Yale University Press, 2005.

Beard, Mary, et al. *Religions of Rome: Volume 1: A History*. Rev. ed. Cambridge: Cambridge University Press, 1998.

Beasley-Murray, George R. *Baptism in the New Testament*. Grand Rapids: Eerdmans, 1962.

Berkhof, Hendrik. *Christ and the Powers*. Translated by John H. Yoder. Scottsdale, PA: Herald, 1962.

Bitner, Bradley. "Acclaiming Artemis in Ephesians: Political Theologians in Acts 19." In *The First Urban Churches 3: Ephesus*, edited by James R. Harrison and L. L. Welborn, 127-70. Atlanta: SBL, 2018.

Block, Daniel I. *For the Glory of God: Recovering a Biblical Theology of Worship*. Grand Rapids: Baker Academic, 2014.

Boesak, Allan A. *Comfort and Protest: The Apocalypse of John from a South African Perspective.* Eugene, OR: Wipf & Stock, 2015.

Borg, Marcus. *Convictions: How I Learned What Matters Most.* New York: Harper One, 2014.

———. *Jesus: Uncovering the Life, Teachings and Relevance of a Religious Revolutionary.* San Francisco: Harper San Francisco, 2006.

Borg, Marcus, and John Dominic Crossan. *The First Christmas: What the Gospels Really Teach About Jesus's Birth.* New York: Harper One, 2007.

Boring, M. Eugene. *1 Peter.* Abingdon New Testament Commentaries. Nashville: Abingdon, 1999.

Bosch, David J. *Transforming Mission.* New York: Orbis, 1991.

Boyd, Gregory A. *God at War: The Biblical and Spiritual Conflict.* Downers Grove, IL: InterVarsity, 1997.

Brooks, Oscar S. *The Drama of Decision: Baptism in the New Testament.* Peabody, MA: Hendrickson, 1987.

Brown, Raymond E. *The Birth of the Messiah: A Commentary on the Infancy Narratives in Matthew and Luke.* New York: Doubleday, 1977.

Bruce, F. F. *The Book of the Acts.* New International Commentary on the New Testament. Grand Rapids: Eerdmans, 1988.

———. "The 'Christ Hymn' of Colossians 1:15–20." *Bibliotheca Sacra* 141 (1984) 99–111.

———. *The Epistles to the Colossians, to Philemon, and to the Ephesians.* Grand Rapids: Eerdmans, 1984.

———. *The Epistle to the Hebrews.* The New International Commentary on the New Testament. Grand Rapids: Eerdmans, 2018.

———. *The Gospel of John.* Grand Rapids: Eerdmans, 1983.

Buchanan, George Wesley. *To the Hebrews: Translation, Comment, and Conclusions.* Anchor Bible 36. Garden City, NY: Doubleday, 1972.

Buffa, Cristina. "The Magnificat and the Song of Hanna: Comparing Social Conditions." *Revue des sciences religieuses* 92 (2018) 377–92.

Caird, G. B. *Principalities and Powers: A Study in Pauline Theology.* London: Oxford University Press, 1956.

Campbell, Brian. *The Romans and their World: A Short Introduction.* New Haven, CT: Yale University Press, 2012.

Campbell, William S. *The Nations in the Divine Economy: Paul's Covenantal Hermeneutics and Participation in Christ.* Lanham, MD: Lexington/Fortress Academic, 2018.

Carson, Donald A. *The Gospel of John.* Grand Rapids: Eerdmans, 1991.

Carter, Warren. "Jesus the Good Shepherd: An Intertextual Approach to Ezekiel 34 and John 10." In *Biblical Interpretation in Early Christian Gospels*, edited by Thomas R. Hatina, 4:45–56. London: T. & T. Clark, 2020.

———. "Jesus the Good Shepherd: John 10 as Political Rhetoric." In *Come and Read: Interpretive Approaches to the Gospel of John*, edited by Alicia Myers and Lindsey S. Jodrey, 97–110. Lanham, MD: Fortress Academic, 2020.

———. *Matthew and Empire: Initial Explorations.* Harrisburg: Trinity, 2001.

———. *Telling Tales About Jesus.* Minneapolis: Fortress, 2016.

Carter, Warren, and Amy-Jill Levine. *The New Testament: Methods and Meanings.* Nashville: Abingdon, 2013.

Charlesworth, James H. *The Earliest Christian Hymnbook: The Odes of Solomon.* Eugene, OR: Cascade, 2009.

————. *Jesus and the Temple: Textual and Archaeological Explorations.* Minneapolis: Fortress, 2014.

————. *The Old Testament Pseudepigrapha.* Anchor Yale Bible. Vol 2. New York: Doubleday, 1985.

————, ed. *The Old Testament Pseudepigrapha.* Anchor Yale Bible. Vol. 1. New York: Doubleday, 1981.

Chilton, Bruce. *Pure Kingdom: Jesus' Vision of God.* Grand Rapids: Eerdmans, 1996.

Collins, Adela Yarbro. *Crisis and Catharsis: The Power of the Apocalypse.* Philadelphia: Westminster, 1984.

————. "Psalms, Philippians, and the Origins of Christology." *Biblical Interpretation* 11 (2003) 361–72.

Collins, John J. *The Apocalyptic Imagination: An Introduction to Jewish Apocalyptic Literature.* Grand Rapids: Eerdmans, 1998.

————. "Sibylline Oracles." In *The Old Testament Pseudepigrapha,* edited by James H. Charlesworth, 1:317–472. New York: Doubleday, 1983.

Collins, Raymond F. "The Pastoral Epistles." In *Letters that Paul did not Write: The Letter to the Hebrews and the Pauline Pseudepigrapha.* Good News Studies 28: 88–131. Wilmington, DE: Michael Glazier, 1988.

Copenhaver, Adam. "Echoes of a Hymn in a Letter of Paul: The Rhetorical Function of the Christ-Hymn in the Letter to the Colossians." *Journal for the Study of Paul and His Letters* 4 (2014) 235-55.

Corley, Kathleen E. *Maranatha: Women's Funerary Rituals and Christian Origins.* Minneapolis: Fortress, 2010.

————. *Private Women Public Meals: Social Conflict in the Synoptic Tradition.* Peabody, MA: Hendrickson, 1993.

Corwin, Virginia. *St. Ignatius and Christianity in Antioch.* New Haven, CT: Yale University Press, 1960.

Cotter, Wendy. "Greco–Roman Apotheosis Traditions and Resurrection Appearance in Matthew." In *The Gospel of Matthew in Current Study,* edited by David E. Aune, 127–53. Grand Rapids: Eerdmans, 2001.

Crenshaw, Ben. *Roman Worship and the New Testament.* Master of Arts thesis, Denver Seminary, 2017.

Cross, F. L. *1 Peter: A Paschal Liturgy.* Bristol: Mowbray, 1957.

Crossan, John Dominic, and John L. Reed. *In Search of Paul: How Jesus' Apostle Opposed Rome's Empire with God's Kingdom.* New York: Harper One, 2005.

Culpepper, R. A. "The Pivot of John's Prologue." *New Testament Studies* 27 (1980) 1-31.

Dalton, William J. *Christ's Proclamations to the Spirits: A Study of 1 Peter 3:18—4:6.* Rome: Pontifical Biblical Institute, 1989.

Danker, Frederick W. *Benefactor: Epigraphic Study of a Graeco-Roman and New Testament Semantic Field.* Saint Louis: Clayton, 1982.

deSilva, David A. *Honor, Patronage, Kinship and Purity: Unlocking New Testament Culture.* Downers Grove, IL: IVP Academic 2000.

————. *An Introduction to the New Testament: Contexts, Methods and Ministry Formation.* 2nd ed. Downers Grove, IL: IVP Academic, 2018.

————. *Seeing Things John's Way: The Rhetoric of the Book of Revelation.* Louisville: Westminster John Knox, 2009.

Dibelius, Martin, and Hans Conzelmann. *The Pastoral Epistles.* Translated by Philip Buttolph and Adela Yarbro. Philadelphia: Fortress, 1972.

Dreissman, G. Adolf. *Biblical Studies*. Edinburgh: T. & T. Clark, 1901.

Dunn, James D. G. *The Epistles to the Colossians and Philemon: A Commentary on the Greek Text*. Grand Rapids: Eerdmans, 1996.

————. *Jesus and the Spirit*. Grand Rapids: Eerdmans, 1975.

————. *New Testament Theology: An Introduction*. Nashville: Abingdon, 2009.

Ehrman, Bart D. *The New Testament: A Historical Introduction to the Early Christian Writings*. Oxford: Oxford University Press, 2014.

Elliott, Neil. "Anti-Imperial Message of the Cross." In *Paul and Empire: Religion and Power in Roman Imperial Society*, edited by Richard Horsley, 67–88. Harrisburg: Trinity, 1997.

Farris, Stephen. *The Hymns of Luke's Infancy Narratives: Their Origin, Meaning, and Significance*. 3rd ed. London: Bloomsbury Academic, 2015.

Fee, Gordon D. *Paul's Letter to the Philippians*. New International Commentary on the New Testament. Grand Rapids: Eerdmans, 1995.

Ferguson, Everett. *Baptism in the Early Church: History, Theology, and Liturgy in the First Five Centuries*. Grand Rapids: Eerdmans, 2013.

————. "The Herodian Dynasty." In *The World of the New Testament: Cultural, Social, and Historical Contexts*, edited by Joel B. Green and Lee Martin McDonald, 54–76. Grand Rapids: Baker, 2013.

Fitzmyer, Joseph A. *Gospel According to Luke I–IX*. Anchor Yale Bible. New Haven, CT: Yale University Press, 1970.

Flint, Peter W. "Psalms and Psalters in the Dead Sea Scrolls." In *The Bible and the Dead Sea Scrolls*, edited by James Charlesworth, 1:233–72. Waco, TX: Baylor University Press, 2006.

Friesen, Steven. "Poverty in Pauline Studies." *Journal for the Study of the New Testament* 26 (2004) 323–61.

Gantz, T. N. "Lapis Niger: The Tomb of Romulus." *La Parola del Passato* 29 (1974) 350–61.

Garland, David E. *Luke: Exegetical Commentary on the New Testament*. Grand Rapids: Zondervan, 2011.

Goldingay, John. *Psalms, Vol 1: Psalms 1–41*. Baker Commentary on the Old Testament and Psalms. Grand Rapids: Baker, 2006.

Gordley, Matthew E. *New Testament Christological Hymns: Exploring Texts, Context, and Significance*. Downers Grove, IL: IVP Academic, 2018.

Gorman, Michael J. *Elements of Biblical Exposition*, Rev. ed. Peabody, MA: Hendrickson, 2009.

————. *Inhabiting the Cruciform God*. Grand Rapids: Eerdmans. 2009.

Grabiner, Steven. *Revelation's Hymns: Commentary on the Cosmic Conflict*. Library of New Testament Studies. London: T. & T. Clark, 2015.

Green, Joel B. *The Gospel of Luke*. The New International Commentary on the New Testament. Grand Rapids: Eerdmans, 1997.

Green, Richard G. "Crossing Paths: Te Ata and Eleanor Roosevelt in the Twenties and Thirties." *Journal of Chickasaw History* 1 (1991) 13–30.

Gritz, S. H. *Paul, Women Teachers, and the Mother Goddess at Ephesus: A Study of 1 Timothy 2:9–15 in Light of the Religious and Cultural Milieu of the First Century*. Lanham, MD: University Press of America, 1991.

Gundry, Robert H. "The Form, Meaning and Background of the Hymn Quoted in 1 Timothy 3:16." In *Apostolic History of the Gospels, Biblical and Historical Essays*

Presented to F. F. Bruce, edited by Ward Gasque and Ralph P. Martin, 203–22. Exeter: Paternoster, 1970.

Hansen, G. Walter. *The Letter to the Philippians*. Pillar New Testament Commentaries. Grand Rapids: Eerdmans, 2009.

Harden, Justin K. *Galatians and the Imperial Cult: A Critical Analysis of the First-Century Social Context of Paul's Letter*. Tübingen: Mohr Siebeck, 2008.

Harland, Philip A. *Associations, Synagogues, and Congregations*. Minneapolis: Fortress, 2003.

Harris, Murray J. *John: Exegetical Commentary of the Greek New Testament*. Nashville: B & H, 2015.

———. *Prepositions and Theology in the Greek New Testament: An Essential Reference Resource for Exegesis*. Grand Rapids: Zondervan, 2012.

Hauerwas, Stanley, and William H. Willimon. *Resident Aliens: Life in the Christian Colony*. Nashville: Abingdon, 2014.

Hawthorne, Gerald F. *Philippians*. Word Biblical Commentary 43. Waco, TX: Word, 1983.

Hay, David M. *Glory at the Right Hand: Psalm 110 in Early Christianity*. SBL Monograph Series 18. Nashville: Abingdon, 1973.

Hazlett, Lisa A. "The Use of British Nursery Rhymes." https://files.eric.ed.gov/fulltext/EJ864823.pdf.

Heen, Erik M. "Phil 2:6–11 and Resistance to Local Theocratic Rule." In *Paul and the Roman Imperial Order*, edited by Richard A. Horsley, 125–54. Harrisburg, PA: Trinity, 2004.

Heiser, Michael S. *The Unseen Realm: Recovering the Supernatural Worldview of the Bible*. Bellingham, WA: Lexham, 2015.

Hengel, Martin. "Hymn and Christology." In *Papers on Paul and Other New Testament Authors*, edited by E. A. Livingstone, 173–79. Journal for the Study of the New Testament: Supplement Series 3. Sheffield: Sheffield Academic, 1980.

Herzog, William R., II. "Onstage and Offstage with Jesus of Nazareth: Public Transcripts, Hidden Transcripts, and Gospel Texts." In *Hidden Transcripts and the Arts of Resistance: Applying the Work of James C. Scott to Jesus and Paul*, edited by Richard A. Horsley, 42–80. Atlanta: SBL, 2004.

Holloway, Paul A. *Philippians*. Hermeneia. Minneapolis: Fortress, 2017.

Horsley, Richard A. *The Liberation of Christmas: The Infancy Narrative in Social Context*. New York: Continuum, 1993.

———. *The Prophet Jesus and the Renewing of Israel: Moving Beyond a Diversionary Debate*. Grand Rapids: Eerdmans, 2012.

Horsley, Richard A., and John S. Hanson. *Bandits Prophets and Messiahs: Popular Movements at the Time of Jesus*. New York: Harper and Row, 1988.

Howard, George. "Phil 2:6–11 and the Human Christ." *Catholic Biblical Quarterly* 40 (1978) 368-87.

Howard-Brook, Wes, and Anthony Gwyther. *Unveiling Empire: Reading Revelation Then and Now*. Maryknoll, NY: Orbis, 2008.

Hurtado, Larry W. *Lord Jesus Christ: Devotion to Jesus in Earliest Christianity*. Grand Rapids: Eerdmans 2005.

Jeffers, James S. *The Greco-Roman World of the New Testament Era: Exploring the Background of Early Christianity*. Downers Grove, IL: IVP Academic, 1999.

John Paul VI, Pope. "Lumen Gentium." *Dogmatic Constitution of the Church*, 1965. https://www.vatican.va/archive/hist_councils/ii_vatican_council/documents/vat-ii_const_19641121_lumen-gentium_en.html.

Kahl, Brigitte. *Galatians Re-Imagined: Reading with the Eyes of the Vanquished*. Minneapolis: Fortress, 2014.

Käsemann, Ernst. *On Being a Disciple of the Crucified Nazarene*. Translated by Roy A. Harrisville. Grand Rapids: Eerdmans, 2010.

———. *The Wandering People of God: An Investigation of the Letter to the Hebrews*. Translated by Roy A. Harrisville and Irving L. Sandberg. Augsburg: Fortress, 1984.

Kelly, John N. D. *Epistles of Peter and Jude*. Black's New Testament Commentary. London: A & C Black, 1969.

Kloppenborg, John S. *Christ's Associations: Connecting and Belonging in the Ancient City*. New Haven, CT: Yale University Press, 2019.

Kloppenborg, John S., and Stephen G. Wilson, eds. *Voluntary Associations in the Graeco-Roman World*. New York: Routledge, 1996.

Knight, George W., III. *The Pastoral Epistles: A Commentary on the Greek Text*. Grand Rapids: Eerdmans, 1992.

Koester, Craig R. *Revelation and the End of All Things*. Grand Rapids: Eerdmans, 2001.

———. *Revelation: A New Translation with Introduction and Commentary*. Anchor Yale Bible. New Haven, CT: Yale University Press, 2005.

Kraybill, J. Nelson. *Apocalypse and Allegiance: Worship, Politics, and Devotion in the Book of Revelation*. Grand Rapids: Brazos, 2010.

Laansma, Jon C. "Hebrews." In *Theological Interpretation of the New Testament*, edited by Kevin J. Vanhoozer, 186–99. Grand Rapids: Baker Academic, 2008.

Lendon, J. E. *Empire of Honour: The Art of Government in the Roman World*. Oxford: Oxford University Press, 2001.

Lenski, R. C. H. *St. Paul's Epistles to the Colossians, to the Thessalonians, to Timothy, to Titus and to Philemon*. Philadelphia: Fortress, 1937.

Lincoln, Andrew T. *Ephesians*. Word Biblical Commentary 42. Grand Rapids: Zondervan, 1990.

Locke, Hubert G., ed. *Exile in the Fatherland: Martin Niemöller's Letters from Moabit Prison*. Translated by Ernst Kaemke et al. Grand Rapids: Eerdmans, 1986.

Lohmeyer, Ernst. *Der Briefe an die Philipper, Kolosser und an Philemon*. Gottingen: KEK, 1962.

———. *Kyrios Jesus: Eine Unntersuchung zu Phil 2, 5-11*. Sitzungen der Heidelberger Akademie der Wissenschaften 18. Heidelberg: C. Winters, 1928.

Lohse, Eduard. *Colossians and Philemon: A Commentary on the Epistles to the Colossians and to Philemon*. Translated by W. R. Poehlmann and R. J. Karris. Hermeneia. Philadelphia: Fortress, 1971.

Long, Fredrick. "Ἐκκλεσία on Ephesians, as Godlike in the Heavens, in the Temple, in γάμος and in Armor: Ideology and Iconography in Ephesians and Its Environs." In *The First Urban Churches 3: Ephesus*, edited by James R. Harrison and L. L. Welborn, 193–234. Atlanta: SBL, 2018.

Lührmann, Dieter. *Das Markusevangelium*. Tübingen: Mohr Siebeck, 1987.

Lyons, Stuart. *Music in the Odes of Horace*. Liverpool: Liverpool University Press, 2010.

Magee, Gregory S. "Uncovering the 'Mystery' in 1 Timothy 3." *Trinity Journal NS* 29 (2008) 247–65.

Maier, Harry O. *Picturing Paul in Empire: Imperial Image, Text and Persuasion in Colossians, Ephesians and the Pastoral Epistles*. London: Bloomsbury/T. & T. Clark, 2013.

Malina, Bruce J., and Richard L. Rohrbaugh. *Social-Science Commentary on the Gospel of John*. Minneapolis: Fortress, 1998.

Malina, Bruce J., and John J. Pilch. *Social-Science Commentary on the Book of Revelation*. Minneapolis: Fortress, 2000.

Marohl, Matthew J. "Hebrews." In *T. & T. Clark Social Identity Commentary on the New Testament*, edited by Brian J. Tucker and Aaron Kuecker, 487–514. London: T. & T. Clark, 2018.

Marshall, I. Howard. *A Critical and Exegetical Commentary of the Pastoral Epistles*. London: T. & T. Clark, 1999.

Martin, Michael W. "Philippians 2:6-11 As Subversive Hymnos: A Study in the Light of Ancient Rhetorical Theory." *Journal of Theological Studies NS* 66 (2015) 90-138.

Martin, Ralph P. *Colossians: The Church's Lord and the Christian's Liberty*. Exeter, England: Paternoster, 1972.

———. "An Early Christian Hymn — (Col. 1:15-20)." *The Evangelical Quarterly* 36 (1964) 195-205.

———. *A Hymn of Christ: Philippians 2:5-11 in Recent Interpretation and in the Setting of Early Christianity*. Grand Rapids: IVP, 1997.

———. *Worship in the Early Church*. Grand Rapids: Eerdmans, 1974.

McKnight, Scot. *The Letter to the Colossians*. New International Commentary on the New Testament. Grand Rapids: Eerdmans, 2018.

Medley, Mark S. "Subversive Song: Imagining Colossians 1:15-20 as a social protest hymn in the context of Roman Empire." *Review and Expositor* 116 (2019) 421-35.

Michaels, J. Ramsay. *The Gospel of John*. New International Commentary on the New Testament. Grand Rapids: Eerdmans, 2010.

———. *1 Peter*. Word Biblical Commentary. Waco, TX: Word, 1988.

Micou, R. W. "On ὤφθη ἀγγέλοις, 1 Tim. iii.16." *Journal of Biblical Literature* 11 (1892) 201-5.

Middleton, J. Richard. *A New Heaven and a New Earth: Reclaiming Biblical Eschatology*. Grand Rapids: Baker Academic, 2014.

Millar, Patrick. *Four Centuries of Scottish Psalmody*. London: Oxford University Press, 1947.

Miller, Amanda C. *Rumors of Resistance: Status Reversals and Hidden Transcripts in the Gospel of Luke*. Minneapolis: Fortress, 2014.

Miller, Andrew M. *Greek Lyric: An Anthology in Translation*. London: Hackett, 1996.

Moo, Douglas. *The Letters to the Colossians and to Philemon*. Pillar New Testament Commentary. Grand Rapids: Eerdmans, 2008.

Moses, Robert E. *Practices of Power: Revisiting the Principalities and Powers in the Pauline Epistles*. Minneapolis: Fortress, 2014.

Moyise, Steve, and Maarten J. J. Menken, eds. *The Psalms in the New Testament*. London: T. & T. Clark, 2004.

Muir, Steven. "Social Identity in the Epistle of Hebrews." In *T & T Clark Handbook to Social Identity in the New Testament*, edited by J. Brian Tucker and Coleman A. Baker, 425–39. London: Bloomsbury/T. & T. Clark, 2014.

Norman, Naomi J. "Imperial Triumph, Funeral and Apotheosis: The Arch of Titus in Rome." In *Koine: Mediterranean Studies in Honor of R. Ross Holloway*, edited by D. B. Counts and A. S. Tuck, 41–52. Oxford: Oxbow, 2009.

O'Brien, Peter T. *Colossians, Philemon*. Word Biblical Commentary 44. Waco, TX: Word, 1981.

———. *The Epistle to the Philippians: A Commentary on the Greek Text*. Grand Rapids: Eerdmans, 1991.

———. *The Letter to the Ephesians*. Grand Rapids: Eerdmans, 1999.

Painter, John. "Inclined to God: The Quest for Eternal Life." In *Exploring the Gospel of John: In Honor of D. Moody Smith*, edited by R. Alan Culpepper and C. Clifton Black, 346–68. Philadelphia: Westminster John Knox, 1996.

Pate, C. Marvin. "Revelation 2–19 and the Roman Imperial Cult." *Criswell Theological Review NS* 17 (2019) 67–85.

Pillar, Edward. *Resurrection as an Anti-Imperial Gospel*. Minneapolis: Fortress, 2013.

Powell, Mark Allan. *Introducing the New Testament: A Historical, Literary, and Theological Survey*. 2nd ed. Grand Rapids: Baker Academic, 2018.

———. *Jesus as a Figure of History: How Modern Historians View the Man from Galilee*. Louisville: Westminster John Knox, 1998.

Price, Simon R. F. *Rituals and Power: The Roman Imperial Cult in Asia Minor*. Cambridge: Cambridge University Press, 1984.

Putnam, Michael C. J. *Horace's Carmen Saeculare: Ritual Magic and the Poet's Art*. New Haven, CT: Yale University Press, 2000.

Pyke, James A. "The Red Redeemer." *World Vision* 14 (1970) 5–7.

Quinn, Jerome D., and William C. Wacker. *The First and Second Letters to Timothy: A New Translation with Notes and Commentary*. Eerdmans Critical Commentary. Grand Rapids: Eerdmans, 1999.

Reicke, Bo. *Disobedient Spirits and Christian Baptism: A Study of 1 Peter 3:19 and Its Context*. Eugene, OR: Wipf & Stock, 2005.

———. *Epistles of James, Peter, and Jude*. Anchor Bible 37. New York: Doubleday, 1964.

Rendsburg, Gary A. "The Psalms as Hymns in the Temple of Jerusalem." In *Jesus and Temple: Textual and Archeological Explorations*, edited by James H. Charlesworth, 95–122. Minneapolis: Fortress, 2014.

Reumann, John. *Philippians*. Anchor Bible 33B. New Haven, CT: Yale University Press, 2008.

Rhoads, David, et al., eds. *Luke-Acts and Empire: Essays in Honor of Robert L. Brawley*. Eugene, OR: Pickwick, 2011.

Richard, Pablo. *Apocalypse: A People's Commentary on the Book of Revelation*. Maryknoll, NY: Orbis, 1995.

Rogers, Guy MacLean. "An Ephesian Tale: Mystery Cults, Reverse Theological Engineering, and the Triumph of Christianity in Ephesus." In *The First Urban Churches 3: Ephesus*, edited by James R. Harrison and Laurence L. Welborn, 69–91. Atlanta: SBL, 2018.

———. *The Mysteries of Artemis of Ephesos: Cult, Polis, and Change in the Graeco-Roman World (Synkrisis)*. New Haven, CT: Yale University Press, 2013.

Sanders, E. P. *Judaism: Practice and Belief, 63 BCE–66 CE*. Minneapolis: Fortress, 2016.

Santelli, Robert. *This Land Is Your Land: Woody Guthrie and the Journey of an American Folk Song*. Philadelphia: Running Press, 2012.

Sartre, Maurice. *The Middle East under Rome*. Translated by Catherine Porter and Elizabeth Rawlings. Cambridge, MA: Harvard University Press, 2005.

Schmidt, Dietmar. *Pastor Niemöller*. Translated by Lawrence Wilson. Garden City, NY: Doubleday, 1959.

Schnackenburg, Rudolf. *The Gospel According to St. John*. Vol 1. New York: Crossroad, 1980.

Scott, James C. *Domination and the Arts of Resistance: Hidden Transcripts*. New Haven, CT: Yale University Press, 1990.

Silva, Moises. *Philippians*. 2nd ed. Baker Exegetical Commentary on the New Testament. Grand Rapids: Baker Academic, 2005.

Smith, Dennis E. *From Symposium to Eucharist: The Banquet in the Early Christian World*. Minneapolis: Fortress, 2003.

———. "Greco-Roman Banquet as a Social Institution." Paper presented at the annual meeting of the SBL, Atlanta, GA, November 2003.

Stegemann, Ekkhard W., and Wolfgang Stegemann. *The Jesus Movement: A Social History of its First Century*. Minneapolis: Fortress, 1999.

Stevenson, Gregory M. "Conceptual Background of the Golden Crown Imagery in the Apocalypse of John (4:4, 10; 14:14)." *Journal of Biblical Literature* 114 (1995) 257–72.

Stokes, Ryan E. "Not over Moses' Dead Body: Jude 22–24 and The Assumption of Moses in their Early Jewish Context." *Journal for Study of the New Testament* 40 (2017) 192–213.

Streett, R. Alan. *Caesar and the Sacrament: Baptism a Rite of Resistance*. Eugene, OR: Cascade, 2018.

———. *Subversive Meals: An Analysis of the Lord's Supper under Roman Domination during the First Century*. Eugene, OR: Pickwick, 2013.

Talbert, Charles H. "The Problem of Pre-Existence in Philippians 2:6–11." *Journal of Biblical Literature* 86 (1967) 141–53.

Taussig, Hal. *In the Beginning was the Meal*. Minneapolis: Fortress, 2009.

Thatcher, Tom. *Greater than Caesar: Christology and Empire in the Fourth Gospel*. Minneapolis: Fortress, 2009.

Thielman, Frank. *Ephesians*. Grand Rapids: Baker Academic, 2010.

Thompson, J. A. *Handbook of Life in Bible Times*. Downers Grove, IL: InterVarsity, 1986.

Thompson, Leonard L. *Revelation*. Abingdon New Testament Commentaries. Nashville: Abingdon, 1998.

Tommasi, Chiara O. "Apotheosis." In *Encyclopedia of Religion*, edited by Lindsey Jones, 437–41. New York: Macmillan, 2005.

Towner, Philip H. *The Letters to Timothy and Titus*. New International Commentary on the New Testament. Grand Rapids: Eerdmans, 2006.

Valentine, Kendra H. *Worlds at War, Nations in Song: Dialogic Imagination and Moral Vision in the Hymns of the Book of Revelation*. Eugene, OR: Wipf & Stock, 2015.

Vearncombe, Erin, et al. *After Jesus Before Christianity: A Historical Exploration of the First Two Centuries of Jesus Movements*. New York: Harper One, 2021.

Vendler, Helen. *The Odes of John Keats*. Cambridge, MA: Belknap, 1985.

Vermes, Geza. *Who's Who in the Age of Jesus*. New York: Penguin, 2005.

Vos, Geerhardus. *The Teaching of the Epistle to the Hebrews*. Grand Rapids: Eerdmans, 1956.

Walsh, Brian J., and Sylvia C. Keesmaat. *Colossians Remixed: Subverting the Empire*. Downers Grove, IL: IVP Academic, 2004.

Webb, Robert L. "Intertexture and Rhetorical Strategy in First Peter's Apocalyptic Discourse." In *Reading First Peter with New Eyes: Methodological Reassessments of* the Letter of First Peter, edited by Betsy Bauman-Martin and Robert Webb, 72–110. London: T. & T. Clark, 2007.

Wengst, Klaus. Pax Romana and the Peace of Jesus Christ. Philadelphia: Fortress, 1987.

Wink, Walter. Naming the Powers: The Language of Power in the New Testament. Philadelphia: Fortress, 1984.

Winn, Adam. An Introduction to Empire in the New Testament. Atlanta: SBL, 2016.

Witherington, Ben, III. The Letters to Philemon, the Colossians, and the Ephesians: A Socio-Rhetorical Commentary on the Captivity Epistles. Grand Rapids: Eerdmans, 2007.

Woodard, Roger D., ed. Cambridge Companion to Greek Mythology. Cambridge: Cambridge University Press, 2007.

Woodchuck, Eldon. "Images of Hell in the Tours of Hell: Are They True?" Criswell Theological Review NS 3 (2005) 11–42.

Wright, N. T. "Paul's Gospel and Caesar's Empire." In Paul and Politics: Ekklesia, Israel, Imperium, Interpretation, edited by Richard A. Horsley, 160–83. Harrisburg, PA: Trinity, 2000.

———. The Resurrection of the Son of God. Minneapolis: Fortress, 2003.

Wright, N. T., and Michael F. Bird. The New Testament in its World. Grand Rapids: Zondervan Academic, 2019.

Yoder, John Howard. The Politics of Jesus. Grand Rapids: Eerdmans, 1972.

Scripture Index

2 Kings

2:1	45
2:11–12	45

1 Chronicles

6:31–32	29
13:8	30
15:16–24	30
15:16	29
16:4–6	30
23:5	29

2 Chronicles

5:11–14	30
7:1	86
20:22–24	30
20:26–28	30
23:18	30
30:25–30	30
36:22–23	31

Ezra

2:64–65	31
3:10–12	32
7:7	32

Nehemiah

7:44	31
7:67	31
12:27–29	32

Job

38:4	27
38:7	27

Psalms

2	33, 35, 45, 136n8
2:1–3	34
2:1–2	33
2:4–6	34
2:7–9	34
2:7	34
2:8–9	154
2:8	34, 137
2:9	34
2:10–12	35
2:10–11	34
2:12	35, 36
8	45, 63n5, 136n8
11	33
19	63n5
23:5	67
29	63n5
33	63n5, 160
33:3	29
33:6	81
40	160
40:3	29
68	45
69	33, 45
89:20	114
89:27	114
92	24n7
96	160
96:1	29
98	160
98:1	29
98:4–6	29
100	63n5
103	63n5
104	63n5
105:2	29
110	45, 136n8
110:1	138
110:4	138
111	63n5
113–118	24
113	63n5
114	63n5
115–118	24
117	63n5
135	63n5

Dead Sea Scrolls

1QS

Early Christian Writings

Didache

Made in the USA
Monee, IL
19 October 2023

44841738R00122